UNDER DOCUMENTARY BILLS AND CREDITS

Croner.CCH Group Limited
145 London Road
Kingston upon Thames
Surrey KT2 6SR
Tel: 020 8547 3333

Published by
Croner.CCH Group Limited
145 London Road
Kingston upon Thames
Surrey KT2 6SR
Tel: 020 8547 3333

First published April 1990
Third Edition 2000

Although great care has been taken in the compilation and preparation of this book to ensure accuracy, the publishers cannot in any circumstances accept responsibility for any errors or omissions.

Readers of this book should be aware that only Acts of Parliament and Statutory Instruments have the force of law and that only the courts can authoritatively interpret the law.

British Library cataloguing in Publication Data. A CIP Catalogue Record for this book is available from the British Library

ISBN 1 85524 560 4

Printed by Creative Print and Design, Wales.

AUTHORS

Frank W Dow ACIB

Revised and Rewritten by Sandra Strong and Brian Herd
Strong & Herd, International Trade Consultants

CONTRIBUTORS

PREFACE TO REVISION
(Year 2000)

It is now 10 years since Frank Dow's *Understanding Documentary Bills and Credits* was first published; the revision in 1994 was largely to include the effects of UCP 500, the new *ICC Uniform Customs and Practice for Documentary Credits* published in May 1993. The purpose of this latest revision is to take account of other changes that have an effect on customs and practice in this field and also in international trade generally.

Significant changes occurring since the revised reprint of Frank Dow's book in 1994 include the following.

- The publication of a revised *ICC Uniform Rules for Collection* (URC522) which came into effect in 1996 introducing a new set of rules included in 26 Articles with an Article by Article commentary as a complementary publication (ICC publication No. 550). This revision clarified and restated the procedures and interpretation of the rules for collections.

- Then in 1998 came ISP98, a much needed set of Rules on International Standby Practices covering all aspects of standby letter of credit transactions previously inadequately covered in UCP500.

- A further significant change which has required the amendment of the 1994 reprint, has been the publication of *Incoterms 2000* (ICC publication No. 560) the first revision of these internationally recognised trade terms since 1990. In this year 2000 revision, the 13 Incoterms, although remaining the same in number and title, have been adjusted or modified to clarify some anomalies in the previous set.

Other major trade and political changes have occurred since 1990, the single market in the EC has led to a "Customs Union" between the 15 Member States; the iron curtain has disappeared leading to significant changes to trading with Eastern Europe; China has become involved in international trade after years of isolation; and e-commerce marches on apace with Internet trading growing daily. Notwithstanding these major changes the world of Documentary Bills and Credit retains many of its original features such as the "Doctrine of Strict Compliance", and rejections of presentations to the banks are still rife. Nothing changes? Well not quite. There is a quiet revolution in the use of electronically transmitted data which will surely percolate through to the most dusty corners within the next decade. In fact, the ICC (International Chamber of Commerce) Commission on Banking Trade & Settlement) are at work on URGETS (ICC Rules and Guidelines for Electronic Trade & Settlement) and ICC National Committees are contributing to the formulation of these rules which will define the playing field, so to speak. Issues such as confidentiality and protection of, and recording and storage of, electronic data will be part of the guidelines which should be published in mid to late 2000.

Frank Dow's book has proved its worth over the years in helping those involved in the sometimes complicated world of Bills and Credits to understand the reasons why certain actions and procedures are required and the publishers are anxious that the book will continue to find a place on the bookshelf of all involved in International Trade.

Contents

x

Index

Introduction

As an instrument designed to provide a compromise between the conflicting interests of buyers and sellers in trade transactions, it is difficult to imagine anything which could adequately replace the documentary letter of credit. Thousands of importers, exporters, bankers and forwarders are handling credits each working day in every country in the world, yet time and again the essential basic understanding of the concept of the credit is simply not there. As a result, someone suffers. That someone may be the buyers who receive the wrong goods, or the right goods at the wrong time (which is sometimes worse), or it may be (and most frequently is) the sellers, who have to wait for cripplingly long periods of time to receive payment for their goods.

The blame for such inconveniences almost invariably falls upon the bank. Yet nearly every letter of credit and application for the issue of a credit carries wording to the effect that it is issued subject to the *Uniform Customs and Practice for Documentary Credits* (UCP) issued by the International Chamber of Commerce (ICC). Similarly, a high proportion of collections are stated to be subject to the ICC's *Uniform Rules for Collections* (URC). How many exporters and forwarders can honestly say that they or their staff have a working knowledge of what those rules say? Sadly, the majority have never read them and do not even have a copy available to be consulted.

"Rules is rules" has a Dickensian sound to it but is very relevant to the subjects contained within this publication. Rules such as UCP500 are designed to provide a secure framework for the conduct of transactions in international trade; they are designed to protect the traders, the banks, underwriters, lawyers, indeed, all who have involvement in the process. Without a clear, understandable set of rules chaos would reign. It is sad that it often seems as if a form of chaos does reign and the finger of blame is regularly pointed at the banks who are the arbiters of the collections process.

Is it fair to blame banks for adhering to the very rules which traders would demand as a protection against fraud and malpractice? No, of course not, but the criticism has been propagated that levels of training and understanding on this discipline within banks generally are inadequate. The same criticism could be levelled at traders and again at freight forwarders but, like all blanket criticism, it would be difficult to substantiate if it wasn't for the stark statistic of rejected documentary presentation, these are still running at high percentage levels (circa 65%). Is it the rules themselves that are at fault? Are they too complex for the average citizen? Whatever the reason for the difficulties experienced by traders, you would expect them to look at the costs they incur in getting it wrong and attempt to improve their procedures. Forwarders would surely benefit from helping their customers achieve an acceptable level of successful compliance.

Do banks benefit from non-compliance? Clearly they do to some extent, but to assist their clients in reducing it would seem to be a better long-term policy. There are signs that some banks are taking steps to help their clients by, for example, issuing checklists, "idiot" guides and even organising free of charge training sessions.

It is the aim of this book to try to bring these varying and often conflicting interests together in a deeper understanding of how the documentary letter of credit and, to a lesser extent, the documentary bill for collection, works. Only by achieving this is there any hope of reducing the high incidence of rejected drawings under credits, and the vast quantities of unwanted goods offered for sale at huge discounts simply to get rid of them.

The target audience is large. The book is not written from the particular standpoint of any one of the parties involved in the international trade transaction, but is intended to be read by all who need to know: export/import clerks, bank clerks, forwarders, students, etc. It does not set out to be an exhaustive guide to trade documentation; many books have appeared on this subject and have admirably achieved their objectives. We will, however, be looking at various documents and examining their function and format, but only from the point of view of their effect on the achievement of the underlying purpose of the documentary credit or bill — the exchange of correct goods for prompt payment.

One apology must be made. Many aspects of international trade are truly international, and this includes the various codes drawn up by the International Chamber of Commerce to standardise actions and interpretations in certain situations on a global basis. Sometimes, however, domestic laws, and in particular bill of exchange legislation, can affect the international aspect of a transaction. It is impossible in a work of this size to examine in detail all the possible variations in attitudes within the courts to a particular problem. What it is hoped will be achieved is that far fewer such transactions will come before the courts at all. However, as this book is written in English in the UK any venture into the legal background to international trade will be based largely upon English law and statute.

Above all, the book is intended to equip the reader with the knowledge and understanding to deal with practical situations as they arise. The variety of these situations can be quite astonishing, and no work of this kind could possibly provide a codified answer to each and every problem, not least because many of them have not yet arisen and are therefore not identified as problems at all.

The world of international commerce is dynamic and change is under way even as these words are written. Although from time to time, as the situation indicates it as desirable, the book will be updated, it must be left to the reader to keep abreast of developments. In this, such publications as Croner's *Export Digest* and the periodic issue by the International Chamber of Commerce of significant opinions of their Banking Committee relating to letters of credit are invaluable.

CHAPTER 1

Methods of payment in international trade

Before looking at the two methods of settlement in international trade which most concern us — the bill for collection and the documentary letter of credit — it will be useful to examine the options which are available to buyers and sellers and the factors which influence their decision to prefer one method over another. Sometimes the domestic regulations in one or other of the countries involved will dictate that a particular method be used, and can be the case where a documentary credit is opted for, as can normal trade usage, whether within a country, a trading community or an individual company. More frequently, however, the most influential factor is the degree of trust which exists between the principals in the transaction, since different methods of settlement provide correspondingly different degrees of protection to the interests of one or the other of them.

Open account trading

International transactions which may involve distance, language, legal and cultural differences bring a fresh set of situations and questions to answer. For example:
- as the seller, how do I protect myself from bad debt, non-payment or excessively slow payment?
- as the buyer, how do I prevent failure to supply or the supply of faulty or incorrect type of goods, or additionally failure to supply to time?
- how do I assess the credit status of the potential customer or supplier and determine the honesty and solidity of that company?

- whether buying or selling, both parties in the international transaction will look to secure their own interests but will be driven by the need to trade
- how do I get my money and what about currency fluctuations?

The most common form of settlement in domestic transactions, Open Account Trading, requires trust, transparency and common accounting procedures to make it work satisfactorily. Credit is given by the seller and mechanisms such as credit status checks, credit limits, proforma invoicing, stop-lists, etc all come into play.

Of the various methods of settlement that are available to the buyer or seller in international trade, open account is quite high on the risk league table. The sellers generally only will extend credit when they are satisfied as to the status of their client(s) and where inter-country transaction rules and traditions allow trading relationships to form. Trading between companies who are part of a multinational organisation is an example of a secure situation where open account is acceptable and normal. Geographical proximity and common cultural tradition is another.

Other methods of payment can and do provide for control and performance mechanisms which are often necessary for the prudent trader, however as in the case of the EC, which is a Customs Union for its members and with shared legislation such as CE Marking, there is a growth in open account trading as trust and shared trade grow. Competition for market share may be a spur to offering open account status if it is offered by your competitors. Would we have become a great trading nation without taking some risk? Probably not.

Payment in advance

One of the traps to avoid in discussing trading and business arrangements in international trade, is to make statements that cannot be borne out by evidence. Hence, in assessing payment in advance, it would be wrong to say that this was a relatively rare method of payment without having the facts to support the statement. In fact, it is probable, that advance payment is used more frequently than you would imagine.

Examples of situations where advance payment would occur are the following.
1. Single source supplier who demands advance payment against proforma invoice. This supplier, eg a manufacturer of spares for previously exported capital equipment, is known to the buyer as

reliable and trustworthy with a market reputation to maintain. Advance payment therefore loses its risk factor and is less costly than more tedious methods, such as letter of credit devices.

2. Advance payment required to fund the manufacture of the goods in question, security for the transaction being secured for the buyers by performance bonds or guarantees (ICC Publication No. 458, *ICC Uniform Rules for Demand Guarantees*) or under a Standby Credit (see Chapter 10).

3. Country of supply currency controls can mean release of currency is limited to certain periods and advance payment during one of those periods is used to ensure supply at a later date. Security may be needed within the contract by some device such as a bond or guarantee.

4. Advance payment of a percentage of the selling price is a common trade practice where the value of the contract warrants it. In fact, many major international contracts may involve more than one method of payment with stage payments being made over a period of many months, in some cases years.

The prudent and commercially acute trader does not need to be reminded of the risk factor in paying for goods before receiving them. Fraud and embezzlement are alive and well in the international market place and greed on the part of the buyers often matches that of the perpetrator. Caution is the rule.

The documentary collection

Both methods of settlement discussed so far deal with extremes; open account represents almost the ideal situation for the buyer and advance payment provides similar advantages for the seller. Between the two come the compromise solutions which will form the subject of the remainder of this book: the documentary bill for collection and the documentary letter of credit. Both methods involve the intervention of an agent and because of the nature of the transaction, which basically involves the remittance of money, and because of their worldwide networks of correspondent agreements, the banks have traditionally filled the role of that agent. With the bill for collection the principals are the sellers, with the credit it is the buyers. But whichever is used, it should always be remembered that it is very often the law of agency which is cited in any dispute, rather than specific laws or other rules dealing with either bills or credits.

Where the level of trust between buyers and sellers is not so high as to make an open account arrangement advisable, yet remains reasonably good, it is very often the collection which will be selected by the parties to achieve settlement of the transaction, whilst going some way towards protecting the interests of both parties. Briefly, since the process will be described in some detail in a later chapter, the sellers despatch the goods and then assemble all the documents which will be required by the buyers in order to import and take delivery of those goods on arrival. The documents, often though not invariably accompanied by a demand for payment addressed to the buyers — a bill of exchange — are then handed to the sellers' bank together with full instructions for their disposal. These instructions are repeated by the bank to its own agent in the buyers' country, which will then release the documents to the buyers in accordance with the instructions received, usually against either payment of the invoice value or against an undertaking to make such payment on an agreed date in the future. Thus the interests of both parties are protected to an extent; the sellers, through their agent the bank, retain control of the documents which are necessary to the buyers before they can take delivery, while the buyers are not obliged to pay before having had an opportunity to inspect those documents and possibly the goods themselves.

To the sellers, the greatest disadvantage of the bill for collection as a method of settlement is that it is slow. The effects of this defect can frequently be overcome, however, by arranging with the bank which is handling the collection to provide finance, on agreed terms, to cover the period during which payment is outstanding. Advantages of a collection to the sellers are that it is a relatively simple and, where bank finance is not required, cheap method. For the buyers, the main advantage is that payment can be deferred at least until arrival of the documents, which can then be inspected before a decision is reached, and frequently, either by agreement or by custom, until arrival of the goods themselves.

A disadvantage for buyers is the possibility of delays when the supplier fails to give adequate instructions to the collecting/presenting banks. Poor communication can lead to documents being held by the banks involved either because they do not have clear contact details or the exporter has instructed the banks to collect monies in addition to the value of the bill of exchange, eg interest, expenses or other charges. These delays can incur storage and prevent the buyer from obtaining an expeditious release of the goods.

The documentary letter of credit

Frequently, the level of security provided to the sellers by the bill for collection is insufficiently high. Although they may retain control of the relative documents they lose physical possession of the goods, although of course retaining legal ownership until payment is received. Legal ownership, however, may be of small consolation to sellers whose goods are eight thousand miles away and must be disposed of by an agent in a forced sale in an unreceptive market. In theory, of course, such goods could be shipped back, but the cost of such an operation is usually prohibitive.

Such exporters are likely to insist on payment being by means of a letter of credit. This is a document issued by the buyers' bank to the sellers promising that they, the sellers, will be paid provided that they comply with all the terms and conditions stipulated by the buyers as expressed in the letter of credit. Thus, the sellers' reliance on the standing and integrity of the buyers is replaced by a promise from a bank that payment will be made under certain specified conditions, and this before the goods have been shipped or, perhaps, even produced.

To the sellers, this system brings the undoubted and obvious advantage of certainty of payment subject to compliance with certain conditions. It brings other advantages to both parties, however, which are perhaps not quite so obvious. Before investigating these advantages it is necessary to consider how the system actually proceeds after the issue of the credit.

Having received the credit, the sellers ship the goods and put together the documents stipulated in the letter of credit, ensuring of course, that any special requirements regarding documents in the letter of credit must be borne in mind. These are then presented to a bank in the sellers' own country, which carefully checks the documents against the terms of the credit and, if they are in order, pays the seller. Two more advantages to the sellers are therefore immediately apparent:

(a) the documents are checked before they leave the exporting country, and therefore if anything is found to be wrong it can very often be put right quickly, whereas with a collection the chances are that such discrepancies remain undetected until documents are checked by the buyers

(b) payment may, if the credit terms make it possible, be made to the sellers immediately upon presentation of documents in their own country after shipment of the goods.

For the buyers, the advantages in using a credit lie in the ability to control the circumstances under which suppliers will receive payment by making presentation of correct documentation a prerequisite for that payment to take place. By careful consideration of the dates which are specified in the credit for certain events to occur, they can also attempt to control the time at which goods are received and the time at which the documents themselves are received, both potentially important factors as we shall see later. Finally, because the issue of the letter of credit is instigated by the buyers, the banks intervening in the operation are acting as their agents and not as those of the sellers, as is the case with a bill for collection.

Disadvantages to the sellers in the use of a credit are few, but significant. The most important is that the method, once set up, is comparatively inflexible and altered circumstances, which might not be considered sufficiently important to frustrate the contract where any other payment method is used, may render the credit null and void and therefore deprive the sellers of all their advantages at a stroke. Also, because banks require 100% compliance with the credit terms any error, however minor the seller may think, will delay payment. To the buyers the greatest disadvantage is probably that payment will have to be made or guaranteed from the time when documents are presented to the issuing bank with no facility for awaiting arrival of the goods as is often the case when using a collection. The credit is also relatively expensive; security must usually be paid for.

Inflexible though the credit may be when things go wrong, an advantage to all concerned is its extreme flexibility in catering for different circumstances. The credit in its many forms will be looked at more closely in a later chapter, but, where security of payment is an important factor, there are few occasions when a letter of credit in one form or another cannot be adapted to meet the particular requirements of that occasion.

Summary

These, then, are the options available to partners in international trade when agreeing between themselves how settlement will be made. Many exporters seek to protect themselves from the risk of non-payment by taking out credit insurance. Although outside the scope of this book, credit insurance is important as it allows exporters to trade in markets otherwise thought of as unstable. For the purposes of this book it is sufficient to say that under the above circumstances most credit insurance policies will insist that exporters obtain a more secure form of payment, eg bills of exchange or letters of credit, before the risk is covered by the insurers. This, therefore, removes the element of choice when selecting the method of payment.

The ascending order of security offered, at least to the sellers, is: open account, bill for collection, documentary letter of credit and cash in advance. From the point of view of the banks, both bills and credits provide a good steady income from handling commissions, with credits being the more lucrative, but also the most expensive to operate in terms of intensity of labour involved and carrying by far the greater risk. Both also offer opportunities for further business in the form of export finance for bills, and import finance for both, but especially for credits, because of the earlier payment, mentioned above, which is often implied by this method of settlement. Such considerations, however, will form the subject material of later chapters.

CHAPTER 2

The international trade contract

This book is not a legal text book and Contract Law and other such legal frameworks are not examined in detail. It is necessary, however, to see documentary collections and credit against the backdrop of contractual agreement between seller and buyer.

Trade contracts, whether international or domestic, are amazingly varied; the international variety where agreement is formed between parties separated by differences of language, culture and geographical distance arguably require the most attention in ensuring that both parties have the same understanding of their responsibilities as each other. The almost infinite variety of these contractual arrangements, whether written into a formal contract, verbally agreed or commonly included in routine quotations, order acceptance and acknowledgement procedures, can be supported in the commercial sense by the use of model contracts such as those formalised in the International Chamber of Commerce publication *ICC Model International Sale Contract* (ICC Publication No. 556) for example, or by a host of protective contract clauses.

The basis of difficulties between buyer and seller in international trading has been caused by various differences between international and domestic business aspects, for example:

    (a) transportation complexity — passage of cost and risk from one party to the other
    (b) documentation responsibilities, eg export and import licences, etc
    (c) difficulty of defining a legal point of delivery
    (d) insurance responsibilities
    (e) document of title and responsibilities for handling same
    (f) export packing.

The responsibilities of buyer and seller in such transactions have major impact on pricing the goods; without knowing what costs you were responsible for it was often difficult to accurately price for export, confusions and dispute often arose in respect of duties and taxes at import into the destination country.

It came as a great boon then in 1936 when the International Chamber of Commerce introduced Incoterms, a set of International Commercial Terms created to provide buyers and sellers with a set of terms designed to show the parties what to do with respect to:

(a) carriage of goods from seller to buyer, and

(b) export and import clearance.

These terms, 13 in all, are examined in detail a little further on, but should be appreciated as an internationally recognised set of delivery terms for international transactions that provide clear definition to those questions of who is responsible for what in terms of cost and risk in delivering goods internationally.

Since 1936, these terms have been amended 7 times to keep pace with changes in trade practices, eg containerisation, electronic trading, etc. The latest set is Incoterms 2000. Traders are encouraged (even urged) to become familiar with Incoterms which are known throughout the world and which leave less margin for error than "home grown" contract clauses. The 1980 United Nations Convention on Contracts for the International Sale of Goods did not deal with interpretation of trade terms, believing that the ICC was better equipped to provide such guidance in its Incoterms publication.

Before looking individually at the 13 terms, it should be emphasised that if you are buying or selling, to or from overseas, it is a worthwhile exercise making yourself familiar with the terms, remember that they are a genuine set of working rules invaluable to export buyers and sellers. Incoterms 2000 are published by the ICC in two books; a basic reference book *Incoterms 2000* (Publication No. 560) and a larger more detailed *Guide to Incoterms 2000*. You can obtain a copy from either your local Chamber of Commerce or from the ICC offices in London.

INCOTERMS: International Commercial Terms

ExWorks named place (EXW)

The two extremes which are possible are where the sellers pay all costs involved in transporting the goods to the buyers, and where the buyers pay all those costs. For the purposes of international invoicing the basic selling price of goods reflects the first situation where the buyers are responsible. This basic selling price is known commonly as the ExWorks price and the ICC has followed common usage in calling this type of contract ExWorks. The sellers' risk and responsibilities end when the goods are packed, ready for export at their premises; they are not responsible even for loading the collecting vehicle. This means buyers must organise the transport of the goods, pay all costs and bear the full transit risk plus undertake to perform any export formalities in the seller's country.

Free alongside ship (FAS) named port of shipment

Where the traditional method of sea carriage is being used it is the duty of the buyers to nominate the ship on which the goods will be conveyed, but because of the difficulties which the buyers may encounter in arranging transportation of the goods to that ship at the port where it is loading cargo and negotiating export customs clearance (where applicable), it is often convenient for the sellers to undertake these arrangements. This is covered contractually by FAS... . Risk of loss or damage and all further responsibilities are the buyer's once the goods are alongside the nominated ship. Note that, under Incoterms 2000, it is the sellers who are responsible for export customs formalities — a major change since the 1990 set of terms.

Free carrier (FCA) named place

This term can be used for any mode of transport; risk of loss or damage is the buyers once the goods are in the hands of the first carrier in the exporter's country. FCA can now be used in two different ways.

FCA sellers' premises

This use of FCA mean that the sellers deliver the goods, and transfer risk once the goods have been loaded on to the buyers' transport at the sellers' premises — similar to ExWorks except loading is now, under FCA..., the sellers' responsibility. In addition, it is the sellers' obligation to clear the goods for export and, if the buyers do not give specific transport instructions, this term protects the sellers by allowing them to arrange transport on behalf of the buyers but at the buyers' risk and cost.

FCA named place of shipment

Under this use of FCA, delivery takes place and risk passes to the buyers when the goods are placed at the disposal of the first carrier at the named point though the sellers do not bear the risk of off-loading the goods at that point. The sellers' costs include delivery to the named point and customs clearance. This makes the term a suitable replacement for FOB... when the goods are not moving by conventional sea freight. First carrier is defined as "any person who, in a contract of carriage, undertakes to perform or to procure the performance of transport" by the appropriate method.

Free on board (FOB) named port of shipment

Under a FOB contract, the sellers' responsibility is to deliver the goods at their own expense to the ship nominated by the buyers, clear the goods for export and pay for their loading on board the vessel. Although the full cost of loading is borne by the sellers it is interesting that the actual point at which the risk in the goods passes from the sellers to the buyers is where they cross the ship's rail. Technically, therefore, if the hawser of a crane breaks the resulting insurance claim will be under the sellers' policy if the goods hit the dock, and under the buyers' policy if they hit the deck; insurance will be discussed in detail in Chapter 5.

This legal delivery point, "loaded across the ship's rail", is not an arbitrary term but the actual physical point at which sellers' fulfil their obligations and has been used for centuries in accordance with sea freight convention. Although the notion under FOB to deliver the goods "across the ship's rail" nowadays may seem inappropriate in many cases, it is nevertheless understood by merchants and applied in a manner which takes account of the goods and the available loading facilities. FOB terms are not suitable for anything other than shipment by sea or inland waterway, and even then the use of a container or trailer, or delivery to the carriers at any point other than the port of loading may make them inoperable. An FCA term should be considered in such circumstances.

As evidence of fulfilment of their obligations, the sellers must provide the buyers with documentary evidence of the loading of the goods on to the ship. In practice, this would normally be a "shipped" bill of lading but in some cases might be a lesser document such as a mate's receipt. It is worth noting that in all cases where documentary evidence of delivery at any point is required, that the document must be "clean", ie it must not contain any notation to the effect that the goods or packaging appear to be defective in any way and if this is not so the sellers are technically in breach of contract. Bills of lading and the clauses which may appear in them relating to the condition of the goods, form the subject of Chapter 3.

Cost and freight to (CFR) named port of destination

Where shipment by sea is concerned, the next major cost which must be allocated is the sum of money which will be charged by the owner of the carrying vessel as consideration for delivering the goods to their port of destination. This charge is referred to as freight or carriage and CFR... is the first term under which payment of freight is the responsibility of the sellers. A CFR contract does not extend the sellers' risk or delivery point, as with FOB. These are responsibilities that are transferred to the buyers once the goods pass the ship's rail at loading. The sellers are, in fact, paying the freight purely as a service to the buyers and usually at the buyers' request. The costs of getting the goods to the named port of destination do not generally include off-loading at the arrival port unless this was part of the contract of carriage agreed between the sellers and the freight company. Payment of freight by the sellers (eg freight prepaid) must be evidenced, either by means of annotation of the bill of lading or by the carrier's signed receipt. The remarks above regarding continued incorrect use of the FOB contract apply equally to the CFR contract, still occasionally abbreviated as C&F though this term ceased being an Incoterm in the 1990 set. Again, it is only suitable for shipment by sea and is inappropriate where goods are containerised or are received by the carriers other than at the port of loading; in those cases, the more appropriate contract terms are likely to be CPT, described below.

Carriage paid to (CPT) named place of destination

This term can be used for any mode of transport. Delivery takes place and risk is transferred to the buyers when the goods are placed at the carrier's disposal at the place of shipment from the UK — similar to FCA named place. The difference is that under CPT the seller must pay all costs to get the goods to the named place of destination, which could be an airport, sea port, road or rail terminal. It is also the sellers' obligation to provide the buyer with transport documents applicable to the mode of transport used and the buyer must accept delivery of the goods on arrival at the named place.

Cost, insurance and freight to (CIF) named port of destination, and Carriage and insurance paid to (CIP) named place of destination

These terms are similar to CFR... and CPT... respectively, except under the CIF and CIP terms the sellers must take out transit insurance cover for the goods on behalf of the buyer. These are the only terms that indicate which party must legally insure the goods, though all Incoterms indicate where risk transfers from the seller to the buyer.

Under these terms the sellers must pay for insurance under the minimum cover of the Institute Cargo Clauses for 110% of the value of the shipment. Usually, this means the sellers raise an Insurance Certificate on their normal marine insurance policy rather than take out a new policy specifically for this movement (although, if they do not have an insurance policy or it does not cover your buyers' country, a specific policy would have to be obtained). The Certificate is issued on behalf of the buyers and should be sent to them if a claim has to be made because it is the buyers' risk once the goods have passed the ship's rail at loading (CIF) or once they are in the hands of the first carrier at the named place in the sellers' country (CIP). If the buyers wish to have more protection than the Institute Cargo Clause for Minimum Cover states, they must expressly instruct the sellers to take out greater insurance cover, eg maximum cover with war risk.

Delivered at frontier (DAF) named place

Under the final group of Incoterms — the D group — the sellers undertake to pay all costs to the named place of destination and, unlike the C terms listed above, also undertake to bear the risk for loss or damage to the destination place. The first D term to consider is DAF..., used when goods are being delivered across a land frontier point so it is not applicable to sea freight shipments.

The seller bears all risk and costs up to the named place, at which point delivery is made. Sellers are responsible for export customs formalities. Off-loading of the goods at the named place and import customs clearance are the responsibilities of the buyers. It is important under DAF to clearly define the named point. It is possible to have DAF country of export, though being an arrival term it is more suited for delivery to the buyers' country.

Delivered ex-ship (DES) named port of destination

This term should only be used if the goods are being moved by conventional sea freight (like FOB, CFR and CIF). Delivery takes place, risk transfers to the buyers and the sellers have no further costs when the goods arrive at the named port available for collection by the buyers, still in the ship but alongside the quay at the port of discharge. It is the buyers' responsibility to arrange for the discharge of the goods from the ship and their clearance through customs.

Delivered ex-quay (DEQ) named point of destination

Again, this term only relates to the goods moved by conventional sea freight. This is one step further in the proceedings than DES.... It is the seller who is now responsible for, and bears the risks of, off-loading the goods from the vessel at the port of destination. Under the 1990 set of Incoterms it was the responsibility of the seller to organise import customs clearance and pay relevant import duties — this has been changed in the new set (Incoterms 2000). The buyers are now responsible for import customs formalities. All costs once the goods are off-loaded, including terminal charges and import clearance, duties and taxes are for the account of the buyers. If the buyer wants the exporter to pay terminal fees they may be added into the contract term.

Delivered duties unpaid (DDU) named place of destination

This delivered term can be used for any mode of transport. All charges are paid by the sellers up to the named point except import duties or taxes. Sellers have no obligation to off-load the goods at the named point. This term, like FCA, can have two uses.

DDU named place of arrival

In affect, this is similar to CPT except the sellers bear all risks and have only legally delivered when the goods have arrived at the named place of arrival in the buyer's country, eg an airport, sea port, road or rail terminal.

DDU buyers' premises

This use of DDU... means the sellers must pay for delivery to the buyers' premises and it is commonly used if goods are shipped by courier on their "door-to-door" services. Import customs clearance and the payment of duties (where applicable) are the buyers' responsibilities; if the buyers do not act expeditiously in carrying out the customs formalities, so incurring delays or costs, it is the buyers who bear all risk and/or costs for these delays.

Delivered duties paid (DDP) named point of arrival

We now reach the furthest extreme regarding the sellers' responsibility, that where they agree to deliver the goods to the buyers' warehouse free of any extra charge. Again, as with DDU... this term can be used for any mode of transport.

DDP differs from DDU... in that all duties and taxes must be paid by the sellers. The buyers have very few responsibilities. It is generally unwise for sellers to take responsibility for import duties and taxes in the destination country as these charges are sometimes difficult to identify accurately or at best guarantee their stability. In addition buyers can usually offset the equivalent of VAT under domestic regulations whereas the sellers would not be able to unless registered in the buyers' country. Therefore, this term should not be used if sellers are unable directly or indirectly to obtain any necessary import licence or complete the import customs formalities.

Documentation

Thus far, we have been concerned only with the aspects of the contract which relate to the actual movement of the goods and the division between the contracting parties of the costs and responsibilities relating to such movement. There are, however, many other aspects which should be covered in the contract. One of these is the question of supplementary documentation. It is, of course, the buyers' responsibility to ensure that all the required documents are called for in the contract. At best, an omission will cause inconvenience; at worst, it could mean that the goods cannot be imported at all. The different types of document used in international trade are examined in detail at a later stage, but only buyers in individual countries can know for certain which documents they require for their own purposes and which are required by the authorities in those countries. For the latter, a regularly updated publication such as Croner's *Reference Book for Importers* is invaluable for British importers, while for forwarders, bankers, and many others, the companion *Reference Book for Exporters* gives similar information for most countries in the world. The same information can usually be obtained from other sources, such as the consulates of the countries concerned, the UK Department of Trade and Industry (DTI) and via the Internet but updating, language and work pressures all combine to make such sources generally unsatisfactory.

Goods

Similarly, the full specification of the required goods must be given by the buyers at the contract stage. Sellers are under no obligation to hold a contract price if the specification is altered at a later stage. Once again, the most common time for such a change to be made, surreptitiously, is in the letter of credit, so it is essential when sellers receive such instruments that they examine them carefully and compare them with the contract terms.

Bank charges

Finally, a word about bank charges. They are not usually very high in comparison to the value of the consignment, but nonetheless are a frequent source of dispute between sellers and buyers as they are almost invariably overlooked at the contract stage. Consequently, when they arise, there is no guidance, either from Incoterms or from the contract itself, regarding who is responsible for their payment. Common sense suggests that each party should bear that portion of any bank charges which relates to their own side of the transaction, but the law of agency says that principals are responsible for reasonable costs incurred by their agents; since in a collection transaction the seller is the principal, and in a credit transaction the buyer is the principal, and all the banks involved are acting as agents forming a continuous chain from the principal, it follows that, legally speaking, all bank charges are for the seller under a collection and for the buyer under a credit. All too frequently, however, the choice of a particular method of settlement is not the result of a freely negotiated agreement but is imposed by one or other of the parties acting from a position of strength. When this is the case, resentment is often engendered in the other party, and so the seeds of dispute are sown.

Leaving aside financial charges for the moment, the charges which will accrue to a collection will be the commissions (plus any out-of-pocket expenses) charged by each bank involved, with a minimum of one (where a bank uses its own overseas branch as collecting agent and charges merely for the one service) and a possible maximum of four (where a domestic bank uses a local branch of a recognised international bank as its agent, which in turn passes the item to its branch in the buyers' country, which may well present for settlement through the buyers' bank), plus any stamp duty which may be payable on the bill of exchange, and any reimbursement commission if the contract stipulates payment in the currency of a third country.

A letter of credit will certainly attract opening commission, probably advising commission and negotiation commission, with possibly confirmation commission and reimbursement commission as well. In all cases any additional services provided, such as amendment fees, charges for handling, discrepant documents, telex costs and postal charges, may be added.

It is important that agreement is reached at the contract stage regarding who is to pay these charges and any financing fees. Only when such agreement has been reached is it possible for sellers to know exactly what their profit on a transaction will be, and for buyers to know the true cost of the goods which they are purchasing.

These, then, are the aspects of the international trade contract of which every person involved in the handling of a bill or credit transaction should be aware. No attempt has been made to investigate the intricacies of contract law in this chapter, and for the most part there is no need to do so, but in the remainder of this book reference will be made when it has a direct bearing on the subject under discussion.

CHAPTER 3

Marine bills of lading

It is necessary to consider the marine bill of lading separately from other documents because of its immense importance as a security document. This importance arises because, apart from being a receipt for the goods, it has one quality which is unique among transport documents in that it can be a document of title to the goods which it covers.

Negotiability

This is made possible by the bill of lading's quality of negotiability. Just as title to the proceeds of a cheque which is made out to the order of the payee can be transferred by simple or specific endorsement, so can title to the goods covered by a bill of lading be transferred, if the consignee is shown as "order". Since the carrier will not deliver the goods without production of the bill of lading, its transfer for value amounts to a sale of the goods and, furthermore, if a buyer refuses to pay for them, the holder of the bill of lading can obtain possession of the goods.

Features of a bill of lading

Please refer to the example of an ocean bill of lading illustrated overleaf.

Shipper

Frequently the name of the sellers of the goods will appear here, although occasionally the name of a forwarding agent or, if the sellers are merchants, the name of the actual manufacturers may be substituted. This is the counterparty to the carriers in the contract of carriage and it is important to remember that the carriers owe no contractual obligation

Face of Bill of Lading

BILL OF LADING

Shipper		B/L No.
		Reference No.

OT AFRICA LINE

74-01-073-000

OT Africa Line Limited
Marc House
13/14 Great Saint Thomas Apostle
London EC4V 2BB
Telephone: 0171 332 6000
Fax: 0171 332 6003

| Consignee |
| Notify Address |
| Place of Receipt* |
| Vessel/Voyage | Port of Loading |
| Port of Discharge | Place of Delivery* |

Container - Trailer Vehicle Number/Plate Marks and Numbers	Number and Kind of Packages, description of Goods	Gross Weight in Kilos	Measurement in Cubic M (M³)
CONTAINER NO: SEAL NO:	1 X 20FT CONTAINER STC 2 PALLETS & 201 DRUMS	6500	

"SHIPPED ON BOARD"
"FREIGHT PREPAID"

Freight details, Charges, etc

FCL/FCL CONTAINER PIER/PIER
Ship not responsible for any discrepancy of
Contents nor any loss or damage to contents

Particulars furnished by the Merchant

SHIPPED on board in apparent good order and condition unless otherwise stated and to be discharged at the port of discharge or so near thereto as the vessel may safely get and be always afloat. Weight, measure, quality contents, value, marks and numbers, if mentioned in the Bill of Lading are to be considered unknown unless the contrary has been expressly acknowledged and agreed to. The signing of this Bill of Lading is not considered as such an agreement. Subject always to the exceptions, limitations, conditions and liberties whether written, printed or stamped on both pages of this Bill of Lading, to which the merchant agrees by accepting this Bill of Lading.

In witness whereof the number of original Bills of Lading stated below have been signed, all of this tenor and date, one of which being accomplished the others to stand void.

The Carrier does not be held responsible for any missing/incorrect IDR Number. The responsibility remains with the Merchant/Importer. Any fines or penalties levied against the Carrier are for the account of the Merchant/Importer.
Shipper Company agency export charges - as per the shipping line's export tariff (copy available on request) payable at Port of Export

Ocean Freight Payable at	Place and Date of Issue
Birmingham	BIRMINGHAM 10/02/99
Number of Original Bills of Lading	
3 (Three)	

* Applicable only when document used as Combined Transport B/L. Place of delivery always to be an address if Notify address not applicable.

O.T. AFRICA LINE LTD. (Carrier)

For the Carrier

Reverse of Bill of Lading

CONDITIONS

to any other party. Since the shippers are the party to whom the carriers address the bill of lading in its capacity as a receipt for the goods, it is their endorsement which must appear first on an "order" bill of lading to constitute it as a negotiable instrument.

Consignee

As stated above, the word "order" must be inserted here to confer negotiability on the bill of lading. If the name of an actual consignee is substituted, the document (known as a "straight" bill of lading) is no longer negotiable, nor is it a document of title, since the carrier will deliver the goods to the named party without production of the bill of lading. For practical purposes a straight bill of lading is little more than a sea waybill, which will be discussed in the following chapter.

Notify party

Although they will accept the word "order" as the consignee, the carriers still require the name and address of someone whom they can contact when the goods arrive at their destination, since goods remaining on the quay or at a container depot for undue time waste valuable space, which, of course, costs money. It is also worth noting that, *prima facie*, the notify party is considered to be the party responsible for the goods after they have been loaded on board the carrying vessel (see section on FOB/CFR contract terms, Chapter 2) and this can have embarrassing consequences for banks who have their own name inserted as notify party, having deluded themselves that this will give them extra security.

Name of carrying vessel

Often there is also provision for the name of a local vessel which carries the goods to a main port for shipment on the ocean vessel. In this instance, and in the case where the preamble to the bill of lading states "received for shipment" rather than "shipped" or "loaded" (see below), the name of the ocean vessel can only be taken as an indication of intention, unless there is a separate signed and dated endorsement on the document stating that goods have been loaded on that vessel.

Port of loading; port of destination

Note that the carriers reserve the right to vary the destination of the goods if they see fit ("... or as near thereto as she may safely come"). This right is one which is frequently exercised in time of war, or where strikes or port congestion make a call at the intended port of destination an uneconomical or unsafe proposition.

Marks and numbers

Packages usually have stencilled on them in large characters an abbreviated form of the consignee's name to assist in identification at the port of destination. The name of the port of destination and port of transhipment, if applicable, is similarly stencilled so that cargo for discharge at a particular port is readily identifiable in the ship's hold. Finally, each package within a consignment is given an individual number for identification purposes. When goods are received at the docks for loading, marks and numbers are copied from the packages themselves on to a mate's receipt or similar document, and it is from this that the details inserted on the bill of lading are derived. The bill of lading is thus the definitive document and it is important that all other documents agree with it in respect of marks and numbers. With containerised freight the bill of lading will show the Container Unit Reference Number.

Number and type of packages

If the carriers notice that either the goods or the packages are defective or damaged in any way, they will protect themselves by clausing the bill of lading appropriately, making it a claused or "dirty" bill of lading. This obviously makes it unattractive to any subsequent holder and may also affect the insurance cover. Many disputes have arisen in the past over what constitutes a dirty bill of lading and the problem has been addressed by the ICC in Incoterms, and in *Uniform Customs and Practice for Documentary Credits* (see Chapter 12 Article 32). They stress that to be considered as not clean, a bill of lading must specifically refer to an observed defect in the goods or packing. Clauses which simply describe the packing, such as "second-hand drums", clauses which reserve the carriers' rights where specific types of packing are used (cartons are a frequent cause of the use of this clause) and clauses whereby the carriers disclaim responsibility for weight, quality, number of pieces, etc ("shipper's load and count") do not turn a clean bill of lading into a dirty one. To this list should be added the various clauses which carriers often use which relate to particular trade routes or ports; these seldom affect the cleanness of the bill in any way.

There are some clauses, however, which must be regarded as transforming the bill of lading into a dirty one. Where such clauses are to be expected from the particular trade, such as "surface rust" if the goods are unprotected steel girders, then sellers and buyers are well advised to agree between them at the contract stage that such clauses are acceptable and to incorporate a provision to this effect in any letter of credit which may be involved.

A relatively common practice among shipowners has been the provision of a clean bill of lading where it would otherwise have been claused, in exchange for the provision of an indemnity stating that the shippers will reimburse the carriers in respect of any claims which may be made against them for goods delivered in a damaged condition. This practice is potentially damaging to the interests of the buyers and of any intermediate endorsee of the bill, and is considered by many to be illegal, since the bill of lading usually contains a statement that the goods have been received in "apparent good order and condition". Since this could involve the carriers and the shippers in being sued jointly or individually for misrepresentation, it is difficult to see who benefits from the procedure in the long term, and it should be discouraged as much as possible. Certainly no bank should ever agree to add its counter-signature to such an indemnity, as has sometimes happened, since it could be the agent of the buyer and may well also be an intermediate holder of the bill.

Description of goods

This need not be detailed, provided that it is consistent with the description given in the commercial invoice and letter of credit, if applicable, and also provided that the regulations of the importing country do not call for a full description to appear on the bill. Upon the description given, the carriers will base the rate of freight which they apply to the consignment and it will usually include the gross and nett weights and cubic measurements of the packages. This information is required by the carriers both for calculation of freight and for safe stowage of the goods in the ship.

Freight

The money payable to the carrier for transportation of the goods — freight — is payable even if the ship and goods fail to arrive at the destination. The bill of lading will state whether it has been paid (*prima facie* evidence of CFR, CIF, DDP, etc contract terms) or is to be paid at destination, either by those words or "freight forward", "freight collect", etc (contract terms ExWorks, FAS, FOB, FCA). Many countries insist that full freight details appear on the bill of lading.

Number of original bills of lading

Bills of lading are usually issued in a set of two or more "originals" plus any number of copy or non-negotiable bills of lading for record purposes. Historically, this was to cater for the uncertainty of international mails when all such material was sent by sailing ships, which were far more susceptible to delay or even total loss than are more modern forms of transport. One original would be (and often still is) dispatched to the consignee and the second similarly mailed two or three days later to ensure that it would be transported on a different conveyance. The originals are equal in all respects and the goods will be delivered against production of any one of them. It is important, therefore, to account for the whereabouts of all of the original bills of lading in the set if title to the goods is to be retained. The Bill of Lading will state how many originals have been issued, eg Originals 3 (three), so that the banks will have the security of knowing that a full set is in their possession on presentation.

Signature of the master or agent

Most carriers have appointed agents for various purposes, including the signing of bills of lading, in every port at which their vessels call. Each of these agents will probably have a number of persons who are authorised to sign. Normally the signature, or rather, the capacity in which it is given is only important when a dispute exists as to whether a particular document is a carrier's bill of lading in the traditional sense, or a house bill of lading issued by a forwarding agent. This matter is discussed further in Chapter 4.

Date

The date of a "shipped" bill of lading is taken to be the date of shipment of the goods. It should be remembered that carriers are frequently very accommodating in the matter of dating bills of lading where their customer, the shipper, is contractually obliged to ship the goods by a certain date. Banks, however, are often in a position to check on the apparent authenticity of the date given and, if it is obviously a misrepresentation, may well reject documents if presented under a letter of credit, since, as we have seen, they are acting as agents for the buyers and must do all they can to protect that party's interests.

"Shipped"/"received"

Many bills of lading bear the word "shipped" printed on them, and this may be taken as evidence that the goods are actually on board the named vessel. Where the bill of lading merely states that goods have been received for shipment it can be converted into a "shipped" bill by the insertion of an appropriate clause by the carrier. This cause should confirm the name of the ship and include the place and date of shipment, although in practice ship and place of loading are often omitted, the assumption being that confirmation of shipment is as described elsewhere on the bill of lading.

Terms in common use to describe bills of lading

Charter party bill of lading

When a ship has been hired to perform a specific task or voyage, the document forming the contract between the hirer and the owner is called the *charter party*. There are two distinct types of charter, the *time charter* and the *voyage charter*. Time charters usually cause little or no problem, since they are frequently the result of fleet owners supplementing the tonnage available to them in order to cover short-term deficiencies due to such causes as repairs and maintenance. Voyage charters, however, are, as the name suggests, entered into with the intention of covering one or a limited number of voyages only, and bills of lading issued while they are in force are subject to their terms. They are not, therefore, evidence of the full conditions of the contract of carriage, since the charter party may perhaps provide for deviation from the voyage under certain circumstances, a possibility which is undesirable from the point of view of holders of bills of lading who are waiting to receive their goods.

Example of Face of Charter Bill of Lading

CODE NAME: "CONGENBILL" . EDITION 1978

Page 2

Shipper

ULSTER MEAT EXPORT CO. LTD.
Antrim Road
BELFAST

BILL OF LADING
TO BE USED WITH CHARTER-PARTIES

B/L No. A1.

Reference No.

ORIGINAL

Consignee
To the order of
ALEXANDRIA COMMERCIAL AND
MARITIME BANK

Notify address
HASSAN HASSAN
Trading Partnership,
P.O. Box XL239
CAIRO

Vessel 'PACIFIC MARCHIONESS' **Port of loading** DUN LAOGHAIRE
Port of discharge
ALEXANDRIA / Egypt

Shipper's description of goods

3765 cartons of fresh frozen
bnoless (boneless) beef
forequarters

Gross Wt.

103,681 Kgs.

Gross weight

Nett Wt.

99,784 Kgs.

Clean on Board
L/C no.: 86159
Carrying temperature not warmer than -20 degrees C
Freight Prepaid

(of which XXXXXX on deck at Shipper's risk; the Carrier not being responsible for loss or damage howsoever arising)

Freight payable as per
CHARTER-PARTY dated 4th July, 1986.

FREIGHT ADVANCE.
Received on account of freight:

– nil –

Time used for loading .... days .... hours.

S H I P P E D at the Port of Loading in apparent good order and condition on board the Vessel for carriage to the Port of Discharge or so near thereto as she may safely get the goods specified above.

Weight, measure, quality, quantity, condition, contents and value unknown.

IN WITNESS whereof the Master or Agent of the said Vessel has signed the number of Bills of Lading indicated below all of this tenor and date, any one of which being accomplished the others shall be void.

FOR CONDITIONS OF CARRIAGE SEE OVERLEAF

Freight payable at
FREIGHT PREPAID

Place and date of issue
DUN LAOGHAIRE, 7th July, 1986.

Number of original Bs/L

3 (three)

Signature

Printed and Sold by S. STRAKER & SONS LTD.
23A Lime Street, London, E.C.3
By Authority of the Baltic & International Maritime Conference
Copenhagen

Reverse of Charter Party Bill of Lading

BILL OF LADING

TO BE USED WITH CHARTER-PARTIES
CODE NAME: "CONGENBILL"
EDITION 1978
ADOPTED BY
THE BALTIC AND INTERNATIONAL
MARITIME CONFERENCE (BIMCO)

Conditions of Carriage.

(1) All terms and conditions, liberties and exceptions of the Charter Party, dated as overleaf, are herewith incorporated. The Carrier shall in no case be responsible for loss of or damage to cargo arisen prior to loading and after discharging.

(2) General Paramount Clause.
The Hague Rules contained in the International Convention for the Unification of certain rules relating to Bills of Lading, dated Brussels the 25th August 1924 as enacted in the country of shipment shall apply to this contract. When no such enactment is in force in the country of shipment, the corresponding legislation of the country of destination shall apply, but in respect of shipments to which no such enactments are compulsorily applicable, the terms of the said Convention shall apply.

Trades where Hague-Visby Rules apply
In trades where the International Brussels Convention 1924 as amended by the Protocol signed at Brussels on February 23rd 1968 – the Hague-Visby Rules - apply compulsorily, the provisions of the respective legislation shall be considered incorporated in this Bill of Lading. The Carrier takes all reservations possible under such applicable legislation, relating to the period before loading and after discharging and while the goods are in the charge of another Carrier, and to deck cargo and live animals.

(3) General Average.
General Average shall be adjusted, stated and settled according to York-Antwerp Rules 1974, in London unless another place is agreed in the Charter.

Cargo's contribution to General Average shall be paid to the Carrier even when such average is the result of a fault, neglect or error of the Master, Pilot or Crew. The Charterers, Shippers and Consignees expressly renounce the Netherlands Commercial Code, Art. 700, and the Belgian Commercial Code, Part II, Art. 148.

(4) New Jason Clause.
In the event of accident, danger, damage or disaster before or after the commencement of the voyage, resulting from any cause whatsoever, whether due to negligence or not, for which, or for the consequence of which, the Carrier is not responsible, by statute, contract or otherwise, the goods, Shippers, Consignees or owners of the goods shall contribute with the Carrier in general average to the payment of any sacrifices, losses or expenses of a general average nature that may be made or incurred and shall pay salvage and special charges incurred in respect of the goods.

If a salving ship is owned or operated by the Carrier, salvage shall be paid for as fully as if the said salving ship or ships belonged to strangers. Such deposit as the Carrier or his agents may deem sufficient to cover the estimated contribution of the goods and any salvage and special charges thereon shall, if required, be made by the goods, Shippers, Consignees or owners of the goods to the Carrier before delivery.

(5) Both-to-Blame Collision Clause.
If the Vessel comes into collision with another ship as a result of the negligence of the other ship and any act, neglect or default of the Master, Mariner, Pilot or the servants of the Carrier in the navigation or in the management of the Vessel, the owners of the cargo carried hereunder will indemnify the Carrier against all loss or liability to the other or non-carrying ship or her Owners in so far as such loss or liability represents loss of, or damage to, or any claim whatsoever of the owners of said cargo, paid or payable by the other or non-carrying ship or her Owners to the owners of said cargo and set-off, recouped or recovered by the other or non-carrying ship or her Owners as part of their claim against the carrying Vessel or Carrier. The foregoing provisions shall also apply where the Owners, operators or those in charge of any ship or ships or objects other than, or in addition to, the colliding ships or objects are at fault in respect of a collision or contact.

For particulars of cargo, freight,
destination, etc., see overleaf.

Incoterms require the sellers, where they are obliged to provide a transport document under the contract and that transport document is a charter party bill of lading, to provide additionally a copy of the charter party itself. Whilst this may or may not satisfy holders of the bill of lading, it is unlikely to change the attitude of banks, who will be unwilling to take on the additional responsibility of examining the small print of the charter party to ascertain the degree of risk which it imports to the transaction. Where letters of credit are concerned, this attitude is spelled out in Article 25 of *Uniform Customs and Practice for Documentary Credits (UCP)*.

Combined transport bill of lading

This is increasingly used nowadays when many goods are shipped in containers. Container depots have been established in many areas remote from the docks and the carrier takes the goods in charge and delivers them at these depots. The bill of lading therefore covers one or more trips by rail, road or inland waterway besides the main ocean voyage. A combined transport bill of lading will normally state merely that the goods have been received for shipment rather than shipped and the name of any vessel given on them can only be taken as evidence of intent rather than fact. Where it is essential under the contract to provide a "shipped" bill of lading, a combined transport bill can be satisfactorily converted by the addition by the carriers' agent of a clause to the effect that goods have actually been shipped. This clause should confirm the name of the carrying vessel, and be separately dated by the carriers in addition to the date which is already on the bill in its capacity as a receipt for the goods. To avoid the difficulties and inconvenience which often attend the securing of the addition of this clause, it is common sense that where such mode of transport is intended, buyers and sellers at the contract stage agree that the terms of the contract shall be one of the types specifically intended to cover multi-modal transport, ie FCA, CPT, CIP, DDU or DDP. If this is done, and the method of settlement is to be a letter of credit, buyers should be careful that they do not spoil the whole thing by allowing their bank to then issue a credit calling for "shipped" bills of lading. Too many bank application forms for credits bear this requirement as a preprinted clause: this does not mean that it cannot be deleted.

House bill of lading

See the section in Chapter 4 on "Other transport documents".

Liner bill of lading

A liner vessel is one which sails regularly between specified ports, departing and arriving on published dates regardless of whether or not she is filled with cargo. Such a service is obviously preferable in most circumstances to that offered by a "tramp" vessel which can await a full cargo before sailing and can deviate from the voyage if sufficient inducement is offered. For some cargoes, however, particularly bulk ones or those requiring specialised accommodation, or where the contemplated voyage is not covered by a liner service, the only practical form of transport is a tramp ship, often operating under a voyage charter, and the already-mentioned problems with bills of lading issued under such circumstances should be remembered.

There was a tendency in the late 1980s and early 1990s for liner owners grouping together in "conferences" associations, which allocated sailing schedules with guaranteed frequency of sailing from and to nominated ports at rates agreed and set by all members of the conference (according to the type of freight being carried). Conference lines still exist, but the practice of offering inducements to shippers to use only conference line vessels is not as common as in previous years. Some shipping lines have left the "conference" to allow them flexibility in rating freight charges. Be cautious if the banks ask for a "conference bill of lading" this is not synonymous with a "liner bill of lading", since not all liner operators are conference members.

Ocean bills of lading

These are issued by the carrier responsible for the main ocean voyage. Where goods are carried to the ocean vessel in feeder vessels, bills of lading issued by the owners of these vessels, even if they purport to be "through" bills of lading (see below), are of no value since they will not be accepted in exchange for the goods at the port of destination, nor indeed can they be evidence that the goods are even on board the ocean vessel. The only exception to this rule is where the owner of the local vessel is an accredited agent of the owner of the ocean vessel, but even then the bill of lading must be the ocean carriers' standard form and, to be acceptable as a "shipped" bill of lading, must bear the same additional clause as a combined transport bill relating to actual shipment on the ocean vessel.

Completed "Received" Bill of Lading

Hapag-Lloyd Aktiengesellschaft	Bill of Lading	Page 2
Hamburg/Bremen	FOR MULTIMODAL TRANSPORT OR PORT TO PORT SHIPMENT	

SHIPPER:	VOYAGE-NO. W88	B/L-NO. 12345
PRINCETON PIPES LTD. MALDON, ESSEX.	SHIPPER'S REFERENCE	

CONSIGNEE:
ORDER

Hapag-Lloyd
Europe – North America Services

NOTIFY ADDRESS (carrier not responsible for failure to notify; see clause 22 hereof):	Place of receipt (Applicable only when document used for MULTIMODAL transport; see clause 2c):
EASTERN TUBE SUPPLIES LTD., P.O.BOX 890045 BUFFALO,N.Y.	RAINHAM FREIGHT TERMINAL

*Local vessel:	*From:	Place of delivery (Applicable only when document used for MULTIMODAL transport; see clause 2c):
OCEAN VESSEL: NURNBERG EXPRESS	PORT OF LOADING: LIVERPOOL	BROOKLYN CONTAINER YARD NEW YORK
PORT OF DISCHARGE: NEW YORK	*For transhipment to:	

Container Nos. Seal Nos. Marks and Nos.	Number and kind of packages, description of goods	Gross weight (kg)	Measurement (cbm)
CNTR.NO.0987654321 SEAL NO. 1234 ETSL NEW YORK 1/34	34 CARTONS PLASTIC TUBING	185	8.5
	FREIGHT PREPAID		

COPY NOT NEGOTIABLE

ABOVE PARTICULARS AS DECLARED BY SHIPPER

Total No. of containers/packages: 1 CONTAINER	Shipper's declared value (see clause 3 hereof) $

Movement:

Received by the carrier from the shipper in apparent good order and condition (unless otherwise noted herein) the total number or quantity of containers or other packages or units indicated (see Box opposite), stated by the shipper to comprise the goods specified above, for carriage subject to all the terms hereof (INCLUDING THE TERMS ON PAGE 1 HEREOF AND THE TERMS OF THE CARRIER'S APPLICABLE TARIFF) from the place of receipt or the port of loading, whichever is applicable, to the port of discharge or the place of delivery, whichever is applicable. In accepting this Bill of Lading the merchant expressly accepts and agrees to all its terms, conditions and exceptions whether printed, stamped or written, or otherwise incorporated, notwithstanding the non-signing of this Bill of Lading by the merchant.

IN WITNESS WHEREOF the number of original Bills of Lading stated below all of this tenor and date has been signed, one of which being accomplished the others to stand void.

Freight and Charges	Prepaid	Collect
Ocean freight		
Multimodal Through Freight		
Origin Landfreight		
Destination Landfreight		
Origin Terminal Charges		
Destination Terminal Charges		

Freight payable at LONDON	Place and date of issue LONDON 15TH.MAY 1990
Number of original Bs/L: TWO (2)	For the carrier:

Appropriate columns to be marked with "X"

* Applicable only when document used for transhipment (see clause 2 b)

15/0002 51 Printed in the Federal Republic of Germany

Short form bills of lading

These do not contain the full terms of the contract of carriage. Provided that they are not defective in any way, however, they remain documents of title and are almost universally accepted as good tender under contracts and letters of credit. A glance at the mass of densely-packed small print on the reverse of a standard bill of lading will make the reason for the genesis of the short-form alternative obvious to anyone familiar with printing and typesetting costs; the principle of the short-form bill is similar to the clause on the back of a bus ticket (another transport document) which says that the full terms of carriage will be made available at the request of the holder, a request which is, of course, seldom necessary.

Stale bills of lading

A bill of lading is usually considered to be stale when it is received at the port of destination later than the arrival date of the goods, although local regulations may require its presentation even earlier. Goods which are uncollected beyond a specified period after discharge incur charges called *demurrage* which must be paid by the holder of the bill of lading before they will be released. The level of such charges varies considerably, usually in line with the degree of congestion normally experienced in that particular port. Where they are high, even a short demurrage period may make the total cost of the goods an unattractive proposition to the buyers, causing them to seek avoidance of the contract. It should be noted that the staleness or otherwise of a bill of lading is irrelevant where it is presented under a letter of credit, for reasons which will be discussed in Chapter 13.

Through bills of lading

These cover voyages where goods must be transhipped from the ocean vessel to another vessel in order to reach their destination. The ocean carrier takes responsibility for the transhipment and for the selection of the oncarrying vessel. The term is also sometimes used to describe combined transport bills of lading.

Summary

From the above, the reasoning may be seen behind the common stipulation, both in contracts and in letters of credit, for presentation of a full set of clean, shipped, ocean bills of lading made out to order and endorsed in blank:

(a) a full set, because if one of the originals is in the possession of someone else, they may get possession of the goods first

(b) clean, because an unclean bill bears a clause which states that the carriers have observed the goods or the packaging to be defective in some way on delivery to them

(c) shipped, because it is often important to the buyers to know that their goods are on board a specific vessel and will, all being well, arrive at a predeterminable time

(d) ocean, because that is the bill of lading which must be presented at the port of destination in order to secure possession of the goods

(e) to order, because that gives the bill of lading its quality of negotiability

(f) endorsed in blank, because that enables the holder of the bill to obtain the goods when they arrive at their destination.

A number of countries impose special regulations relating to bills of lading covering goods which they are importing. Often these relate to the minimum amount of information which must appear on the bills, but sometimes the requirements are more unusual. Also, a number of countries require all bills of lading relating to their imports to be presented to their embassy or consulate in the exporting country for legalisation. As has been mentioned before, Croner's *Reference Book for Exporters* is invaluable in determining what, if any, special regulations apply to any particular country.

To sum up this chapter, we will briefly trace the life history of a bill of lading which conforms with the above description. Goods, space for which will previously have been booked by the shippers, or their freight forwarder, on that vessel, are presented at the advertised place for receiving cargo. In exchange, the carriers will issue a dock receipt, wharfinger's receipt, or the like, a copy of which will be retained by the carriers. It will state the number of packages received and their visible marks and numbers, and will comment on their apparent condition. The freight forwarder (occasionally the shipper) will then prepare the bill of lading and submit it to the carriers for signature after the goods have been loaded on the carrying vessel.

The carriers will carefully check the details declared on the bill of lading against those on their copy of the dock receipt and will add to or amend the bill as appropriate, at the same time adding any clauses applicable to the particular type of goods or packing (not necessarily derogatory though almost invariably protective of the carriers' interests). They will then sign the original copies (not a contradiction in this context), date the bill, usually with the sailing date of the ship, and release it to the forwarder or shippers against payment of the freight due, unless freight is to be paid at destination. The bill will then be endorsed either in blank by simple signature or specifically in favour of a named party (usually either a bank or the consignees) by the shippers and sent, possibly through the banking system if a collection or a letter of credit is the agreed method of settlement, to the buyers, who on arrival of the ship will present it to the carriers and receive the goods in exchange.

CHAPTER 4

Other transport documents

The house bill of lading

When the first edition of this book was published the house bill of lading was perhaps one of the most controversial documents involved in international trade. This was because it was, with certain exceptions, not acceptable under a letter of credit which called for presentation of a marine bill of lading. This situation was radically changed with the introduction of the 1993 Revision of *Uniform Customs and Practice for Documentary Credits* (UCP500). Basically, the position taken by UCP500 (Article 30) is that, to be acceptable where the credit makes no specific provision for its presentation, a house bill of lading must be signed by the issuer either as carrier or as agent for a named carrier. This is discussed fully in Chapter 12, but the following discussion of house bills should be read with this in mind. Much of what follows now only relates to the drawbacks of a house bill of lading as might be perceived by a bank which has been requested to provide bill finance against it, or where it is presented under a credit but fails to fulfil either of the two conditions mentioned above as being laid down by UCP500.

House bills of lading are generally understood to be those issued by forwarding agents and become necessary when a forwarder is arranging shipment of goods for more than one client on the same vessel and between the same ports of loading and discharge, although for convenience and consistency forwarders often cover all shipments in this way.

Example of a House Bill of Lading

BILL OF LADING

Shipper	B/Lading number
ABLE COFFEE MACHINERY LTD	00000000
	Shipper's Reference
	11111111

Consignee (If 'Order', state Notify Party and Address)
TO ORDER

Notify Party (No claim shall attach for failure to notify)
AFRICAN COFFEE EXPORTERS LTD
BLANTYRE, MALAWI

AFL

Afri-Freight Ltd
Ketts House
30-32 Staines Road
Hounslow
Middlesex
TW3 3JS
United Kingdom
Tel: 01-572 5371
Telex: 264237 AFLLDN
Fax: 01-570 8228

Place of Receipt	Port of Loading
	FELIXSTOWE
First Vessel	Port of transhipment
CHIARA	
Second Vessel	Port of Loading

LUSAKA Tel. 215012 Tlx. 40720, NAIROBI Tel. 23071/22000 Tlx. 22823
KAMPALA Tel. 57328 Tlx. 61324, KITWE Tel. 214981 Tlx. 53250
DAR ES SALAAM Tel. 29403 Tlx. 41625

Port of Discharge	Final Destination	Freight Payable at	Number of original Bs/L
DURBAN	BLANTYRE	LONDON	THREE

Marks and Numbers	Number and kind of packages: description of goods	Gross Weight	Measurement
A.C.E. BLANTYRE MALAWI VIA DURBAN NO.1	1 PALLET said to contain 10 CARTONS COFFEE MACHINERY	260KGS	0.910CBM

FREIGHT TO DURBAN, CHARGES AT DURBAN AND ON-CARRIAGE TO BLANTYRE PREPAID.

LETTER OF CREDIT NUMBER - said to be - 12345/6789

1 4 MAR
AFRI-FREIGHT LTD.

PARTICULARS OF GOODS ARE THOSE DECLARED BY SHIPPER

TO OBTAIN DELIVERY THIS BILL OF LADING, DULY ENDORSED, MUST BE DELIVERED TO —

AFRI - FREIGHT (M) LTD. BLANTYRE, MALAWI

Freight Details, Charges etc	
	RECEIVED by the Carrier the Goods as specified above in apparent good order and condition unless otherwise stated, to be transported to such place as agreed, authorised or permitted herein and subject to all the terms and conditions appearing on the front and reverse of this Bill of Lading to which the Merchant agrees by accepting this Bill of Lading, any local privileges and customs notwithstanding.
	The particulars given above as stated by the shipper and the weight, measure, quantity, condition, contents and value of the Goods are unknown to the Carrier.
	In WITNESS whereof one (1) original Bill of Lading has been signed if not otherwise stated above, the same being accomplished the other(s), if any, to be void. If required by the Carrier one (1) original Bill of Lading must be surrendered duly endorsed in exchange for the Goods or delivery order.
	Place and date of issue _____ LONDON 1 4 MAR
	Signed on behalf of the Carrier: Afri-Freight Ltd
	AFRI-FREIGHT LTD.
	by _____

40

When forwarders have a number of such consignments they consolidate them, which means that, so far as the carriers are concerned, all goods are declared on one bill of lading which shows the forwarders as shippers. To satisfy their individual clients, they then issue their own "bills of lading" which have similar functions to the carriers' bills but with subtle differences.

They act as receipts for the goods addressed to the shippers by the forwarders instead of by the carriers (the word "carrier" is used in its literal rather than its legal sense here, but the legal implications will be discussed later). They may evidence the conditions of the contract between the shippers and the forwarders but not the conditions on which the true carrier is handling the goods. And they act as a means of transferring to a third party the right to take delivery of the goods from the forwarder on arrival at their destination. However, they convey no rights against the true carriers, who, of course, will require presentation of a signed original of their own bill of lading before releasing the goods. Legally, the owner of the goods is the party named as shipper on the marine bill of lading, or the consignee or endorsee of that bill.

The effect of these differences is to reduce the attractiveness of these documents to banks who may be in part relying on their rights against the goods when either providing export finance against collections, issuing letters of credit, or financing imports by trust receipt facilities and the like. Although there are many notable exceptions, generally speaking, forwarding agents are less likely to be well known names than ship-owning companies, and banks may feel that they are relying on the goodwill of an organisation concerning which they have no knowledge and no means of acquiring information at short notice. Their natural tendency in these circumstances is to exercise the caution for which they are renowned and reject the document. The fact is that under a letter of credit or bill of exchange procedure, it must be made absolutely clear in the letter of credit or bill of exchange whether a house bill of lading is acceptable.

Forwarding agents

With modern methods of transportation of goods, particularly containerisation and multi-modal transport, the use of forwarding agents has become increasingly common, since such entities are geared to extract the maximum benefit from these methods. At one time forwarders were merely agents who, for a fee, would take on the responsibility of making all the necessary arrangements for the dispatch of goods; they have now risen in the hierarchy of the transport world to the status of contractual carriers. This is quite possible under English law, where to be a common carrier, a company (or individual) merely has to agree to accept full liability for the goods from the point at which it takes delivery of them to the point at which they are delivered to the holder of the house bill of lading. Thus, whereas the traditional bill of lading was signed "for the master", it is now far more common to find it signed "for the carrier" or simply signed under the name of the issuer.

The problem remains, however, that there is, in many countries, very little statutory control over who can call themselves a forwarding agent. Many are, quite literally, one-person concerns, often established by people who have previously worked for larger forwarders or for shipping companies and who are using the expertise acquired during such employment to make their own way in business. The banks' historical concern about the value of house bills of lading was thus founded upon doubts regarding the status of their issuers.

FIATA

Much of the credit for the recent change in the attitude of banks to the house bill of lading must be given to the Zurich-based International Association of Freight Forwarders (FIATA — Federation Internationale des Associations de Transitaires et Assimiles). The members of FIATA are national forwarders' associations, which in turn are associations of individual companies. FIATA has developed a standard forwarding agents' bill of lading (FBL) using standard conditions of carriage, which affiliates of its member organisations are entitled to use upon the granting of a licence. Before such a licence is issued, the National Association must have satisfied itself upon various relevant subjects, such as capital adequacy of the licensee, the standard of expertise of its management and employees, and, most importantly the level of indemnity insurance cover carried by the company in relation to its average turnover.

The FBL, as used by FIATA licensees, is a very distinctive document, currently a deep blue in colour and bearing the globe and ribbons FIATA logo prominently in its centre. Its format was arrived at in full consultation with the International Chamber of Commerce, and the ICC symbol, accompanied by that of the national association concerned, is prominent towards the top of the document. The licence number of the issuer is also given. The issuer accepts carrier's liability under

Face of Completed FIATA Transport Bill of Lading (FBL)

		Customs Reference/Status	8. Lading number	**GB**
Consignor ABLE COFFEE MACHINERY LTD			00000000	
		Shipper's Reference	11111111	
	FBL	F/Agent's Ref		

Consignee (If Order state Notify Party and Address) TO ORDER	NEGOTIABLE FIATA COMBINED TRANSPORT BILL OF LADING issued subject to ICC Uniform Rules for a Combined Transport Document (ICC publication 298) **ICC**

Notify Party AFRICAN COFFEE EXPORTERS LTD BLANTYRE, MALAWI	**AFL** FIATA Licence No. 1010	AfriFreight Ltd Ketts House 30-32 Staines Road, Hounslow Middlesex TW3 3JS United Kingdom Tel: 01-572 5371 Telex: 264237 AFLLDN Fax: 01-570 8228

Pre-Carriage By	Place of Receipt by Pre Carrier	
Vessel/Trailer CHIARA	Port of Loading FELIXSTOWE	
Port of Discharge DURBAN	Place of Delivery by On-Carrier BLANTYRE	LUSAKA Tel 215012 Tlx. 40720. NAIROBI Tel. 23071/22000 Tlx. 22823 KAMPALA Tel. 57328 Tlx: 61324, KITWE Tel. 214961 Tlx: 53250 DAR ES SALAAM Tel. 29403 Tlx. 41625

Marks and Numbers	Number and Kind of Packages	Description of Goods	Gross Weight	Measurement
A.C.E. BLANTYRE MALAWI VIA DURBAN NO.1	1 PALLET said to contain 10 CARTONS COFFEE MACHINERY		260KGS	0.910CBM

FREIGHT TO DURBAN, CHARGES AT DURBAN AND ON-CARRIAGE TO BLANTYRE PREPAID.

LETTER OF CREDIT NUMBER - saID TO BE - 12345/6789

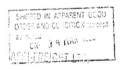

SHIPPED IN APPARENT GOOD ORDER AND CONDITION except as noted ON 4 MAR ... AFRIFREIGHT LTD

according to the declaration of the consignor

The goods and instructions are accepted and dealt with subject to the Standard Conditions printed overleaf

Take in charge in apparent good order and condition, unless otherwise noted herein, at the place of receipt for transport and delivery as mentioned above

One of these Combined Transport Bills of Lading must be surrendered duly endorsed in exchange for the goods. In Witness whereof the original Combined Transport Bills of Lading all of this tenor and date have been signed in the number stated below, one of which being accomplished the other(s) to be void

Freight Amount	Freight Payable at LONDON	Place and date of issue LONDON
Cargo Insurance through the undersigned ☐ not covered ☐ covered	Number of Original FBL's THREE	Stamp and signature
For delivery of goods please apply to AFRI - FREIGHT (M) LTD, BLANTYRE, MALAWI		

OTHER TRANSPORT DOCUMENTS

Reverse of FIATA FBL

Standard Conditions (1984) governing FIATA COMBINED TRANSPORT BILLS OF LADING

Definitions -Merchant- means and includes the Shipper, the Consignor, the Consignee, the Holder of this Bill of Lading, the Receiver and the Owner of the Goods. -The Freight Forwarder- means the issuer of this Bill of Lading as named on the face of it.

The headings set forth below are for easy reference only.

CONDITIONS

1 Applicability
Notwithstanding the heading -Combined Transport Bill of Lading- the provisions set out and referred to in this document shall also apply if the transport as described on the face of the Bill of Lading is performed by one mode of transport only.

2 Issuance of the -Combined Transport Bill of Lading-
2.1 By the issuance of this -Combined Transport Bill of Lading- the Freight Forwarder
a) undertakes to perform and/or in his own name to procure the performance of the entire transport, from the place at which the goods are taken in charge to the place designated for delivery in this Bill of Lading.
b) assumes liability as set out in these Conditions.
2.2 For the purposes and subject to the provisions of this Bill of Lading, the Freight Forwarder shall be responsible for the acts and omissions of any person of whose services he makes use for the performance of the contract evidenced by this Bill of Lading.

3 Negotiability and title to the goods
3.1 By accepting this Bill of Lading the Merchant and his transferees agree with the Freight Forwarder that, unless it is marked -non-negotiable- it shall constitute title to the goods and the holder, by endorsement of this Bill of Lading, shall be entitled to receive or to transfer the goods herein mentioned.
3.2 This Bill of Lading shall be prima facie evidence of the taking in charge by the Freight Forwarder of the goods as herein described. However proof to the contrary shall not be admissible when this Bill of Lading has been negotiated or transferred for valuable consideration to a third party acting in good faith.

4 Dangerous Goods and Indemnity
4.1 The Merchant shall comply with rules which are mandatory according to the national law or by reason of international Convention, relating to the carriage of goods of a dangerous nature and shall in any case inform the Freight Forwarder in writing of the exact nature of the danger before goods of a dangerous nature are taken in charge by the Freight Forwarder and indicate to him, if need be, the precautions to be taken.
4.2 If the Merchant fails to provide such information and the Freight Forwarder is unaware of the dangerous nature of the goods and the necessary precautions to be taken and if, at any time they are deemed to be a hazard to life or property, they may at any place be unloaded, destroyed or rendered harmless, as circumstances may require, without compensation and the Merchant shall be liable for all loss, damage, delay or expenses arising out of their being taken in charge, or their carriage, or of any service incidental thereto.
The burden of proving the Freight Forwarder knew the exact nature of the danger constituted by the carriage of the said goods shall rest upon the person entitled to the goods.
4.3 If any goods shipped with the knowledge of the Freight Forwarder as to their dangerous nature shall become a danger to the vehicle or cargo, they may in like manner be unloaded or landed at any place or destroyed or rendered innocuous by the Freight Forwarder without liability on the part of the Freight Forwarder except to General Average, if any.

5 Description of Goods and Merchant's Packing
5.1 The Consignor shall be deemed to have guaranteed to the Freight Forwarder the accuracy, at the time the goods were taken in charge by the Freight Forwarder, of the description of the goods, marks, number, quantity, weight and/or volume as furnished by him, and the Consignor shall indemnify the Freight Forwarder against all loss, damage and expenses arising or resulting from inaccuracies in or inadequacy of such particulars. The right of the Freight Forwarder to such indemnity shall in no way limit his responsibility and liability under this Bill of Lading to any person other than the Consignor.
5.2 Without prejudice to Clause 6 (A) (2) (c), the Merchant shall be liable for any loss, damage or injury caused by faulty or insufficient packing of goods or by faulty loading or packing within containers and trailers and on flats when such loading or packing has been performed by the Merchant or on behalf of the Merchant by a person other than the Freight Forwarder or by the defect or unsuitability of the containers, trailers or flats, when supplied by the Merchant and shall indemnify the Freight Forwarder against any additional expenses so caused.

6 Extent of Liability
A 1) The Freight Forwarder shall be liable for loss of or damage to the goods occurring between the time when he takes the goods into his charge and the time of delivery.
2) The Freight Forwarder shall however be relieved of liability for any loss or damage if such loss or damage was caused by:
a) an act or omission of the Merchant or person other than the Freight Forwarder acting on behalf of the Merchant or from whom the Freight Forwarder took the goods in charge.
b) insufficiency or defective condition of the packaging or marks and/or numbers.
c) handling, loading, stowage or unloading of the goods by the Merchant or any person acting on behalf of the Merchant.
d) inherent vice of the goods.
e) strike, lockout, stoppage or restraint of labour, the consequences of which the Freight Forwarder could not avoid by the exercise of reasonable diligence.
f) any cause or event which the Freight Forwarder could nor avoid and the consequences whereof he could not prevent by the exercise of reasonable diligence.
g) a nuclear incident if the operator of a nuclear installation or a person acting for him is liable for this damage under an applicable Convention or national law governing liability in respect of nuclear energy.
3) The burden of proving that the loss or damage was due to one or more of the above causes or events shall rest upon the Freight Forwarder.
When the Freight Forwarder establishes that, in the circumstances of the case, the loss or damage could be attributed to one or more of the causes or events specified in b) to d) above, it shall be presumed that it was so caused. The claimant shall however be entitled to prove that the loss or damage was not, in fact caused wholly or partly by one or more of these causes or events.
B When in accordance with clause 6 A 1 the Freight Forwarder is liable to pay compensation in respect of loss or damage to the goods and the stage of transport where the loss or damage occurred is known, the liability of the Freight Forwarder in respect of such loss or damage shall be determined by the provisions contained in any international Convention or national law, which provisions
(i) cannot be departed from by private contract, to the detriment of the claimant, and
(ii) would have applied if the Claimant had made a separate and direct contract with the Freight Forwarder in respect of the particular stage of transport where the loss or damage occurred and received as evidence thereof any particular document which must be issued in order to make such international convention or national law applicable.

7 Paramount Clause
The Hague Rules contained in the International Convention for the unification of certain rules relating to Bills of Lading, dated Brussels 25th August 1924, or in those countries where they are already in force the Hague-Visby Rules contained in the Protocol of Brussels dated February 23rd 1968, as enacted in the Country of Shipment, shall apply to all carriage of goods by sea and, where no mandatory international or national law applies, to the carriage of goods by inland waterways also, and such provisions shall apply to all goods -whether carried on deck or under deck.

8 Limitation Amount
8.1 When the Freight Forwarder is liable for compensation in respect of loss of or damage to the goods, such compensation shall be calculated by reference to the value of such goods at the place and time they are delivered to the Consignee in accordance with the contract or should have been so delivered.
8.2 The value of the goods shall be fixed according to the current commodity exchange price, or, if there be no such price, according to the current market price, or, if there be no commodity exchange price or current market price, by reference to the normal value of goods of the same kind and quality.
8.3 Compensation shall not, however, exceed 2 SDR (SDR = Special Drawing Right) units per kilo of gross weight of the goods lost or damaged, unless, with the consent of the Freight Forwarder, the Merchant has declared a higher value for the goods and such higher value has been stated in the CT Bill of Lading, in which case such higher value shall be the limit. However, the Freight Forwarder shall not, in any case, be liable for an amount greater than the actual loss to the person entitled to make the claim.

9 Delay, Consequential Loss, etc.
Arrival times are not guaranteed by the Freight Forwarder. If the Freight Forwarder is held liable in respect of delay consequential loss or damage other than loss of or damage to the goods, the liability of the Freight Forwarder shall be limited to double the freight for the transport covered by this Bill of Lading, or the value of the goods as determined in Clause 8 whichever is the less.

10 Defences
10.1 The defences and limits of liability provided for in these Conditions shall apply in any action against the Freight Forwarder for loss of or damage or delay to the goods whether the action be founded in contract or in tort.
10.2 The Freight Forwarder shall not be entitled to the benefit of the limitation of liability provided for in paragraph 3 of Clause 8 if it is proved that the loss or damage resulted from an act or omission of the Freight Forwarder done with intent to cause damage or recklessly and with knowledge that damage would probably result.

11 Liability of Servants and Sub-contractors
11.1 If an action for loss of or damage to the goods is brought against a person referred to in paragraph 2 of Clause 2, such person shall be entitled to avail himself of the defences and limits of liability which the Freight Forwarder is entitled to invoke under these Conditions.
11.2 However if it is proved that the loss or damage resulted from an act or omission of this person done with intent to cause damage or recklessly and with knowledge that damage would probably result, such person shall not be entitled to benefit of limitation of liability provided for in paragraph 3 of Clause 8.
11.3 Subject to the provisions of paragraph 2 of Clause 10 and paragraph 2 of this Clause, the aggregate of the amounts recoverable from the Freight Forwarder and the persons referred to in paragraph 2 of Clause 2 shall in no case exceed the limits provided for in these Conditions.

12 Method and Route of Transportation
The Freight Forwarder reserves to himself a reasonable liberty as to the means, route and procedure to be followed in the handling, storage and transportation of goods.

13 Delivery
If delivery of the goods or any part thereof is not taken by the Merchant at the time and place when and where the Freight Forwarder is entitled to call upon the Merchant to take delivery thereof, the Freight Forwarder shall be entitled to store the goods or the part thereof at the sole risk of the Merchant, where upon the liability of the Freight Forwarder in respect of the goods or that part thereof stored as aforesaid (as the case may be) shall wholly cease and the cost of such storage (if paid by or payable by the Freight Forwarder or any agent or sub-contractor of the Freight Forwarder) shall forthwith upon demand be paid by the Merchant to the Freight Forwarder.

14 Freight and Charges
14.1 Freight shall be paid in cash without discount and whether prepayable or payable at destination shall be considered as earned on receipt of the goods and not to be returned or relinquished in any event.
14.2 Freight and all other amounts mentioned in this Bill of Lading are to be paid in the currency named in the Bill of Lading or, at the Freight Forwarder's option in the currency of the country of dispatch or destination at the highest rate of exchange for bankers sight bills current for prepayable freight on the day of dispatch and for freight payable at destination on the day when the Merchant is notified of arrival of the goods there or on the date of withdrawal of the delivery order, whichever rate is the higher, or at the option of the Freight Forwarder on the date of the Bill of Lading.
14.3 All dues, taxes and charges or other expenses in connection with the goods shall be paid by the Merchant.
14.4 The Merchant shall reimburse the Freight Forwarder in proportion to the amount of freight for any costs for deviation or delay or any other increase of costs of whatever nature caused by war, warlike operations, epidemics, strikes, government directions or force majeure.
14.5 The Merchant warrants the correctness of the declaration of contents, insurance, weight, measurements or value of the goods but the Freight Forwarder reserves the right to have the contents inspected and the weight, measurements or value verified. If on such inspection it is found the declaration is not correct it is agreed that a sum equal either to five times the difference between the correct figure and the freight charged, or to double the correct freight less the freight charged whichever sum is the smaller, shall be payable as liquidated damage to the Freight Forwarder for his inspection costs and losses of freight on other goods notwithstanding any other sum having been stated on the Bill of Lading as freight payable.

15 Lien
The Freight Forwarder shall have a lien on the goods for any amount due under this Bill of Lading, including storage fees and for the cost of recovering same, and may enforce such lien in any reasonable manner which he may think fit.

16 General Average
The Merchant shall indemnify the Freight Forwarder in respect of any claims of a General Average nature which may be made on him and shall provide such security as may be required by the Freight Forwarder in this connection.

17 Notice
Unless notice of loss of or damage to the goods and the general nature of it be given in writing to the Freight Forwarder or the persons referred to in paragraph 2 of Clause 2, at the place of delivery before or at the time of the removal of the goods into the custody of the person entitled to delivery thereof under this Bill of Lading, or if the loss or damage be not apparent, within seven consecutive days thereafter, such removal shall be prima facie evidence of the delivery by the Freight Forwarder of the goods as described in this Bill of Lading.

18 Non delivery
Failure to effect delivery within 90 days after the expiry of a time limit agreed and expressed in a CT Bill of Lading or, where no time limit is agreed and so expressed, failure to effect delivery within 90 days after the time within which it would be reasonable to allow for diligent completion of the combined transport operation shall, in the absence of evidence to the contrary, give to the party entitled to receive delivery, the right to treat the goods as lost.

19 Time Bar
The Freight Forwarder shall be discharged of all liability under the rules of these Conditions, unless suit is brought within nine months after.
(i) the delivery of the goods, or
(ii) the date when the goods should have been delivered, or
(iii) the date when in accordance with Clause 18, failure to deliver the goods would, in the absence of evidence to the contrary, give to the party entitled to receive delivery, the right to treat the goods as lost.

20 Jurisdiction
Actions against the Freight Forwarder may only be instituted in the country where the Freight Forwarder has his principal place of business and shall be decided according to the law of such country.

44

internationally agreed rules for the performance of the contract of carriage for loss of or damage to the goods during such performance.

Even with full acceptance of the FIATA FBL, however, there still remains the large number of forwarding agents who do not use it, either through failure or inability to obtain a licence or because they consider that their own document should be acceptable to all concerned without further assurance from FIATA. The banks, understandably, are reluctant to maintain any sort of credit rating table to enable them to decide whether a particular forwarder's house bill should be acceptable or not. Since we are talking of international trade, such a list would have to be worldwide in its scope, and the problems of compiling it and of keeping it updated would be insuperable. The simplest solution, therefore, from the banks' point of view, is to treat all house bills of lading with caution.

Some forwarders have reacted to this attitude by designing their house bills of lading to resemble as closely as possible the traditional form of marine bill, complete with house flags and funnel symbols, in the hope that by making the document appear to be what is required it will be accepted without further query. Some have gone to the lengths of calling the service which they offer by a suitably nautical brand name followed by the word "Line", and it has even been known for forwarders to sign their house bills "For the Master", though this amounts to misrepresentation and could leave them open to legal action.

In many cases, the tell-tale sign of a house bill of lading is the nomination upon it of a clearing agent at the port of discharge to whom application must be made in order to obtain delivery of the goods. It is the task of clearing agents to present to the ship's agents the true ocean bill of lading in order to obtain the goods which were shipped by their principals, the forwarders. Only then are they in a position to release individual consignments to holders of the relative house bills of lading. The principle of transfer of ownership of goods by mere endorsement of the bill of lading makes it difficult to exclude from the bill such vital information as the name of the clearing agent, since in its absence the bill is useless.

Whatever its shortcomings as a security document, in practice the house bill of lading is used in the same way as the marine bill of lading to facilitate transfer of control of goods by simple or specific endorsement. None, with the exception of the FCT, of the transport documents which remain for our consideration has this capability. Some may evidence the conditions of the contract of carriage; all act as a receipt, issued by the carrier to the shipper, for the goods; none, however, can be a document of title. Because of their comparatively low worth, the potential for disputes is correspondingly reduced and less time need therefore be spent in discussing their attributes and shortcomings.

Most non-negotiable transport documents take the form of waybills. All indicate that the sellers have performed their obligations under the contract as far as those obligations relate to the dispatch of goods. All show a named consignee for the goods, and this is the basis of the contract of carriage, with the carriers' obligation being to deliver the goods to that named consignee.

Sea waybill

The sea waybill, at first glance, looks very similar in layout to a bill of lading. The same information is given, in the same places; it may bear the same clauses as the bill of lading, and it is signed, dated, and freight is denoted as either paid or to collect in the same way. It clearly distinguishes itself, however, by announcing in bold print at the top that it is a non-negotiable sea waybill. It was first introduced on the shorter sea routes where use of the traditional bill of lading was rendered impractical by the time constraints involved in getting an original document to the port of destination by the arrival date of the goods. One solution was to arrange for an original bill of lading, in an envelope addressed to the buyers, to be sent with the goods in the "ship's bag", but as this was tantamount to releasing the goods to the buyers it was but a short step to the use of the waybill in which the goods are normally consigned to the buyers anyway.

Air waybill

The air waybill is a very different document in appearance, though not in effect. Again the goods are deliverable to a named consignee, with provision for the details of the goods to be declared by the shippers. Freight particulars are usually shown in some detail, not always the case with sea transport documents, and separate columns are provided for charges which have been paid by the shippers and those which are to be collected from the consignees. Many of the details which are inserted on the waybill when it is typed relate to intended actions rather than accomplished ones, particularly with regard to airports of departure and destination, dates of dispatch and arrival, and to carriers and flight numbers. As much of this information is in code anyway, it is largely unintelligible to anyone not intimately connected with the air transport industry.

It is customary for actual details of dispatch to be added to the waybill after the event by typing or impressing on it the actual flight number and its date. This may or may not be separately signed by the issuers or their agents. As with a bill of lading, the document may be issued by the carriers themselves or their agents, or by forwarding agents (house air waybill, or air consignment note).

So far as UCP500 is concerned, for an air waybill to be accepted under a letter of credit it must appear on its face to indicate the name of the carrier and to have been signed either by the carrier or by a named agent for or on behalf of the carrier. The air waybill must clearly show the flight details and, where the letter of credit calls for an actual date of dispatch, a specific notation (ie stamp) must confirm that the goods did in fact fly on the details shown in the box on the air waybill that indicates the proposed flight number(s) and date.

There are two types of air waybills. The Master Air Waybill (MAWB) is the transport document issued by the carrier/airline, eg British Airways, Lufthansa, Air France, etc. A MAWB shows the exporter's goods moving as an independent consignment on that flight and means that the goods are not grouped or consolidated with other shippers' freight by a freight forwarder. This "direct airline" shipment generally means premium air freight rates are paid (one could compare it to travelling in a taxi).

The other air waybill has been called an "air consignment note" but is commonly known as a House Air Waybill (HAWB). A HAWB is issued to each shipper by the freight forwarder to indicate the movement of one consignment of goods from freight grouped together in a consolidation. The total consolidation (which could involve freight collected together by the forwarder from dozens of exporters) is covered by one MAWB issued by the carrier to the forwarder. This grouping together of freight by a forwarder to move on schedules they have agreed with airlines, means shippers share the cost and pay less than the "direct airline" shipment — in fact it could be compared with a bus service operated by the forwarder.

Until UCP500 banks had problems in accepting an HAWB as a valid air freight transport document, but now, banks will accept an HAWB as long as they comply with the terms of the UCP500 Articles 27 (Air Transport Document) and 30 (Transport Documents Issued by Freight Forwarders).

Road transport

The usual document where goods are sent by road is the international consignment note, known universally as the CMR from the initials (Convention Marchandises Routiers) appearing prominently on its face. Many road hauliers, however, issue their own documents, calling them variously road receipts, truck receipts and the like. The CMR carries the advantage that it is issued subject to a standard set of conditions of carriage laid down by international agreement, whereas the private document may not convey any information on the terms of the contract. The CMR's use, however, is restricted to those countries, all in Europe, which are signatories to the agreement.

Rail transport

A similar standard document for goods sent by rail is the CIM (Convention International Marchandises Chemin de Fers).

Parcel post

No such standard document exists where goods are dispatched by parcel post, although in most cases carriage will be on the globally-recognised conditions laid down by the Universal Postal Union.

Courier consignment notes

Couriers, or air express operators as they prefer to be called, such as DHL, UPS, TNT, Fedex, etc are now handling an increasing number of freight consignments internationally. Though no standard document exists, the transport document — courier consignment note — bears a unique tracking reference number and blanks are usually provided to the shipper by the courier company. It is generally completed by the shipper of the goods on the day of collection and although signed by the driver as a receipt, is not evidence that the goods were exported. Though

Completed International Consignment Note (CMR)

LETTRE DE VOITURE INTERNATIONALE	(CMR) INTERNATIONAL CONSIGNMENT NOTE
Sender (Name, Address, Country) Expéditeur (Nom, Adresse, Pays) 1	Customs Reference/Status Référence et/désignation pour mise en douane 2
Aldgate Warehouse Wholesale Ltd 65/66 Whitechapel High St London E1	Senders/Agents Reference Référence de l'expéditeur/de l'agent 3 BM211644
Consignee (Name, Address, Country) Destinataire (Nom, Adresse, Pays) 4	Carrier (Name, Address, Country) Transporteur (Nom, Adresse, Pays) 5
Habselyem Kötöttárugyár Budapest. XX. Török F.U. 116. Hungary	Hungarocamion Budapest
Place & date of taking over the goods (place, country, date) Lieu et date de la prise en charge des marchandises (lieu, pays, date) 6	Successive Carriers Transporteurs successifs 7
London, 9.9.1985 ~~Budapest~~xxxxxxxx	
Place designated for delivery of goods (place, country) Lieu prévu pour la livraison des marchandises (lieu, pays) 8	This carriage is subject, notwithstanding any clause to the contrary, to the Convention on the Contract for the International Carriage of Goods by Road (CMR). Ce transport est soumis nonobstant toute clause contraire à la Convention Relative au Contrat de Transport International de Marchandises par Route (CMR)
Budapest XX, Hungary	

Marks & Nos, No & Kind of Packages, Description of Goods Marques et Nos, No et nature des colis, Désignation des marchandises 9		Gross weight (kg) 10 Poids Brut (kg)	Volume (m³) 11 Cubage (m³)
Tricotex Budapest Hungary	415 Rolls Cloth	6225	40 circa
	Contract No. 164.19.5.3104 xcxcxcxcxcxcxcxcxcxcxcxcxcxc		
Trailer VR3585/XY9313			

Carriage Charges Prix de transport 12	Senders Instructions for Customs, etc Instructions de l'expéditeur (optional) 13
c&f Budapest	
Reservations Réserves 14	Documents attached Documents Annexés (optional) 15
	Invoices packing lists
	Special agreements Conventions particulières (optional) 16
and unexamined	
Goods Received/Merchandises Reçues 17	Signature of Carrier/Signature du transporteur 18	Company completing this note 19
	for Hungarocamion Co. HUNGAROCAMION Budapest U.K. Sole Agent	London, 9.9.1985 Place and date, Signature 20

49

Example of FIATA Forwarders Certificate of Receipt (FCR)

Suppliers or Forwarders Principals	Customs Reference/Status	FCR Number	**G** **B**
	Shipper's Reference		

FIATA FCR

FORWARDERS
CERTIFICATE
OF RECEIPT

Forwarder's Reference

ORIGINAL

Consignee

Marks and Numbers	Number and Kind of Packages	Description of Goods	Gross Weight	Measurement

R S T

Container no.

Contents, weight and measurement according to the declaration of the consignor.
The goods and instructions are accepted and dealt with subject to the General Conditions printed overleaf.

We certify having assumed control of the above mentioned consignment in external apparent good order and condition.

* Forwarding instructions can only be cancelled or altered if the original Certificate is surrendered to us, and then only provided we are still in a position to comply with such cancellation or alteration

at the disposal of the consignee ☐

With irrevocable instructions*

to be forwarded to the consignee ☐

Instructions authorizing disposal by a third party can only be cancelled or altered if the original Certificate of Receipt is surrendered to us, and then only provided we have not yet received instructions under the original authority.

Special remarks

Instructions as to freight and charges

PREPAID

Place and date of issue

Stamp and signature

Text authorised by FIATA   COPYRIGHT   FIATA/Zurich – Switzerland 2.82

some courier companies may call this document an "air waybill" it is not an air waybill as defined above and will not be accepted by any banks as such under documentary collection procedures.

Forwarders' documents

Finally, mention must be made of two other FIATA creations. The first is the Forwarders' Certificate of Receipt (FCR), which is a non-negotiable document designed to cover forwarders' handling of traffic for which the FBL would not be appropriate, such as overland, short-sea or inland waterway consignments. The second is the Forwarders' Certificate of Transport (FCT) which is designed for multi-modal transport where the facility to transfer title to the goods is required, but where a carrier's document is not a necessity. The latter is issued in a set of originals, as is the FBL, but contains an express statement that the issuer is acting as a forwarder and not as a carrier. As with the marine bill of lading and the FBL, delivery of the goods will only take place on surrender of a properly endorsed original FCT.

Summary

It will be evident that only the first and the last of the documents which have been dealt with in this chapter are of any use where some measure of control over the goods is required as security, whether that security is sought by the sellers or by a bank. Where a non-negotiable transport document is dictated by the mode of transport used, the only method of retaining control over goods until payment is made by the buyers is to consign them to the sellers' agents in the buyers' country, and the agency most frequently used in this connection is the bank itself. Goods are only released to the buyer, in this case, on presentation of an instruction letter issued by the bank evidencing payment has been made. Banks, however, are in the business of handling money and documents, not goods, and are understandably reluctant to become more deeply involved in trade transactions. The charges they make for such services reflect this attitude. As we have seen in a previous chapter, in FOB, CFR and CIF contracts the risk in the goods passes from sellers to buyers at the point of FOB, and if a bank is named as consignee or even as notify party in a transport document, then, *prima facie*, that is where the risk lies as far as the carrier is concerned. Furthermore, if the goods are not taken up on arrival, it falls to the bank to make

British Airways Air Waybill

CSR/ECI

Shipper's Name and Address		Shipper's Account Number	

Not Negotiable
Air Waybill

Issued by
British Airways London
Member of IATA

BRITISH AIRWAYS

Copies 1, 2 and 3 of this Air Waybill are originals and have the same validity

It is agreed that the goods described herein are accepted in apparent good order and condition (except as noted) for carriage SUBJECT TO THE CONDITIONS OF CONTRACT ON THE REVERSE HEREOF. THE SHIPPER'S ATTENTION IS DRAWN TO THE NOTICE CONCERNING CARRIER'S LIMITATION OF LIABILITY. Shipper may increase such limitation of liability by declaring a higher value for carriage and paying a supplemental charge if required.

ISSUING CARRIER MAINTAINS CARGO ACCIDENT LIABILITY INSURANCE

Consignee's Name and Address		Consignee's Account Number	

Issuing Carrier's Agent	Accounting Information

Agent's IATA Code	Account No.

Airport of departure (Addr. of First Carrier) and Requested Routing

To	By First Carrier	Routing and Destination	to	by	to	by	Currency	CHGS WT/VAL	Other	Decld Val for Carr'g	Decld Val for Customs

Airport of Destination	Flight/Date	For Carrier Use Only	Flight/Date						

Handling Information

No. of Pieces RCP	Gross Weight	kg lb	Rate Class / Commodity Item No.	Chargeable Weight	Rate / Charge	Total	Nature and Quantity of Goods (Incl. Dimensions or Volume)

Prepaid	Weight charge	Collect	Other Charges

Valuation Charge	

Tax	

Total Other Charges Due Agent	

Shipper certifies that the particulars on the face hereof are correct and that insofar as any part of the consignment contains dangerous goods, such part is properly described by name and is in proper condition for carriage by air according to the applicable Dangerous Goods Regulations.

Total Other Charges Due Carrier	

....
Signature of Shipper or his agent

Total prepaid	Total collect

Currency conversion rates	CC charges in dest. currency

....

	Executed on (date)	at (place)	Signature of Issuing Carrier or its agent

For Carrier's Use only at Destination	Charges at Destination	Total Collect Charges

Original 3 - (For Shipper)

House Air Waybill

arrangements for their clearance, storage and insurance. Herein lies the reason for the banks' reluctance to be involved unless they require for their own security that the goods be consigned to them.

From the point of view of the sellers, this underlines what was said several times at the beginning of this book: there is no security so good as a knowledge of the standing and integrity of the person with whom one is dealing, and this applies especially if full advantage is to be taken of modern methods of transportation.

CHAPTER 5

Marine insurance

The scope of this subject is immense and it is fortunate that a detailed knowledge is not necessary within the present context of its application to collections and letters of credit. As with any other form of insurance, its basic aim is to provide compensation where a loss is suffered due to circumstances beyond the control of the insured loser. The sellers and buyers of the goods are clearly the parties primarily concerned with the covering of such risks, but banks may also have an interest where they are in any way relying on goods as security for lending or for the issue of credits. As the arrangers of marine insurance cover on behalf of others, forwarders also need a basic understanding of the principles involved.

Marine insurance is divided into two broad categories, hull and cargo. Hull insurance is the insurance of the ships themselves, and does not concern us here. Cargo insurance may be taken out with an insurance company, or with underwriters. "Underwriters" usually means the Corporation of Lloyds in London or similar organisations elsewhere. It should be noted that some countries insist that imports are insured with their own national insurance companies making CIF/CIP contracts impossible with those countries.

Marine insurance is subject to many of the conditions normally applying to other forms of insurance. For example, the insured party must have an insurable interest: that is, they must actually be at risk. All known facts which may affect the underwriters' decision to insure (and, of course, the premium charged) must be disclosed, and all parties must exert the "utmost good faith" (often expressed as the Latin phrase *uberrimae fidei*) which involves eventualities ranging from inadequate packing to fraudulent claims.

Extent of cover

No claim will be met if the loss was caused by a risk not covered. This would seem to be obvious but is not always as simple as it sounds. If a policy covers the risk of fire but not war risks and goods are destroyed by a fire started by an act of war, a claim will probably not succeed. The extent of the cover to be taken out will depend on the contract and on the custom in a particular trade. It is not possible to insure against loss of market due to delay of the carrying vessel, or against inherent vice, such as natural decay of fresh produce, neither are you protected if marking is deemed to be inadequate. Basic cargo insurance covers the goods against loss due to sinking, fire, storm, water damage, piracy, barratry (dishonest acts of the ship's master or crew), pilferage, breakage from mishandling, and jettison (where cargo is thrown overboard to save the ship). These risks are known as particular average and may be varied to suit particular trades. For instance, breakage is usually deleted from the risks covered where the commodity shipped is ordinary glass, since the risk is so great that the premium would be prohibitively expensive.

General average

Also covered is general average. A voyage of a ship is considered as a joint venture involving all who have an interest in the safe arrival of the ship at its destination — basically the shipowner and the individual owners of the cargo. If any of these makes a financial sacrifice which is for the general benefit of the rest, such as salvage costs for the ship or the value of jettisoned cargo, then each of the others is expected to make a *pro rata* contribution to those costs based on the extent of their interest.

War clauses; strikes clauses

War and strikes must be specifically insured against and additional premium will be charged. It will not usually be possible to cover these risks where war or strike conditions actually exist at the time the insurance proposal is made.

Institute cargo clauses

Standard clauses governing the contract of marine insurance have been drawn up by the Institute of London Underwriters (comprising both Lloyd's underwriters and companies), and similar clauses are used by other organisations such as the American Institute of Underwriters. The clauses currently in force are designated A, B and C. Broadly speaking:
  (a) clauses A cover all claims for risks covered and attract the highest premiums
  (b) clauses B cover total loss of individual packages, each package being treated as a separate insured risk
  (c) clauses C cover loss of the whole consignment only and provide the cheapest cover available, being particularly suitable for very durable cargoes such as iron and steel.

These clauses approximate to the old "All Risks", "WA" (with average) and "FPA" (free of particular average) clauses, respectively, but these terms are now obsolete and should not be used.

Franchise

Like any other insurance, marine insurance may be subject to a franchise, ie in return for a reduction in premium, the insured party bears an agreed proportion of the amount of any claim. Such arrangements are common where the nature of the goods would give rise to numerous small claims, such as wine in bottles, crockery and the like.

Lloyd's

The Corporation of Lloyd's is effectively a market place for marine insurance, where the sellers are syndicates of underwriters and the buyers are accredited Lloyd's brokers acting on behalf of customers. Different syndicates cover different types of risk and brokers will take propositions to the appropriate syndicate. If the amount is large a syndicate may not feel able to accept the entire risk but will mark the proposal with the proportion which they are prepared to cover (they literally "write under" hence their name). The broker must then approach other syndicates until the entire risk is covered. To become members of Lloyd's, individuals must undergo exhaustive investigation of their financial position and must put up a bond from an acceptable bank for a substantial sum of money.

Insurance documents

Insurance documents come in two forms, policies and certificates. Marine policies for specific shipments may be the custom in certain countries, such as Japan, or may be issued where the seller does not engage in international trade to an extent where it becomes worthwhile to take out an open cover. Each policy represents a separate contract of insurance and, because to arrange such a contract for every shipment which they make would be onerous and time consuming, regular exporters often seek a more convenient arrangement by obtaining an open or blanket policy to cover all international (and perhaps domestic) movements. This may still produce a policy document, perhaps by an arrangement whereby the exporters are appointed by the insurers as their policy-issuing agents. With this authority, the exporters can issue policies to themselves for each shipment, sending copies to the insurers with payment of premiums due, as would any other issuing agent, but this is not always practical.

An alternative to this arrangement is the certificate of insurance, which is issued under two types of contract:

(a) a floating policy, where the insured pays advance premium for cover up to a certain total amount, then declares individual shipments under the policy until the total cover is used up

(b) open cover, where all consignments falling within the scope of the agreement are automatically covered and the insured pay a premium at an agreed rate as they declare each shipment.

In the United Kingdom, the initial incentive towards the development of the insurance certificate was the *ad valorem* stamp duty which was at one time applied to all policies of insurance. Thus, the issue of but one policy, in the case of the floating type, and the undertaking to issue a policy only in the event of a claim being made, in the case of the open cover, saved a great deal of money, the spending of which achieved no other purpose than the filling of the coffers of the Treasury, since the majority of export consignments reach their destination unharmed. The duty was abolished but the system set up for its avoidance remains, since it is a very convenient way of arranging cargo insurance. Instead of an individual policy for each shipment, the insured are issued with a supply of signed and numbered certificates, each one usually in triplicate. The details are completed by the insured (though brokers will undertake this task), the first copy forming the insurance document to be sent to the buyer, the second being sent to the insurers as a declaration to them of the risks they are assuming, and the third being retained by the insured for their records. Payment of premiums may be made with each declaration, or on an open account basis, according to the terms of the arrangement.

Policies of marine insurance

This, then is the background to marine cargo insurance. We will now consider the attributes of the two types of insurance document, beginning with the policy.

Cover usually attaches, ie becomes effective, from the date when the goods leave the sellers' warehouse or from the date of the policy, whichever is the later. As an insurance policy represents an individual contract of insurance, it is essential that it is dated no later than the date of the bill of lading, since if a cause of loss arises between the bill of lading (shipment) date and the policy date the claim will not be met.

Amount insured

The amount insured must be adequate, the figure in general use being the CIF value (cost of the goods, insurance premium plus freight) of the goods plus a ten percent margin (this figure is in any case stipulated as a minimum level of insurance both by Incoterms and by the UCP). It should be expressed in the same currency as the commercial invoice to guard against adverse fluctuations in exchange rates.

It was stated in Chapter 3 that, because it is based on information taken directly from the goods when they were received for shipment, the bill of lading is the definitive document regarding the actual shipping marks and numbers appearing on the packages. Because these marks and numbers provide positive identification of particular consignments, it is essential that those declared on the policy should agree exactly with the bill of lading, since any difference may cause doubt as to which goods are insured and thus make claims invalid.

The description of the goods as given on the policy need not be detailed but should include all information which may be relevant to the insurance, eg flashpoint of chemicals, etc or as stipulated in the terms of a letter of credit.

MARINE INSURANCE

Example of Face Side Policy of Marine Cargo Insurance

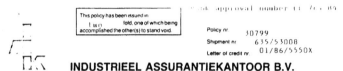

approval number 11 /r . 04

Policy nr   30799
Shipment nr   635/53008
Letter of credit nr   01/86/5550X

INDUSTRIEEL ASSURANTIEKANTOOR B.V.

Be it known that   PHILIPS EXPORT B.V., or order,

as well in their own Name, as for and in the Name and Names of all and every other Person or Persons to whom the name doth, may or shall appertain, in part or in all, doth make Assurance, and cause themselves and them and every of them, to be insured, lost or not lost, at and from

    interior Holland to Rotterdam (Dutch Port)
    to consignee in Limbe.

upon any kind of Goods and Merchandises in the good Ship or Vessel called: "TRANSVAAL"   o.h.c.   (cl cl)

sailing date   20-06-1986 or h.c.

whereof is Master, under God, for this present voyage   N.N.   or whosoever else shall go for Master in the said Ship or by whatsoever other Name or Names the said Ship, or the Master thereof, is or shall be named or called; beginning the Adventure upon the said Goods and Merchandises from the loading thereof aboard the said Ship, as above; and shall so continue and endure her Abode there, upon the said Ship etc , and further, until the said Ship with all her Goods and Merchandises whatsoever shall be arrived at as above, and upon the Goods and Merchandises, until the same be there discharged and safely landed, and it shall be lawful for the said Ship etc. in this voyage to proceed and sail to and touch and stay at any Ports or Places whatsoever without Prejudice to this Assurance. The said Goods and Merchandises etc. for so much as concerns the Assured by Agreement between the Assured and Assurers in this Policy, are and shall be valued at

    JPY 5.624.199,= (FIVE MILLION SIX HUNDRED TWENTY FOUR THOUSAND
    ============== ONE HUNDRED NINETY NINE JAPANESE YEN)
                   so valued on 1555 cartons, containing philips products
                   marked and numbered as per suppliers' invoices.

The insured amount is inclusive of all profit, imaginary or other and cost of freight and insurance.
In case of loss or damage losses to be assessed on the basis of the sound value and the percentage thus found to be applied to the insured value.
Touching the Adventures and Perils which we the Assurers are contented to bear and to do take upon us in this Voyage, they are of the Seas, Men-of-War, Fire, Enemies, Pirates, Rovers, Thieves, Jettisons, Letters of Mart and Countermart, Surprisals, Takings at Sea, Arrests, restraints and Detainments of all Kings, Princes and People, of what Nation, Condition, or Quality soever, Barratry of the Master and Manners, and all other Perils, Losses, and Misfortunes that have or shall come to the Hurt, Detriment or Damage of the said Goods and Merchandises and Ship, & c , or any part thereof; and in case of any Loss or Misfortune, it shall be lawful to the Assured, their Factors, Servant, and Assigns, to sue, labour, and travel for, in and about the Defence, Safeguard and Recovery of the said Goods and Merchandises and Ship, & c., or any part thereof, without Prejudice to this Insurance, to the Charges whereof we, the Assurers, will contribute, each one according to the rate and Quantity of his sum herein Assured And it is especially declared and agreed that no acts of the Insurer or Insured in recovering, saving, or preserving the property insured, shall be considered as a waiver or acceptance of abandonment. And it is agreed by us, the Insurers, that this Writing or Policy of Assurance shall be of as much Force and Effect as the surest Writing or Policy of Assurance heretofore made in Lombard Street, or in the Royal Exchange, or elsewhere in London.

This insurance is governed by English Marine Insurance Law and supplementary customs and further subject to the terms and conditions of the attached clauses, specified as follows:

    Institute Cargo Clauses (A) dated 01.01.1982
    Institute War Clauses (Cargo) dated 01.01.1982
    Institute Strike Clauses (Cargo) dated 01.01.1982
    From warehouse eindhoven to warehouse lime, transshipment risks.

In the event of claim for particular average or loss, the amount insured to be divided as per invoice. In the event of any claim for loss and or damage under this policy, advances shall be treated as increased value of cargo and shall be paid as insured value of cargo.
Now this policy witnesseth that we, the Undersigned Assurers, take upon ourselves the burden of this Assurance, each of us to the extent of the amount underwritten by us respectively, and promise and bind ourselves, each Company for itself only and not one for the other, and in respect only of the due proportion of each Company to the Assured, their Executors, Administrators and Assigns, for the true Performance of the Premises confessing ourselves paid the Consideration due into us for the Assurance by the Assured, at and after the rate as per contract
This insurance has been effected through the intermediary of the Industreel Assurantiekantoor B.V. at Eindhoven and we have debited their account for the premium, thus discharging the Assured.
In the event of accident whereby loss or damage may result in a claim under this policy and under this policy should be paid abroad, immediate notice to be given to

    Claims payable in Malawi.

In witness whereof we, the Assurers, have subscribed our Names and Sums assured
All disputes on the subject of this policy or on the insurance covered thereby are to be decided by the competent judge at Rotterdam, subject to appeal to a higher court.
Issued at EINDHOVEN, 15th June   1986

C 41b

Marine Cargo Reverse

Industrieel Assurantiekantoor B.V.
For One Hundred Percent.
Assurantie Maatschappij
"Nieuw Rotterdam" N.V. at Rotterdam

p.p. PHILIPS EXPORT B.V.

SETTLEMENT OF CLAIMS

In the event of damage, which under this policy may involve a claim apparently in excess of Dutch Guilders 1500,– (or equivalent), **immediate** notice of such damage should be given to the average agent mentioned in the policy. If in the policy no average agent is mentioned or if, on account of the place where the survey should be held, it is not feasible to apply to that average agent, application for survey should be made to

a) the nearest agent of the Marine Underwriters Association in Holland.
b) the nearest Lloyd's agent or
c) another competent average agent of first class reputation.

Failure to comply with these requirements may prejudice any claim under this policy.

Instructions in case of damage or loss

1. The insurance is continuously effective from the time the goods leave the works until they reach your warehouse. This is, however, subject to the condition of your taking delivery of the goods as soon as they are placed at your disposal. In case there is a delay in the delivery of the goods to your premises (e.g. by customs formalities) the cover may be extended another sixty days (air cargo thirty days). In any case the cover ends sixty days (thirty days) after discharge. Therefore, in order that we may try to keep the insurance effective on your behalf, it is necessary for you to advise us immediately:

   a) If you do not want to take delivery as soon as the goods are placed at your disposal.
   b) If for other reasons the goods will not arrive at your warehouse within sixty days from discharge.

2. All containers shipped abroad and sealed with a "one seal-lock" have to be inspected on arrival at the port of destination by consignee or his representative (if possible even before customs formalities) in order:

   a) to examine the condition of the "one seal-lock".
   b) to compare the number of the "one seal-lock" with the seal-lock number on the B's/L (or copies).

   In case it appears that the container has travelled unlocked and unsealed or the seal-lock number (mentioned under b.) does not correspond, an **immediate** inspection should be arranged.

3. On discharge the goods should be externally examined at the port. In case there are visible or audible signs of damage, do not give a clean receipt but hold the carriers immediately responsible and invite them to be present at the inspection of the goods. If the damage is likely to be more than 1500 Dutch guilders or its equivalent, call in the surveyor. Unless contrary instructions are given by the surveyor, this inspection should not be postponed until the goods reach your warehouse.

4. If there is a shortage on discharge, ask the carriers for a certificate of short-landing.

5. To avoid loss and damage, do not allow the goods to remain on the quay or in the port sheds any longer than is strictly necessary. Bring the goods into the safety of your warehouse as quickly as possible.

6. When the goods reach your warehouse, they should be immediately unpacked and inspected irrespective of external signs of loss or damage. If loss or damage is ascertained and the amount thereof is likely to exceed 1500 Dutch guilders or its equivalent, call in the surveyor. Keep the container and inner packing for inspection by the surveyor.

7. The surveyor mentioned in nos 2, 3 and 6, is the representative of Underwriters indicated on the back of the insurance policy. If there is no such representative, Lloyd's Agent should be called in.

8. If it is obvious that damage or loss occured while the goods were in care of a local carrier, this carrier should immediately be held responsible.

9. Losses are not payable abroad, unless otherwise stated in the insurance policy.

10. All claims with the supporting documents must be sent **without delay** to the original shippers who will settle the claim on your behalf through the brokers with Underwriters.

    The following is required:

    a) The report of the surveyor (or if the loss is below 1500 Dutch Guilders or its equivalent your own report)
    b) A copy of the invoice.
    c) Copies of your letters to the carriers and of their replies.
    d) Short-landing certificate, if applicable.
    e) Policy of insurance
    f) Information about condition and identification number of the "one seal-lock"

Risks

The policy must state the risks which are covered (ie Clauses A, B or C, war, strikes, etc), must bear the signature of the insurers, and also the endorsement of the insured, thus enabling subsequent owners of the goods (either in physical possession or as holders of the bill of lading) to claim against the insurer should loss be incurred.

Certificates of marine insurance

Now we turn to the certificate of insurance, be it issued under a floating policy or an open cover. In either case, cover is automatic and the date of the certificate is not important, as it is with a policy. Though banks need evidence that the Certificate was issued prior to or at the time of shipment to satisfy letter of credit claims. Most of the other important aspects of the policy, however, particularly regarding insured value, type of cover, shipping marks and goods description, apply equally where a certificate is used. In addition there are some features of a certificate which are not present in a policy.

Limit per bottom

Firstly, because of the blanket nature of the agreement between the parties to the contract of insurance, at the time of its signature the insurers will have little knowledge of the detail of the risks for which they are taking responsibility. In order that some limiting influence may be exerted over the extent of this risk the certificate may be claused to the effect that no more than a stated total value of goods may be shipped in any one vessel, a restriction known as the "limit per bottom". A similar restriction may also be given relating to locations other than on board ship.

Nature of goods

The certificate will often restrict the nature of the goods which may be declared under the contract, depending on the type of commodity in which the insured party trades. The narrower the scope of goods which may be declared, the easier it is for the insurers to assess their likely risk and therefore a lower premium may well be charged.

Geography of voyage

Similarly, there may well be limitations placed on the geographical extremes of the voyage to be undertaken by goods declared under the contract, and again the greater the restriction, the less potential risk, and so a further premium reduction may be possible.

All these limits will be agreed at the time that the contract of insurance is signed, and it is for the sellers to decide for themselves whether the resulting contract will be adequate to meet their foreseeable needs during the lifetime of the contract, which may span a number of years. Much of the benefit to be derived from an open cover will be nullified if it is frequently necessary to take out specific insurance for consignments, which fall outside the scope of the agreement. Worse is the situation where goods which are outside that scope are shipped in reliance upon it, thereby making the insurance document null and void.

Endorsement by insured party

As with the policy, to enable third parties to the agreement who have obtained an interest in the goods to make valid claims in the event of loss, the certificate requires endorsement by the insured party, unless, as sometimes occurs, it states that claims will be payable to bearer or to the buyer. In addition, because it is a declaration made by the insured, it is usually invalid unless countersigned on its face by them, and the insurers will have specimen signatures of those in the employ of the insured who are authorised to sign.

Expiry date

Finally, where the type of agreement is an open cover, the certificate will normally state the expiry date of the contract of insurance, beyond which date the issue of further certificates is invalid. Because such arrangements are frequently in force for many years, it becomes easy for this date to be overlooked.

Claims

Both policies and certificates will usually state the procedure to be followed in the event of any claims, including the name of the party to be contacted at the port of destination. Frequently use is made of the worldwide network of claims agents maintained by the Corporation of Lloyd's, who also provide detailed reports of ship movements which are collated by the Corporation and published daily as *Lloyd's Shipping Index*.

MARINE INSURANCE

Front of a Completed Standard Lloyd's Certificate of Insurance

LLOYD'S

THIS CERTIFICATE
REQUIRES ENDORSEMENT IN
THE EVENT OF ASSIGNMENT

**CLAIMS SETTLEMENT
INSTRUCTIONS**
1. Lloyd's Agent at LOS Angeles
is authorised to adjust and settle on behalf of
the Underwriters, and to purchase on behalf of
the Corporation of Lloyd's in accordance with
Lloyd's Standing Regulations for the Settlement
of Claims Abroad, any claim which may arise on
this Certificate.
2. In the event that Clause 1 is not completed
claim papers should be sent to J. O. B. Long &
Co., Ltd. 999 Lloyd's Street, Insurance Avenue
London, E C 0

Certificate of Insurance No. C 0000/11111

This is to Certify that there has been deposited with the Committee of Lloyd's a continuous Contract effected by *J. O. B. Long & Co.,
Ltd.,* of Lloyd's, acting on behalf of *The Herne Bay Supply Company* with Underwriters at Lloyd's, and that the said Underwriters have
undertaken to issue to *J. O. B. Long & Co., Ltd.,* Policy/Policies of Insurance at Lloyd's to cover, up to *£10,000 (or equivalent in other currencies)*
in all by any one steamer or sending by air and/or parcel post, *Golf Equipment, other interests held covered,* from any port or ports, place or places
in *the United Kingdom* to any port or ports, place or places in *the World;* and that *The Herne Bay Supply Company* are entitled to declare against
the said Contract insurances attaching thereto on or after the *First* day of *January, 1981.* This Certificate is not valid in respect of insurances
attaching after the *Thirty-first* day of *December,* 1983.

For the Committee of Lloyd's

Dated at Lloyd's London 29th February 1981

Conveyance	From	
"ALEMANIA EXPRESS"	LONDON	
Via To	To LOS ANGELES	INSURED VALUE Currency GBP 24200-00

INSURED VALUE Currency GBP 24200-00
Interest (Twenty four thousand two hundred
Pounds Sterling only.)

Marks and Numbers

R S I   30 cases SPORTS EQUIPMENT

LOS ANGELES

We hereby declare for Insurance under the said Contract interest as specified above so valued subject to the special conditions stated below and on the back hereof

Institute Cargo Clauses (All Risks) excluding rust, oxidisation, discolouration, twisting and bending
Institute Replacement Clause
Institute War Clauses (Cargo) or Institute War Clauses (Cargo) including on carriage by Air) or Institute War Clauses (Air Cargo (excluding sendings by Post) or Institute War Clauses for the
insurance of sendings by Post as applicable
Institute Strikes Riots and Civil Commotions Clauses

Underwriters agree losses, if any, shall be payable to the order of HERNE BAY SUPPLY COMPANY on surrender of this Certificate.

In the event of loss or damage which may result in a claim under this Insurance, immediate notice should be given to the Lloyd's Agent
at the port or place where the loss or damage is discovered in order that he may examine the goods and issue a survey report.
(Survey fee is customarily paid by claimant and included in valid claim against Underwriters.)

SEE IMPORTANT INSTRUCTIONS ON REVERSE

This Certificate not valid unless the Declaration be signed by

for THE HERNE BAY SUPPLY COMPANY

Dated 22.2.82

Signed *Zachariah Clements*

Authorised Signatory

Z. Clements, Director

Brokers J O B Long & Co., Ltd.
999 Lloyd's Street, Insurance Avenue London E C 0

Lloyd's Insurance Reverse

For and on behalf of The Herne Bay Supply Co.

Zachariah Clarendon

Director

IMPORTANT INSTRUCTIONS IN EVENT OF CLAIM

DOCUMENTATION OF CLAIMS

To enable claims to be dealt with promptly, the Assured or their Agents are advised to submit all available supporting documents without delay, including when applicable:—

1. Original policy or certificate of insurance

2. Original or copy shipping invoices, together with shipping specification and/or weight notes

3. Original Bill of Lading and/or other contract of carriage

4. Survey report or other documentary evidence to show the extent of the loss or damage

5. Landing account and weight notes at final destination

6. Correspondence exchanged with the Carriers and other Parties regarding their liability for the loss or damage

IMPORTANT

LIABILITY OF CARRIERS, BAILEES OR OTHER THIRD PARTIES

It is the duty of the Assured and their Agents, in all cases, to take such measures as may be reasonable for the purpose of averting or minimising a loss and to ensure that all rights against Carriers, Bailees or other third parties are properly preserved and exercised. In particular, the Assured or their Agents are required

1. To claim immediately on the Carriers, Port Authorities or other Bailees for any missing packages

2. In no circumstances, except under written protest, to give clean receipts where goods are in doubtful condition

3. When delivery is made by Container, to ensure that the Container and its seals are examined immediately by their responsible official. If the Container is delivered damaged or with seals broken or missing or with seals other than as stated in the shipping documents, to clause the delivery receipt accordingly and retain all defective or irregular seals for subsequent identification

4. To apply immediately for survey by Carriers or other Bailees Representatives if any loss or damage be apparent and claim on the Carriers or other Bailees for any actual loss or damage found at such survey

5. To give notice in writing to the Carriers or other Bailees within 3 days of delivery if the loss or damage was not apparent at the time of taking delivery

Note — The Consignees or their Agents are recommended to make themselves familiar with the Regulations of the Port Authorities at the port of discharge

NOTE.— The Institute Clauses incorporated herein are deemed to be those current at the time of commencement of the risk
It is necessary for the Assured when they become aware of an event which is "held covered" under this Insurance to give prompt notice to Underwriters and the right to such cover is dependent upon compliance with this obligation.
Lloyd's Agents referred to herein are not insurers and are not liable for claims arising on this Certificate. The service of legal proceedings upon Lloyd's Agents is not effective service for the purpose of starting legal proceedings against Underwriters.
This Insurance is subject to English jurisdiction.

MARINE INSURANCE

Example of a Company Certificate of Marine Cargo Insurance

ORIGINAL

Commercial Union Assurance

C U
ASSURANCE

Marine Centre,
Drury House,
19 Water Street, Liverpool L2 0RL

Exporters Reference
Contract No.31442

Marine Open Cover No: M.A.935 - FO065Z
For HALEWOOD CHEMICALS LIMITED.

Insured's Invoice or Reference No.
31442

Certificate of Insurance

INSURANCE CERTIFICATE NO. MAF 32478

Name of Insured
HALEWOOD CHEMICALS LIMITED,
HORTON ROAD, STANWELL MOOR,
STAINES, MIDDLESEX. TW19 6BJ.

This is to Certify that the Commercial Union Assurance Company plc. has insured in the United Kingdom under this Open Cover in the name of this Insured the interest described and valued herein.

Claims payable at destination by nearest branch or agency of Commercial Union Assurance Company plc.

See list of branches and agencies on reverse of this form or by:-

Notwithstanding the description of the voyage stated herein, provided the goods are at the risk of the Assured, this insurance shall attach from leaving the warehouse, premises or place of storage in the interior of the Country of export to interior of destination country as per Institute Clauses if in accordance with the Open Cover and unless stated otherwise hereon.

FROM WAREHOUSE STAINES BY

It is a condition of this Insurance that the Insured shall act with reasonable despatch in all circumstances within their control.

| Conveyance &/or Steamers SEAFREIGHT | From LONDON | Insured Value (in words) ONE THOUSAND SEVEN HUNDRED AND NINETY POUNDS |
| Via/To BANJUL | To WAREHOUSE BANJUL | Insured Value (in figures) £1,790.00 Sterling   ONLY |

Marks and Numbers	Interest
H.C.L. 31442 G.P.L. BANJUL Nos.1-2	2 Ply Cases PHARMACEUTICALS AS PER PROFORMA INVOICE 6578C

Claims Procedure

Insured or their agents must:—
1. Report claims immediately to C.U.'s agent shown above or overleaf.
2. Claim on carrier, Port Authority or any negligent party for damage or omissions.
3. Apply immediately for survey in the docks by carriers' representative if any loss or damage is apparent at the docks.
4. In no circumstances give clean receipt where goods are in doubtful condition except under written protest.
5. Give notice to carriers' representative within three days of delivery if loss or damage was not apparent at time of delivery.
6. Send all correspondence with carriers or other negligent parties when submitting claim to C.U.

This Insurance is subject to the conditions below and extended to cover Marine and War Risks Insurance, including Transhipment Risks.

Extension of Cover

If the ordinary course of transit from ship to destination takes more than 60 days (30 days Air) or is in any way interrupted (within control or knowledge of the Insured) this insurance shall terminate unless prompt notice is given to the CU or their agents for extension of cover and such extension, if agreed, shall be subject to an additional premium.

Conditions of Insurance

The policy to which this insurance attaches is against all risks of loss of or damage to the subject matter insured in accordance with the terms, conditions and exclusions set out in the current issue of the following clauses:

Institute Cargo Clauses (A)
Institute Cargo Clauses (Air)
Institute Classification Clause
Institute Replacement Clause } as applicable
Duty Clause
War & Strikes Riots & Civil Commutions as appropriate
Institute Clauses.

This insurance is subject to English jurisdiction

Special Policy Conditions.

Signed for Commercial Union Assurance Company plc.

JOHN POPE
UK Divisional Director.

GSF1047(c)
(Liverpool)

Registered in England No. 21487
Registered Office, St. Helen's 1 Undershaft, London EC3P 3DQ

THIS CERTIFICATE IS NOT VALID UNLESS COUNTERSIGNED.
Countersignature by or on behalf of the Insured also declared to constitute effective assignment thereof.

Place & Date of issue HALEWOOD CHEMICALS LTD.
3.6.86. Horton Road, Stanwell Moor
Signature STAINES,
E.M. HICKS Middlesex

Reverse of a Company Certificate of Marine Cargo Insurance

HALEWOOD CHEMICALS LTD.
Horton Road, Stanwell Moor,

Principal CU Marine Settling Agencies

	Country	Location	
U.K.		London	Marine Dept. of Commercial Union Assurance Company plc or Marine Centres at Glasgow, Liverpool, Manchester, Leeds, Birmingham, Bristol, London Marine Centre.
Canada		Toronto	Boyd Phillips & Co. Ltd.
		Montreal	Dale & Co. Ltd.
U.S.A.		New York	Marine Dept. of Commercial Union Assurance Companies or at C.U. Marine Centres at San Francisco.
West Indies	Barbados	Bridgetown	Barbados Commercial Insurance Co. Ltd.
	Trinidad	Port of Spain	Huggins Services Ltd.
Central and South America	Argentina	Buenos Aires	Ascoli & Weil
	Bolivia	La Paz	La Britanica S.A.
	Chile	Valparaiso	Compania de Seguros La Republica S.A.
	Ecuador	Guayaquil	The Sociedad General C.A.
	Guatemala	Guatemala City	G.W.F. Franklin Ltd.
	Guyana	Georgetown	Guyana National Shipping Corporation
Europe	Austria	Vienna	Gellatly Hankey Marine Services / Graham Miller Gesellschaft M.b.H.
	Belgium	Antwerp	J. Haenecour & Co. S.A.
	Cyprus	Nicosia	Commercial Union Assurance (Cyprus) Ltd.
	Denmark	Copenhagen	Hansen & Klein
	Eire	Dublin	Hibernian Insurance Co. Ltd.
	Finland	Helsinki	O.Y. Lars Krogius A.B.
	France	Paris	Commercial Union Assurance Company plc c/o A.T.I.C.A.M.
	Germany	Bremen	Lampe & Schierenbeck
	Gibraltar		Solrac & Co. Ltd.
	Greece	Athens	Commercial Union Assurance Company plc
	Italy	Milan	Bevington Assicurazioni S.A.S.
	Malta	Sliema	A & V Von Brockdorff (Insurance) Ltd.
	Netherlands	Amsterdam / Rotterdam	De Vos & Zoon
	Norway	Oslo	Sev Dahl's Assurancekontor S.A.S.
	Portugal	Lisbon	Rawes & Pinto Basto Ltda.
	Spain	Barcelona	Commercial Union Assurance Company plc
	Sweden	Stockholm	Commercial Union Assurance Svenska A/B.
	Switzerland	Basle	Keller Shipping Ltd
Middle East	Bahrein		Bahrein Technical & Trading Co.
	Duba		African & Eastern (Near East) Ltd.
	Kuwait		Kuwait Maritime & Mercantile Co. K.S.G.
	Saudi Arabia	Damman / Dhahran / Jeddah / Riyadh	Arabian Establishment for Trade
	Syria	Lattakia	Syrian Maritime & Transport Agencies S.A.S.
Africa	Egypt	Cairo	Malcolm Sheppard & Co. Commodity Surveys) Ltd.
	Kenya	Nairobi	Lion of Kenya Insce. Co. Ltd.
	Mauritius	Port Louis	L & H. Vigier de Latour Ltd.
	South Africa	Johannesburg	Commercial Union Assurance Company of South Africa Ltd. or at any branch office.
	Tanzania	Dar-Es-Salaam	General Agricultural Products Export Corp. (GAP EX).
Asia	Bangladesh	Chittagong	James Finlay & Co. Ltd
	Hong Kong	Hong Kong	Commercial Union Assurance Company plc
	India	Bombay	Tata Tea Ltd.
		Calcutta	Gillanders Arbuthnot & Co. Ltd.
	Japan	Tokyo	Cornes & Co. Ltd.
	Malaysia	Kuala Lumpur	Commercial Union Assurance (Malaysia) Sdn. Bhd.
	Pakistan	Karachi	Commercial Union Assurance Company plc
	Singapore	Singapore	Commercial Union Assurance Company plc
	Sri Lanka	Colombo	Harrisons & Eastern Export Ltd.
	Thailand	Bangkok	Commercial Union Assurance Company (Thailand) Ltd.
Australia		Melbourne	Associated Marine Insurers Australia Pty Ltd.
New Zealand		Auckland / Wellington	Commercial Union General Insurance Co. Ltd.

IMPORTANT

Please follow the claims procedures shown on the face of this certificate. In the event of difficulty in contacting a local settling agent please contact Commercial Union Assurance Company plc in London for advice
Telex 889135   Cable CUMARINE LONDON EC3

JANUARY 1985

Brokers' cover notes

One last insurance document which must be mentioned is the brokers' cover note, although this will be discussed again in Chapter 12. Insurance brokers are to the world of insurance what forwarding agents are to the world of shipping. In other words, they act as agents who undertake to procure insurance for customers. Because of their deep understanding of the insurance market and because, by bringing new business to particular insurers in quantity they are able to obtain favourable rates of premium which may be passed on to their customers, they perform a valuable service to the insurance community. The problem arises when they issue their own documents which amount to statements that insurance has been, or will be, effected. Such documents are not evidence of the terms, or even the existence, of the actual insurance cover, and are seldom usable by a third party in the event of a claim becoming necessary. Another similarity to the forwarding agent is that in many countries there is little or no control over who may call themselves insurance brokers and thus the trading community, and banks in particular, tend to treat the brokers' cover note with the same circumspection as they display towards the house bill of lading.

CHAPTER 6

Commercial and official documents

Invoices

Confusion often exists in the minds of international traders on this subject. Why? Partly because of the proliferation of names given to the documents; examples are:
- Commercial Invoice
- Shipping Invoice
- Customs Purposes Only Invoice
- Proforma Invoice
- Invoice for Insurance Purposes
- Export Invoice
- Legalised Invoices.

The purpose of the invoice

The purpose of the document also confuses the mind, for example an invoice can be used for one or more of the following:
- charging the customer for the goods
- complying with the Letter of Credit or Bill of Exchange requirements
- part of a customs export declaration
- import entry requirements
- no charge supplies — statement of nature and quantity of goods plus insurance value
- making a legal statement to all authorities in the transportation supply chain — carriers, customs authorities, transport convention authorities.

Destination country requirements

The confusions are then multiplied by the wide variety of destination country requirements such as:

- format and phrasing dictates
- legalisation of invoices demanded by some Middle East countries
- language
- number of copies and signature rules.

Items of information

There then come into play a number of items of information which can be either very useful of vital on the document. This again causes the originator some difficulty is not familiar with such procedures or the information required. For example:

- Commodity Code Number (HS — Harmonised tariff code system)
- Incoterm relating to the supply (if stated correctly will give vital information about responsibilities, mode of transport and price, etc
- value of the goods (World Trade Organisation and World Customs Organisation Rules give the force of law to accuracy of these statements)
- VAT Numbers for EC trade
- Export Licence status for controlled goods
- specific clauses relating to origin
- specific clauses relating to Preference status of shipments
- specific clauses relating to returned goods (USA and Canada particularly)
- specific statement regarding terms of sale, reason for sale and relationships between buyer and seller
- Letter of Credit compliance wording
- certified status of the documents
- Customs Procedure Code
- hazardous goods declaration reference
- forwarder or clearing agent at destination
- packing information; number of pieces and weight plus dimensions, etc.

It is little wonder that confusions reign. Build your own matrix of destination invoice formats, remember the modern exporter takes the last steps in the supply chain very seriously indeed. Until the goods are satisfactorily in the hands of the customer, to type and undamaged, the job is not complete.

Much of the above involves competence and familiarity with export procedures, some computerised document preparation systems are a great help if you have sufficient activity to warrant installing them. Build up a good set of information sources on these subjects. Croner's *Reference Book for Exporters* has country pages which are very useful. The Department of Trade and Industry (DTI) has country desks where free advice can be obtained, the Internet with many countries having introduction pages for potential exporters and, of course, existing customers are all useful on occasion.

It does not help to call your invoice "Invoice for Customs Purposes Only"; the invoice is a vitally important document to foreign Customs authorities as it is the basis for their calculation of revenue required for duty and tax. Customs are alert to mis-statements and to say "for customs purposes" may be interpreted as saying that there is another more realistic invoice in existence and it may provoke a Customs delay. Why not use the word "Invoice" as a stand alone heading. Ensuring your invoices comply completely with the requirements of the letter of credit is vital to successful bank presentations, yet is often beyond the capabilities of exporters, either because of poor training of staff or understanding of the requirements.

Packing list

A packing list a recommended device for showing to the world at large exactly what you have packed into consignments and where a certain item or product is in the number of crates, containers, etc. Remember the more clarity given to the accompanying paperwork that goes with shipment the more you ensure swift transit to the customers. Some foreign Customs require a packing list to accompany the shipment, this should be checked in, for example, Croner's *Reference Book for Exporters*.

If a packing list is required under a letter of credit procedure it should bear the names and addresses of all parties involved (ie the beneficiary, applicant, consignee), a description of goods that complies with the letter of credit and then a more detailed list of products pertaining to the consignment. Of course, a packing list must show weights and dimensions and indicate any packing case numbers, container number or seal numbers that relate to the consignment. Most banks like to see a packing list dated though it need only be signed if it is specifically required by the letter of credit.

Certificate of origin

Certificates of origin of goods take many forms and are required for many reasons. In their simplest form, they are merely a statement on the commercial invoice as to the country from which the goods originate and may require simply to reassure the buyers that they are receiving goods which have been made in a country in whose products they have confidence. More often, however, the buyers require a certificate of origin in order to provide evidence to the customs authorities in their country that the goods qualify for a preferential rate of import duty.

Preferential and reciprocal trade agreements exist between groups of countries, eg between the 15 Member States forming the EC and the 4 countries forming EFTA (European Free Trade Association) consisting of Switzerland, Norway, Iceland and Liechtenstein. Goods consigned between these countries will receive a preferential (usually zero) rate of duty if a preference statement is made by the exporter. This may be on a form called a Movement Certificate or EUR1 or may be a statement made in the appropriate style on the invoice. Customs authorisation can be obtained to make regular invoice declarations. An unusual exception to the normal preference rules is that existing between Turkey and the EC where an ATR Form is used indicating that the goods are in free circulation with the EC.

Important: A Movement Certificate (EUR) is not a simple statement of origin but a declaration that the goods qualify for preferential status under the rules as laid down in the agreement between the country groups and spelt out in HM Customs Public Notices numbered 826, 827, 828 and 829. To qualify for preference and to issue the EUR, which is a legally binding document, it is vital for the originator to understand the rules for preference as failure to comply is a serious offence and is punishable under the law. The list of countries and the preference arrangements are published in HM Customs & Excise Integrated Tariff of the United Kingdom (the Tariff) Volumes 1–3.

Certificates of origin, as such, may be as simple as a statement on the invoice, a statement made in a prescribed format dictated by the country to which the goods are being despatched or a separately signed document issued on company letterhead by the seller. More formally, a certificate of origin may be a document specifically designed for the purpose evidencing the origin of goods, such as the standard forms issued by Chambers of Commerce within the EC and that required by the Middle East countries issued by the Arab/British Chamber of

Commerce in the UK. These documents must be purchased from the relevant Chamber of Commerce and, in the case of the Middle East countries, may also have to be certified by the Arab/British Chamber and legalised by the relevant country's Embassy (both subject to the payment of fees).

It is important to understand the essential difference between "origin" and "preferential status". The latter requires understanding of the preference arrangements contained within the Public Notices. Beware!

Another form of "origin" declaration may be requested which is, in fact a negative statement; instead of certifying origin in a particular country, it states that goods do not originate in a named country. Obviously, the necessity for such documents changes with the winds and tides of international relations and it is interesting to note that the issuance of such "negative" statements is illegal under USA law. At the present time, such statements may be required by Middle East buyers to state goods do not originate in Israel and India with regard to Pakistan. These so-called blacklist certificates occasionally go further than the origin of the goods and touches upon whether the sellers have been known to trade with, employ, the proscribed state or have shipped the goods on a vessel or aircraft belonging to the stated country and that the goods will not be transhipped via that country.

As mentioned, some countries require these certificates, as they may other documents, to be legalised by the embassy or consulate in the sellers' country, these being chiefly among the Middle East countries with the addition of some Latin American countries. Checking in a reference book such as Croner's *Reference Book for Exporters* is essential to establish when this legalisation is required.

Certificate of conformity (Certificate of quality)

This is a certificate certifying that a particular consignment or supply of goods meet an industry standard, and example of this is the *Air Worthiness Certificate* or *Release Note* used in the supply of aircraft equipment. The demand for such a certificate will generally be included within the contract as a requirement of the customer, but it is also necessary for exporters to be aware of restrictions that may be imposed on their goods on arrival in the country of destination. The following section deals with what can also be called a qualify certification procedure, but one which may generally be mandated by the rules of the importing country for reasons, not only of quality, but also of control for currency and anti-fraud reasons.

Pre-shipment inspection

A number of developing countries require by law that all imports be subject to Pre-Shipment Inspection (PSI), which is usually in the form of a Comprehensive Import Supervision Scheme (CISS) working under the rules laid down by the GATT (General Agreements on Tariffs and Trade) and monitored by the World Trade Organisation (WTO) which was established in 1995.

The purpose of such schemes is broadly to ensure that the importing country receives value for the foreign exchange it expends on its imported goods or that they are not being used as a market to "dump" sub-standard products. As such, a PSI comprises of:

(a) a physical inspection covering quality and quantity aspects
(b) a price evaluation to ensure that the price being charged is within the normal export market price range for the particular country of supply and complies with the GATT Valuation Rules
(c) legality checks to ensure that the transaction complies with the laws of the importing country and international trading regulations.

This is the traditional mandatory form of pre-shipment inspection which because it has been made mandatory by the government of the particular country is a cost chargeable by the exporter to the customer. There are other forms of this PSI such as the following.

1. Pre-shipment inspection required under the contract. This can be imposed by the buyer for a number of reasons relating to the nature of the goods, in determining the quality of the product, even to confirming the existence and status of the supplier. The procedure is similar to that of the mandatory PSI outlined below.
2. GOST Certification. This is a certification procedure operated under the mandates of GOSSTANDART the Russian authority for standardisation, certification and metrology. As the requirement for a certificate to be issued by the inspection authority is operated by the first 6 digits of the tariff classification of the goods (under the Harmonised System — HS) it is essential that you verify your classification at an early stage. Currently (May 2000) this procedure

has been adopted by Kazakhstan, Uzbekistan, Moldova and Romania as well as Russia itself with possible application in Belarus and Azerbaijan.

Procedure

In the procedure below, the "Inspection Agent" will be an independent inspection contractor such as SGS, Cotecna or ITS whose professional status is based on conducting professional examination of goods to be exported to the country demanding the PSI.

In a typical transaction, the inspection agent covering the country of supply of the goods will receive from the importers' bank or direct from the buyers, their official pre-shipment inspection request form. Upon receipt, the inspection agent will contact the exporter to arrange the pre-shipment inspection. This is normally organised by the exporter completing the official Request For Information (RFI) and returning it to the PSI agent. As soon as the inspection agent receives adequate information the PSI activities can proceed (usually between 3–5 working days after receipt of the RFI) with all elements taking place concurrently. If all aspects are satisfactory, and subject to receipt of satisfactory final documents (including, in some cases, a certified copy of the original bill of lading or air waybill) a Clean Report of Findings (CRF) will be issued. This is the means by which the inspection agent informs its principal (the government of the importing country, generally) of the results of its PSI activities. The format of the CRF may vary from country to country, depending upon the exact information the inspection agent is required to provide. The sellers might not see this CRF, they are usually left with a "docket" to verify a satisfactory inspection has taken place a copy of which must be sent to the PSI company, with any supporting documents required, for the issuance of the CRF.

If some aspect of the PSI remains unsatisfactory after consultation between inspection agent and exporter, a non-negotiable report of findings is issued, but this is likely to result in non-payment.

Increasingly, such schemes also include some form of import duty and tariff code assessment to ensure that the importing country receives the correct amount of import duty due on a consignment. This information may be included on the CRF or a separate report may be produced — an Import Duty Report (IDR). Where an IDR scheme exists, the original of the Report will normally be required by the importers in order to clear the goods through customs.

The PSI contract, in mandatory situations, is between the inspection agent and the government of the importing country whereas, when PSI is demanded by the buyers, the PSI contract is between the buyers and the inspection agent and such charges are billed to the buyer. This is dictated under Incoterms 2000, where all 13 of the terms make payment of PSI an obligation of the buyers. In the vast majority of PSI schemes, though, it is the government which pays the inspection agent's fees, which are more than covered by the economic benefits accruing to the client country; there is normally no direct cost to either importer or exporter. Countries which currently require PSI include those in Africa, Latin America as well as Eastern Europe. Up-to-date information on which countries require PSI and the nominated PSI inspection agency can be found in the country pages of Croner's *Reference Book for Exporters*. **Cautionary Note**: If there is a requirement under a letter of credit for the Clean Report of Findings (CRF) or other documents associated with PSI to be included with the presentation of documents to the bank be careful that you can comply. Remember that the PSI is done not at your instruction by the overseas party, whether governmental or private, and the CRF will generally not be released to the sellers but to the overseas party directly by the inspection agent. To evidence PSI has taken place for letter of credit purposes, the PSI agency will endorse and stamp the commercial invoice to that affect. Ensure that this is acceptable under the terms of the letter of credit or payment may be frustrated — any PSI clause that you cannot comply with must be rejected or amended.

Conclusion

This section covers Commercial and Official Documents as far as they relate to the subject title "Understanding Documentary Bills and Credits" and is comprehensive in that sense. Nevertheless, the complex world of international trade has a devotion to certificates and forms, some of which are omitted here because they do not usually impinge on the payment process. Examples of these documents are export licences, export declaration (ie C88 forms), import licences, etc any of which if faulty of omitted could have a negative effect on other procedures leading to non-payment.

Example of Commercial Invoice

Seller (name, address VAT reg. no.)	Vendeur (nom, adresse, no. d'immatriculation TVA)	**COMMERCIAL EXPORT INVOICE**	RECHNUNG FACTURA	FACTURE فاتورة

Invoice number	Numéro de facture		
Invoice date (tax point)	No. de facture et date	Seller's reference	Référence du vendeur
Buyer's reference	Référence de l'acheteur	Other reference	Autres références

Consignee (name, address VAT reg. no.)	Destinataire (nom, adresse, no. d'immatriculation TVA)	Buyer (if not consignee) (name, address VAT reg. no.)	Acheteur (s'il est différent du destinataire) (nom, adresse, no. d'immatriculation TVA)

PRO
I2

Country of origin of goods	Pays d'origine	Country of destination	Pays de destination
Terms of delivery and payment		Conditions de livraison et de paiement	

Vessel/flight no. & date Identité du moyen de transport	Port/airport of loading	Lieu de chargement
Port/airport of discharge Lieu de déchargement	Place of delivery	Lieu de livraison

Shipping marks; container number Marques d'expédition et numéro de conteneur	No. and kind of packages; description of goods Nombre et nature des colis; désignation des marchandises	Commodity code Code des marchandises	Total gross wt. (kg) Poids brut total (kg)	Total cube (m³) Cubage total (m³)
			Total net wt. (kg) Poids net total (kg)	

Item/packages Article/colis	Gross/net/cube Poids brut/poids net/cubage	Description Description	Quantity Quantité	Unit price Prix unitaire	Amount Montant

Invoice total Total de la facture

Name of signatory	Nom du signataire
Place and date of issue	Lieu et date d'émission
Signature Signature	

It is hereby certified that this invoice shows the actual price of the goods described, that no other invoice has been or will be issued, and that all particulars are true and correct.

Il est certifié que la présente facture reprend le prix réel des marchandises décrites, qu' aucune autre facture n' a été ni ne sera émise et que tous les renseignements fournis sont exacts.

Example of a Customs Invoice — currently used for Nigeria

In accordance with Nigerian Government Notice 1989 of 1970

FEDERATION of NIGERIA

Combined Certificate of Value and of Origin and Invoice of Goods for
Exportation to Nigeria

C.16

CERTIFICATE OF VALUE

I, ...

of ....

*Manufacturers/Suppliers/Exporters of the goods enumerated in this invoice amounting to ....

....

hereby declare that I have the authority to make and sign this certificate on behalf of the aforesaid
*Manufacturers/Suppliers/Exporters and that I have the means of knowing and I do hereby certify as follows:-

(1) That this invoice is in all respects correct and contains a true and full statement of the price actually paid or to be paid for the said goods, and the actual quantity thereof.

(2) That no different invoice of the goods mentioned in the said invoice has been or will be furnished to anyone.

(3) That no arrangement or understanding affecting the purchase price of the said goods has been or will be made or entered into between the said exporter and purchaser or by anyone on behalf of either of them either by way of discount, rebate, compensation or in any manner whatever other than as fully shown on this invoice.

CERTIFICATE OF ORIGIN

(1) That all the goods mentioned in this invoice have been wholly produced or manufactured in ....

....

(2) That all the goods mentioned in this invoice have been either wholly or partially produced or manufactured in

....

(3) That as regards those goods only partially produced or manufactured,
(a) the final process or processes of manufacture have been performed in ....

(b) the expenditure in material produced and/or labour performed in .... calculated subject to qualifications hereunder, in the case of all such goods is not less than 25 per cent of the factory or works costs of all such goods in their finished state. *See note below.

(4) That in the calculation of such proportion of material produced and/or labour performed none of the following items has been included or considered:-
Manufacturer's profit, or remuneration of any trader, agent, broker or other person dealing in the goods in their finished condition; royalties; cost of outside packages; or any cost of packing the goods thereinto; any cost of conveying, insuring, or shipping the goods subsequent to their manufacture.

Dated at .... this .... day of .... 19 ....

(Signature) .... (Signature of Witness) ....

Note: (1) The person making the declaration should be the principal or manager, chief clerk, secretary, or responsible employee.

(2) The place or country of origin of imports is that in which the goods were produced or manufactured and, in the case of partly manufactured goods, the place or country in which any final operation, has altered to any appreciable extent the character, composition and value of goods imported into that country.

(3) In the case of goods which have at some stage entered into the commerce of, or undergone a process of manufacture in a foreign country, only that labour and material which are expected in or added to the goods after their return to the exporting territory, shall be regarded as the produce or manufacture of the territory in calculating the proportion of labour and material in the factory or works cost of the finished article.

(4) *Delete the inapplicable.

Enumerate the following charges and state whether each amount has been included in or excluded from the above selling price to purchaser:-	Amount in currency of exporting country	State if included in above selling price to purchaser
(1) Cartage to rail and/or docks		
(2) Inland freight (rail or canal) and other charges to the dock area, including inland insurance		
(3) Labour in packing the goods into outside packages		
(4) Value of outside packages		
(5) If the goods are subject to any charge by way of royalties		
(6) OCEAN FREIGHT		
(7) OCEAN INSURANCE		
(8) Commission, establishment and other charges of a like nature		
(9) Other costs, dues, charges and expenses incidental to the delivery of the articles		
State full particulars of Royalties below:-		

Form No
73.150   Published and sold by FORMECON SERVICES Ltd., Gateway House, Ellesmere Port, Cheshire. 051-355 5255

Example of a Standard Invoice

*INVOICE of

.... 19 ....
(Place and Date)   consigned

by   of

*State here general nature or class of goods

to   of

to be shipped per

Order Number ....

Country of Origin	Marks and numbers on packages	Quantity and description of goods	Selling price to purchaser	
			₤	Amount

Example of a Packing List

		PACKING LIST	LISTE DE COLISAGE ESPECIFICACION DE EMBALAJE VERSANDLISTE

Seller (name, address)

Invoice number

Invoice date (tax point) — Seller's reference

Buyer's reference — Other reference

SITPRO 1992

Consignee

Buyer (if not consignee)

Country of origin of goods — Country of destination

Terms of delivery and payment

Vessel/flight no. and date — Port/airport of loading

Port/airport of discharge — Place of delivery

Shipping marks; container number — Number and kind of packages; description of goods — Commodity code — Total gross wt. (kg) — Total cube (m³)

Total net wt. (kg)

Item/packages — Gross/net/cube — Description — Quantity — Other details

Additional packing information

Name of signatory

Place and date of issue

Signature

Form No. 44/80 Published and sold by FORMECON SERVICES Ltd., Gateway, Crewe CW1 6YN Tel: (01270) 500800 SITPRO Approved Licensee No. 21

CHAPTER 7

The bill of exchange

Although the role of the bill of exchange in international trade has diminished somewhat in recent years, it is probably true to say that the majority of collections and drawings under letters of credit still involve its use. It is perhaps questionable whether the use of the bill of exchange is always justified, since on occasions where it is expedient to dispense with it (such as where it attracts heavy stamp duty), trade seems to manage quite adequately without it. As a general rule, however, the comprehensive legislation which remains in force in many countries, which is designed to protect the holder of a bill of exchange from loss, makes its use attractive to any party involved in the financing of a trade transaction, whether they be the sellers themselves or an intermediary bank. To the latter, a bill of exchange payable at some date in the future can also be useful as an instrument of liquidity owing to the thriving markets in such documents in many financial centres.

Definition

A good starting point in any study of the bill of exchange is the legal definition of the instrument as set out in the **Bills of Exchange Act of 1882** (s.3). This states that a bill of exchange is "an unconditional order in writing, addressed by one person to another, signed by the person giving it, requiring the person to whom it is addressed to pay, on demand or at a fixed or determinable future time, a sum certain in money to or to the order of a specified person or to bearer".

If at first this description makes the reader's head spin, it is worth a second reading, since, in order that a holder of the bill may qualify for the protection given by the Act and referred to above, it is important that it complies with the legal definition in all respects. The courts take the logical view that if a particular piece of paper fails in any way to meet the requirements then it is not a bill of exchange and therefore the further provisions of the Act are irrelevant.

Negotiability

The basis of the bill of exchange is that it is a written request for payment. In this respect it is similar to, and in addition to, the invoice. Unlike that document, however, it can, and frequently does, have an existence completely independent from the other documents to which it relates, since it is a negotiable instrument. The concept of negotiability has been previously referred to in Chapter 3 in connection with bills of lading, but whereas in that case the transfer of title which took place related to goods, in the case of the bill of exchange what is transferred is the right to receive payment of money. The actual transfer is effected in the same way as with a bill of lading, by including the word "order" in the payment instructions followed by endorsement, simple or specific, by the holder.

An important aspect of negotiability is that purchasers of negotiable instruments, provided that they act in good faith and without knowledge of any defect in title of previous holders, can acquire a better title to the instrument than was possessed by the person from whom they obtained it. This is in direct contrast to the situation regarding, for example, stolen goods, which may be traced and recovered from the holders even though they might have purchased in good faith.

Parties

The various parties to a bill of exchange are as follows.
1. The *drawers* are the issuers of the bill and therefore evidently the prime creditors in the transaction, usually the sellers.
2. The *payees* are the people whom the drawers instruct that the debt be paid to. Normally, of course, this would be themselves, but it may be a third party, particularly where that third party is providing finance to the sellers, such as a bank.
3. The *drawees* are the debtors, usually the buyers of the goods.

4. The *acceptors* of a bill are the drawees of that bill where it is payable at a future date, after they have indicated on the bill their promise to pay it when due.

5. The *endorser* of a bill is anyone who has transferred title to the proceeds of the bill by endorsement, simple or specific. Simple endorsement is achieved initially by the payee signing it on the back. Specific endorsement is where that signature is accompanied by a specific instruction that payment be made to a named party.

6. The *endorsee* of a bill is anyone to whom title to the bill has been transferred by specific endorsement. Although seldom seen at the present time, it is possible to create more space on the back of a bill of exchange for further endorsements by the attachment of a piece of blank paper called an *allonge*. This is also sometimes used to accommodate the revenue stamps which must be attached to the bill in many countries before it is legally valid.

7. The *holder* of a bill may be the drawer, payee or any endorsee. Under English law, perfect title is enjoyed by a *holder in due course*. To qualify for the maximum protection afforded by the Act (s.29) to such holders, they must:

   (a) hold a bill which is "complete and regular on the face of it"; completeness implies that no essential ingredient is missing, such as the date, the drawer's signature, or any necessary endorsement (the latter even though an endorsement would normally appear on the back, rather than literally "on the face" of the bill); regularity means the absence of such discrepancies as differing words and figures, endorsements in which the name of the endorser is incorrectly given, and so on

   (b) have acquired their rights to the bill before it became overdue

   (c) have had no notice that the bill had been previously dishonoured

   (d) have taken the bill in good faith

   (e) have given value for the bill, and

   (f) have had no notice of any defect in the title of the person from whom they acquired it.

If holders cannot prove that they can fulfil all of these conditions, they become *holders for value*, which still gives them a certain amount of protection but effectively destroys the bill's negotiability in that they are unable to obtain a better title to it than was possessed by the party from whom they acquired it. Thus, if one of a chain of endorsements on a bill is proved to be a forgery, subsequent holders for value of that bill would be unable to enforce it in the courts against the original drawer or against any endorsers prior to the forgery, though they would still have rights of recovery against subsequent holders. The latter is likely to be of small consolation where the bill was taken for value from the forgers themselves. In these circumstances, holders in due course would have the option of suing any one of the previous holders, or all or any of them collectively, and their claims would be supported by the law.

One of the most significant features of a bill of exchange is the date on which it will be due for payment. This is known as the *tenor* of the bill. It may be payable on demand, in which case it is known as a *sight bill*. If the sellers are granting the buyers time to pay, or, in other words, extending credit to them, these circumstances may be met by making the bill payable on the expiry date of the agreed credit period. In these circumstances, it is known as a *usance* bill. In most cases, usance bills are presented to the drawees first for acceptance, by which the drawees indicate on the bill their willingness to pay it on its maturity date.

Acceptance

The acceptance to a usance bill must be signed in precisely the same name as that shown on the bill as the drawee. It is desirable, but not essential, that the word "accepted" precedes the signature, the signature in itself being regarded as sufficient acknowledgement of the debt. Thus, individual drawees need merely sign their name across the face of the bill; partners the name of the firm, and company representatives their names under words indicating that they sign on behalf of the company. The date of the acceptance is essential only where necessary to establish the maturity date of the bill, as when it is drawn payable at a stated period after sight, and when this is the case the date should be that of presentation. Acceptance of a bill is perfectly valid if it is indicated on the reverse of the instrument, but the internal rules of discount markets usually require it to be on the face.

Maturity

The due date of a usance bill may be expressed in a number of ways. It may be payable on a fixed date in the future, or it may be specified as payable at the expiry of a stated period from its date of drawing. In neither of these cases is presentation for acceptance strictly necessary, since the maturity of the bill is known. Such presentation is usually made, however, if for no other reason than reassurance that the debt will

A Typical Form of Bill of Exchange

N°. REFERENCE

DATE .... 19 .... For AMOUNT IN FIGURES

At TENOR

Pay this ....

of Exchange

to the Order

of ....

PAYEE

AMOUNT IN WORDS

Value Received ....

which place to Account

To DRAWEE

DRAWER'S SIGNATURE

PRINTED AND SOLD BY
BOWENA COURT LTD. 7 GARDNER INDUSTRIAL ESTATE KENT HOUSE LANE BECKENHAM KENT

85

THE BILL OF EXCHANGE

Example of a Completed Sight Draft

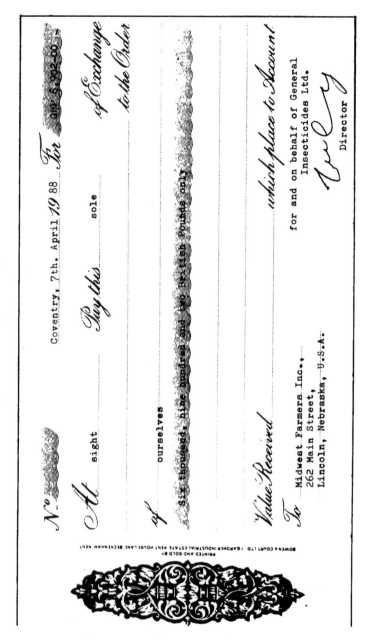

be met when due, and is essential if it is desired to *discount* the bill in the market, a process which is discussed in Chapter 18. Far more usually, the usance is stated to be a given period after sight of the bill, which means that the period will not start to run until the drawee has accepted the bill, and dated such acceptance.

Qualification as bill of exchange

Technically, until such a bill has been so accepted, it is not possible to determine its maturity date and, therefore, it is not payable at "a fixed or determinable future time". Thus, such a bill is not a bill of exchange within the meaning of the Act, and it is not possible to become a holder in due course of an unaccepted usance bill where the usance is expressed as a particular period after sight. This is perhaps a good point at which to consider the other ways in which a bill of exchange might fall foul of the legal definition, and leave its holders with less protection than they might have thought that they had.

So, to consider the requirements of s.3 of the **Bills of Exchange Act 1882** phrase by phrase, the first stipulation which may affect the bill is the word "unconditional". Thus, a clause on the bill such as "pay, subject to satisfactory inspection of goods on arrival" would mean that the instrument would not be a bill of exchange. Note that where a bill of exchange is issued in a set, the whole is regarded as one bill, and the words "pay this first of exchange, second unpaid", or similar, have no such disqualifying effect. "Fixed or determinable future time" has already been mentioned in connection with unaccepted usance bills, but there are other circumstances where these words may be important, such as where the bill is payable "at x days after bill of lading date" or "x days after arrival of goods". In the former case the bill could be validated by the drawees accepting it for payment on a fixed date calculated in accordance with the stated tenor, but the last-mentioned event may, of course, never happen, and therefore the bill's usance period could never commence to run. Such dates are conjectural. Finally, the bill must be for "a sum certain in money", a requirement which would disqualify a bill which bears an interest clause such as "payable with interest from date hereof until approximate date of receipt of proceeds by sellers, at the rate ruling in London at maturity", since it is impossible to foretell either what the rate will be at maturity or how long it will take for proceeds to reach the drawers.

A Bill of Exchange Payable at a Fixed Date in the Future

Nº

Coventry, 7th. April 19 88

For UK£ 6,900.00

Of Exchange

to the Order

At 31st. July 1988

Pay this first

(second unpaid).

of ourselves

Six thousand nine hundred and two British Pounds only

Value Received .... *which place to Account*

for and on behalf of General
Insecticides Ltd.

Director

To Midwest Farmers Inc.,
262 Main Street,
Lincoln, Nebraska, U.S.A.

PRINTED AND SOLD BY
BOWEN & COURT LTD 7 GARDNER INDUSTRIAL ESTATE KENT HOUSE LANE BECKENHAM KENT

88

A Bill of Exchange Payable at a Stated Period from its Date of Issue

Nᵒ

Coventry, 7th. April 19 88 For USD 8,892.00

Pay this second *of Exchange to the Order*

At 30 days date

(first of exchange not being paid)

of Warwickshire Bank Ltd.

Six thousand, nine hundred and two British pounds only

Value Received which place to Account

for and on behalf of
General Insecticides Ltd.

Director

To Midwest Farmers Inc.,
262 Main Street,
Lincoln, Nebraska, U.S.A.

The Commonest Form of a Usance Bill of Exchange

Nº

Coventry, 7th. April 19 88   For

At   120 days sight

Pay this   sole   of Exchange
to the Order

of   Warwickshire Bank Ltd.

six thousand, nine hundred and two British Pounds only

which place to Account

Value Received

for and on behalf of General
Insecticides Ltd.

Director

To   Midwest Farmers Inc.,
262 Main Street, Lincoln,
Nebraska, U.S.A.

PRINTED AND SOLD BY
BOWEN & COURT LTD   1 GARDNER INDUSTRIAL ESTATE, KENT HOUSE LANE, BECKENHAM, KENT

90

A Simple and Perfectly Valid Acceptance

A Domiciled Acceptance

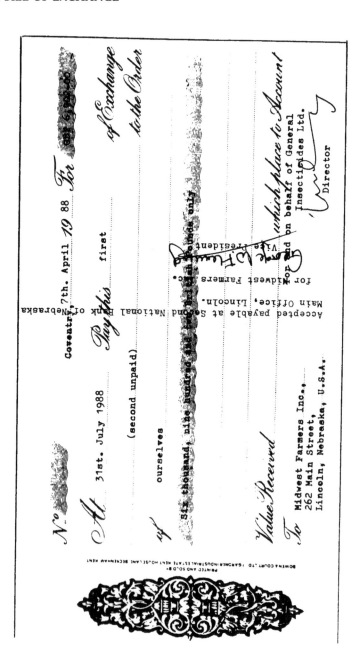

No.

Coventry, 7th. April 19 88 For

At 31st. July 1988

Pay this first of Exchange

(second unpaid) to the Order

of ourselves

Six thousand, nine hundred Pounds only

Value Received

To Midwest Farmers Inc.,
262 Main Street,
Lincoln, Nebraska, U.S.A.

Accepted payable at Second National Bank of Nebraska
Main Office, Lincoln.

for Midwest Farmers Inc.

Frank D. Truman
Vice President

For and on behalf of General
Insecticides Ltd.

Director

which place to Account

PRINTED AND SOLD BY
BOWERS COURT LTD, 'GARDNER INDUSTRIAL ESTATE KENT HOUSE LANE BECKENHAM KENT

92

An Accepted Usance Bill

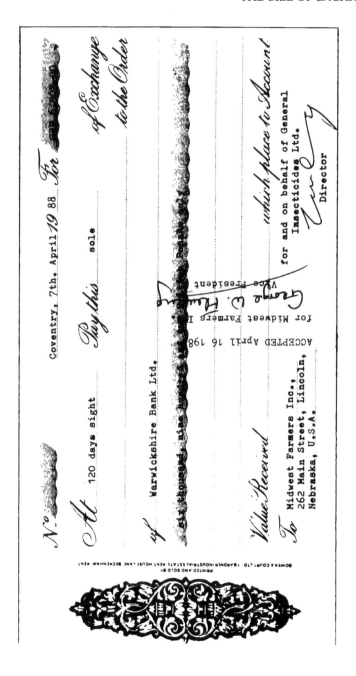

No.

Coventry, 7th. April 19 88

At 120 days sight Pay this sole of Exchange to the Order

of Warwickshire Bank Ltd.

.... five thousand six hundred ....

Value Received

To Midwest Farmers Inc.,
262 Main Street, Lincoln,
Nebraska, U.S.A.

which place to Account

for and on behalf of General
Insecticides Ltd.

Director

ACCEPTED April 16 198

for Midwest Farmers I....

George W. Fleming

Vice President

PRINTED AND SOLD BY
BOWEN & COURT LTD   7 GARDNER INDUSTRIAL ESTATE KENT HOUSE LANE BECKENHAM KENT

A Domiciled and Dated Acceptance

N⁰

Coventry, 7th. April 19 88 For

At 120 days sight sole of Exchange

Pay this to the Order

of Warwickshire Bank Ltd.

ACCEPTED 4.16.88 payable at Second National Bank
of Nebraska, Main Office, Lincoln.

for Midwest Farmers Inc.

George E. Hering

Vice President

which place to Account

for and on behalf of General
Insecticides Ltd.

Director

Value Received

To Midwest Farmers Inc.,
262 Main Street, Lincoln,
Nebraska, U.S.A.

PRINTED AND SOLD BY
BOWENA COURT LTD 1 GARDNER INDUSTRIAL ESTATE KENT HOUSE LANE BECKENHAM KENT

Presentation for payment

Once a bill has been accepted its maturity date must be determined in accordance with the laws of the country in which it is payable. Normally, if maturity falls on a non-working day, that maturity is automatically extended until the next working day. It remains the case in some countries of the world, particularly in the British Commonwealth, that days of grace are allowed to the acceptors before the bill may be regarded as overdue, the most common period being three days. It is important, if full rights under the bill are to be retained, to present the bill for payment on the maturity date so calculated, and, what is more, to present it at the correct place. This will be the address of the drawees as stated on the bill if their acceptance was in plain form, ie a simple signature, dated if necessary, across the face of the bill. If, however, the acceptance is a domiciled one it will nominate a place, usually a bank, at which the bill must be presented for payment at maturity and this stipulation must be complied with.

Where a bill of exchange is domiciled for payment by the acceptors' bankers it has exactly the same effect as if they had drawn a cheque on those bankers. Provided that the acceptance is signed in accordance with the mandate which the paying bank holds from its customers, that the bill is in order and that sufficient funds are available to meet it, the bank may pay the bill without reference or advice to the customers.

Protest

Where a bill is dishonoured by either non-acceptance or non-payment, further action may be necessary to preserve the rights of the holders against the acceptors and any other parties to the bill. Usually this takes the form of *protest*, the object of which is to establish beyond doubt for the benefit of the courts that the bill was properly presented at the right place on the correct maturity date. A second presentation is made, this time by a notary public or similar official, although, in the absence of such a dignitary, presentation may be made by any householder in the presence of two witnesses and the resulting deed of protest later sworn in the presence of a notary public. The deed of protest, whatever its source, testifies to the time and place of presentation and to the answer received, if applicable, this answer being, *prima facie*, the reason for refusal of acceptance or payment. From that point on the protest becomes an integral part of the bill of exchange and if the bill is later paid, the notary's charges must be paid in addition to its face amount and any interest or other charges which may be payable as a result of clauses on it. Without such a process being followed it would be almost impossible to satisfy the courts that the bill was properly presented. Under English law, protest must be made not later than the next working day following the bill's maturity date. Protest for non-acceptance is only required where it is necessary to establish a date from which the bill's maturity can be calculated. The date of such protest becomes the equivalent of the date of acceptance for this purpose.

It should be noted that protest of a bill is not always as desirable a course of action as it might at first seem. In many countries the publicity accompanying the protest can spell commercial ruin to the acceptors and bring about their bankruptcy. In extreme cases, particularly in Middle Eastern countries, non-payment of an accepted bill is a criminal offence which attracts the same penalties as outright theft. Careful thought should therefore be given to the particular circumstances surrounding each case. The remedy for such a dilemma is often to be found in a thorough knowledge of the *bona fides* of the buyers at the pre-contract stage. If sellers have confidence in the integrity of the buyers then they may feel that refusal of payment is probably well-justified and any dispute will be amicably and honourably settled without the intervention of the courts.

Another practical disadvantage of protest is that it is expensive. A deed of protest is a legal document which is completed under seal and as such may well be subject to stamp duty in addition to the fees charged by the notary public and other expenses. If the reason for non-payment is lack of funds, then the fact of protest is unlikely to improve the bill's chances of being paid and its cost may well prove to be money thrown away. Furthermore, particularly where the bill must be presented at a place which is remote from the necessary legal facilities, presentation for protest may prove impossible given the time constraints laid down by the law.

Noting

In the UK and in a very limited number of countries within the Commonwealth, a cheaper form of protection is available by having the unpaid bill *noted*. Presentation must still be made by a notary public but instead of drawing up a legal document to evidence such presentation the notary will merely attach a slip of paper to the bill recording the time and date of presentation, the answer received and the notary's charges. As with the protest, this slip thenceforward forms part of the bill, and the charges must be paid in addition to the face amount before the bill is discharged. The courts will not accept a noted bill as evidence of proper presentation but what noting does achieve is the preservation of the right to take out a full protest at a later date should it prove desirable. Thus, not only are the legal charges reduced but stamp duty on the deed is not due until the decision to protest is taken. Where the refusal of payment is likely to be temporary, this alternative to protest is often much more attractive and it is a pity that a similar option is not available in more countries.

Promissory notes

The legislation enacted by most countries to govern the rights of the various parties to bills of exchange also encompasses promissory notes. Most of the qualities of a bill apply equally to a note. The latter is a fully negotiable instrument, the chief difference being that it emanates from the debtor, known in this context not as the drawee but as the *maker*, instead of the creditor, who becomes the *beneficiary*. A very simple form of promissory note, payable to bearer, is the ordinary banknote.

Aval

English law recognises the rights of no parties to a bill of exchange other than the drawer, payee, drawee and intermediate holders in due course or for value. Many other countries, however, allow for the intervention of a guarantor of payment. The existence of such a guarantee is indicated on the bill (or note) by the signature of the guarantors *por aval*. The system of avalisation has formed the basis for the growth of the specialised form of bill finance known as *forfaiting*, which will be discussed more fully in Chapter 18.

Summary

To summarise the bill of exchange from the point of view of the drawers, or sellers, the bill must be complete and regular in that it must be dated and signed, the amount shown in words must agree with that in figures, it must be for a specific sum of money, must not include any conditions as regards payment, and there must be no doubt as to when it is payable, although where the bill is payable at a stated period after sight by the drawee such doubt will remain until it has been accepted. If the money the bill represents is to be received by any party other than the payees, it must be properly endorsed by those payees. If it is a usance bill it is probably desirable and may be essential for it to be presented first for acceptance by the drawees. Presentation for payment at maturity must be made in business hours on the correct date at the place named on the bill as the drawee's address or at the place named in the acceptance if it is a domiciled one. In practice, of course, such presentation will frequently be carried out by the holder's bankers, and the responsibilities of such agents will be discussed in the next chapter, dealing with collections.

From the buyers' point of view, it is important to remember that once the bill has been accepted, it acquires an existence independent from the contract to which it relates. It may be presented for eventual payment by a holder who was not a party to and has no knowledge of that contract and the rights of such a holder will be rigidly enforced by the law. Conversely, a flaw in a bill of exchange, or an irregularity in its presentation, does not mean that the buyers' obligations under the commercial contract may be evaded, but merely that the bill cannot be used to enforce those obligations.

CHAPTER 8

Collections

In the majority of international trade transactions, the fact of the geographical distance which separates sellers from buyers means that, where a bill for collection is the agreed method of settlement, the physical collection of the debt must be entrusted to an agent. That agent may, of course, be the sellers' commercial representative in the buyers' country, but because of their worldwide networks of correspondents which involve the exchange of lists of authorised signatories and the agreement of test arrangements for electronic communications systems, the role of the collecting agent is almost invariably filled by a bank.

Clean collections

The action required of the sellers' bank may be merely to arrange for the presentation of the bill for payment or acceptance without any accompanying documents, in which case the item is known as a clean collection. Whether or not such an item is honoured depends very much upon the drawee's willingness to pay, and if they refuse there is very little that can be done other than to protest the bill, if considered appropriate. Since no documentation accompanies the bill, it must be assumed that this has been sent direct to the drawees and that they are therefore in a position to obtain control of the relative goods, or that the bill is a usance one being presented for payment at maturity and that documents were previously released against acceptance.

Documentary collections

More often, the documents which the buyers require to obtain delivery of the goods and to clear them through import procedures in their own country are sent with the bill of exchange and the item becomes a documentary collection. By doing this, the sellers can make release of the documents conditional upon the honouring of the bill by the buyers. This is of little help if the buyers have lost interest in the goods altogether, but in normal circumstances provides a considerable incentive to them to pay or accept the bill.

It is very important that when handing the collection to their bankers the drawers provide full instructions as to how that item is to be handled. Where the bill is payable at sight the documents will normally be released only against payment, and the terms of the collection are said to be D/P (Documents against Payment). The sellers may, however, be prepared to make some concessions to the buyers, such as giving them the option to await arrival of the goods before taking up the documents. This is in fact the custom in many parts of the world, particularly in the East, and local banks will automatically allow it to happen unless they are specifically instructed to the contrary. The buyers may be able to inspect the goods before deciding whether or not to honour the bill, and may even be permitted to take away samples for testing. Neither of these privileges will be granted by any bank unless the instructions which it has received expressly authorise it to do so.

Where the bill is at usance, it is vital that the bank be informed by the drawers whether the documents are to be released to the drawees against acceptance (D/A terms) or payment (D/P terms). Buyers will normally ask for D/A terms since this will enable them to clear the goods quickly on arrival, but the granting of these terms means that reliance must thereafter be placed upon the acceptance on the bill, the promise to pay. If that promise is worthless there is little that can effectively be done other than to resort to law, and the exhortation to sellers which has been repeated often in this book, to know the buyers before entering into the contract, must be given yet again. Nonetheless, the vast majority of usance bills sent for collection are handled on D/A terms, since, after all, few would grant a complete unknown a period of months to pay for goods which have already changed hands.

The Collection Process

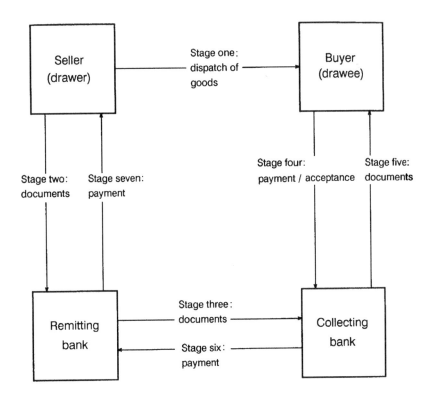

Warehousing and insurance of goods

Despite this, D/P terms are fairly frequently encountered, and are often convenient where the buyers are merchants operating either with restricted storage space or with a very tight cash flow. They may not require to take possession of the goods until they have a firm contract for the onward sale of those goods, or until they are needed for a specific purpose. This arrangement means that the goods may well arrive before the buyers are in a position to pay for them, and as such will need protection for the intervening period. They remain, of course, the property of the sellers, who will need an agent to act on their behalf to clear the goods into a warehouse, to supervise their storage and to attend to insurance while they remain in store. Often that agent is the collecting bank. In these circumstances it is even more important that full instructions are given at the outset as to how that bank is to proceed.

Goods on consignment

A similar situation arises where the goods are sent on a consignment basis. This means that no payment will be made until the buyers have firm contracts for their onward sale, which may constitute all or part of the total consignment. Sometimes a limit is placed on the time allowed for total disposal of the goods. This may involve the buyers in giving an undertaking to pay any remaining balance at the expiry of that period. Once again, it is important that full instructions are given by the sellers at the time of handing the collection to their bankers, since those instructions will determine the actions taken by the collecting bank over what may well be a considerable period of time.

Historically, many banks, particularly in important seaports around the world, maintained their own warehouses and employed their own staff to run them. They were thus well-placed to carry out this type of service on behalf of their correspondents. Although bank warehouses, or "go-downs", are not entirely unknown at the present time, the modern tendency is to subcontract this type of work to a specialist company. What usually happens in practice is that when necessary a bank will release an original bill of lading to its warehousing agents with instructions to clear the goods and to place them in store in the bank's name until further notice. The instructions may also cover insurance of the goods, or the bank may have its own policy under which they may be declared.

It is desirable that periodically a bank bearing responsibility for the safe keeping of goods in this way makes physical checks on those goods to ascertain their continued presence and condition. When the time comes for the goods, or part of them, to be released to the first buyers or their nominees, the bank will, on receipt of payment, issue a delivery order addressed to the warehouse keepers authorising them to deliver the goods to a named party or to bearer. These documents are effectively title to the goods and in some countries have acquired almost the status of negotiable instruments. They fail to achieve this distinction, however, for a number of reasons but particularly because they can convey no better title to the goods than was possessed by the person giving them, unlike a marine bill of lading.

Such involvement of banks in the warehousing of goods is not as unusual as might at first be thought. There are a number of circumstances where goods may be warehoused in the bank's name, of which we have so far considered but two, goods on D/P usance terms and goods on consignment. Another is where acceptance or payment of the bill of exchange has been refused by the drawees and the goods have arrived. Again, the collecting bank in the buyers' country is best placed to ensure that the goods come to no harm, as the holder of the documents of title and as the sellers' already-appointed agent. As will be discussed later in this chapter, the last-mentioned circumstance is often important in determining the course of action which a bank will take in particular circumstances, but to be sure that the sellers' wishes are carried out in case of dishonour of the bill it is important that they include specific instructions at the outset as to what their requirements are.

It may also be necessary for the collecting bank to arrange for storage of the goods where the collection order authorises the drawees to inspect them, or to take away samples, before payment or acceptance of the drawing. In these circumstances, an inspection order or a sampling order will be issued by the bank to the warehouse keepers to enable this to happen.

Protest of dishonoured bill

Storage and insurance of goods are but two of the possible courses open to the sellers where those goods are not taken up following either acceptance or payment of the bill. Protest or noting of the bill, as described in the last chapter, is another, and again it is important in view of the statutory time limits on when this may be done that instructions be given at the outset, before anything has gone wrong. There is then no risk that a bill may be left unprotested and therefore invalid in a court of law merely because no-one was asked to carry out that protest. Great care should be taken, however, to ensure that protest is indeed a desirable remedy in the individual circumstances applying to each collection, since its effect in some countries can be little short of catastrophic for the buyers. On the other hand, the mere threat of it being carried out may be sufficient to induce the buyers to honour the drawing. Only the sellers can make this decision and it should be made clear before the documents leave their control.

Case of need

Another possibility is that the sellers have their own commercial agents in the buyers' country who may be in a position to represent them in negotiations with the buyers in an attempt to reach a settlement. No bank will divulge information regarding its customers' affairs to a third party without written authority to do so. Again, such authority should be given when the drawing is first sent for collection. Furthermore, this should state the precise extent of the powers which may be delegated to the agents, known as the *case of need*, since they are only brought into the transaction in case of the need arising for their services. Such powers may be advisory, in which case their action will be simply to try to use their influence to persuade the buyers to take up the goods. They may be absolute, enabling the agents if they see fit to take documents of title from the bank free of payment and seek to sell the goods elsewhere or even ship them back to the sellers. They may lie anywhere between these two extremes. Whatever they are, there must be no room for doubt on the part of the bank seeking to put the sellers' instructions into effect.

Collection charges

Before leaving the subject of instructions which should be given by the sellers to their bank with the collection, mention must be made of the often vexing question of bank charges. Naturally, banks who are providing the services which have been described above require adequate payment for those services. As was mentioned in Chapter 2, all too often no provision is made at the contract stage regarding who would be responsible for the payment of such charges and it is therefore important that the sellers state clearly in their instructions what, if anything, has been agreed on the subject. If, in their perception, the buyers are responsible for meeting all bank charges, or for perhaps only those levied by the bank or banks handling the collection in the buyers' country, then instructions should be given for the amount of such charges to be collected in addition to the amount of the drawing. Instructions should also give the banks clear guidance as to the action required of them should the buyers' perception of the responsibility be different from that of the sellers. This is usually achieved by stating that charges should be collected but may be waived if refused, or may not be waived as the case may be. Careful consideration should be given to the matter before the latter alternative is used, however, since economically speaking, it is often nonsense to sacrifice payment of the principal amount for the sake of what are usually relatively insignificant charges. Buyers, of course, are well aware of this and many refuse bank charges as a matter of principle. In such cases, the law of agency will apply, and as in a collection the sellers are the principals, so they are the party with ultimate responsibility for reimbursement of expenses incurred on their behalf by their agents.

Effect of the law of agency

It is perhaps time to examine this question of agency in more detail, since in the still significant number of countries where the ICC's Uniform Rules for Collections have not been adopted it is the law of agency which exerts most influence on the actions of the various parties involved in the collection process. All the banks which may become involved in the collection are regarded as acting on behalf of the drawers, though they may have played no part in the selection of those banks other than the first in the chain. This rule applies even where the ultimate collecting bank is presenting the drawing to its own customer for settlement.

The first duty of agents is, of course, to act in accordance with their principals' instructions. There are one or two exceptions to this rule, such as where to carry out such instructions would be detrimental to the interests of the principals, or to those of the agents themselves. But, generally speaking, a bank which acts in a way which is plainly not according to the instructions it has received is taking a very grave risk should its principals incur a loss as a result.

Another important responsibility applying to agents and one which is not so easily definable as the first, is to take any action appropriate to the protection of their principals' interests. This is likely to happen where a situation arises which is not covered by the principals' instructions, such as where goods have arrived and a collecting bank decided to take steps to protect those goods through storage and insurance even though it has no instructions to do so. Since it is plainly of considerable benefit to the owners of the goods that such action be taken, they would not be able to claim that the agents had acted outside the terms of their instructions and would be bound to reimburse the agents for any expenses incurred. Similarly, where a bill is unpaid and the collecting bank arranges for its protest without specific instructions to that effect, such action would be regarded as being in the interests of the drawers in preserving their rights to sue under the bill. The costs (and the consequences) would have to be borne by the drawers. This further underlines what has been said previously in this chapter, that it is important that complete and clear instructions be given at the outset regarding what action is to be taken in particular circumstances, especially in the event of dishonour of the bill.

The prime responsibilities of the drawers, as we have seen, are those of principals towards their agents. Other than these, their chief responsibility is to themselves, since imperfect documentation may well result in delayed payment, unnecessary expense, or even eventual dishonour of the drawing. It therefore makes good sense to ensure that all the documents called for under the contract have been supplied, that they are properly completed, signed and endorsed where necessary, and that any statement regarding the goods or any other aspect of the transaction which is required to be made on the invoice or elsewhere is present.

What of the responsibilities of the other parties in the collection process?

The remitting bank

The first of these parties is the bank to which the collection is entrusted by the drawers, known as the *remitting bank*. Most frequently, this will be the drawer's own bank, though this is not always the case. Too often, the remitting bank sees itself as nothing more than a post office, dispatching the collection to its overseas correspondents, charging its commission, but doing little more to bring the collection to a successful conclusion.

However, it is a good idea to examine the documents, both for completeness and accuracy. It should be alert for such possibilities as missing endorsements or signatures, absence of documents known to be required for the country of destination of the goods or indicated as being required by the contract terms quoted on the invoice and so on. This examination need not be in minute detail, but it is to the benefit of all concerned if obvious discrepancies in the documents are identified and corrected at this stage, rather than when those documents are perhaps ten thousand miles away. The remitting bank, however, is not expected to carry out the exporter's own checking procedures. No legal liability is likely to be incurred by the remitting bank if it fails to detect errors in the documents at this stage. However, if it does detect them its relations both with its customers and its correspondents are enhanced and much correspondence at a later stage is avoided, besides improving the chances of the collection being paid by the drawees.

Endorsement of bill

Since the essence of a collection is usually the bill of exchange and this document may at some later date be required as evidence in legal proceedings, particular attention should be paid to ensure that it fulfils all the requirements of a bill of exchange as laid down in the relevant legislation and described in Chapter 7. If it is made out payable to the order of the drawers, as is usually the case, it should be endorsed by them to enable the proceeds to be paid to a third party, the collecting bank. Such endorsements may be specifically to the remitting bank, which will in turn need to add its own endorsement in favour of the collecting bank. It may be restricted, making the bill payable to "any bank or trust company", or blank, in which case the remitting bank will often close the endorsement by adding words making the bill payable to itself or its correspondent. It is desirable that words such as "value for collection only" be added to the endorsement as an indication that the banks handling the collection are not parties to the financial aspect of the bill or they might find themselves liable to a later "holder in due course" of the bill. Such a qualification should obviously not be used where the bank is providing finance against the bill but will still apply to the endorsement in favour of the collecting bank.

The collection order

Having examined the documents, the remitting bank should next examine the drawer's instructions. If it is not satisfied that they are adequate or, if there are any apparent contradictions, or requirements which might be impossible to comply with or are even to the drawer's detriment should they be complied with, it should take such matters up with its principals immediately rather than slavishly repeating the instructions to its correspondent as is too often the case. Again, by doing so, it is avoiding much needless correspondence and expense at a later date when the bill is unpaid and the collecting bank is unclear as to the action required of it.

It is worth mentioning at this point that great care should be taken by banks when drawers include an instruction that money, usually representing agent's commission, be paid direct from the proceeds of the drawing to a third party. Considerable amounts have been obtained by fraudsters in this way in the past, simply by diversion of relatively insignificant percentages of drawings into their private accounts. Such amounts are easily assumed to have been deducted in the form of bank charges. It is much safer if such commission payments are made as a separate remittance after receipt of proceeds by the drawers. In any case, bill schedules are rarely signed in accordance with the mandate held by the bank for operation of the account, which, of course, they should be if they include payment instructions.

The remitting bank must then give its attention to the instructions which it in turn will give to the collecting bank. For the most part, these will mirror those it has received from the drawers, but it may wish to add its own contribution in such matters as the method by which proceeds of the drawing will eventually be remitted, including the nomination of a receiving bank if the bill is expressed in a foreign currency. It must then send the collection to its selected correspondent by the most expeditious means. Many banks make extensive use of courier services for their international mail and a careful record should be kept of the date on which the item was entrusted to the couriers along with the consignment note number and bag reference, if any. If the documents are despatched by airmail they should be sent by registered post, not so much for the nominal compensation which is paid in case of non-delivery of such mail, as for the means of proof of dispatch which this affords. At least a Post Office registration receipt will be evidence that missing documents have not been accidentally shredded or dropped behind a filing cabinet before they have even left the premises of the remitting bank.

Fate enquiries

Having dispatched the collection, the remitting bank should send a copy of its collection schedule to the drawers, both to act as an acknowledgement of receipt of the drawing and to enable them to verify that the instructions which have been given to the collecting bank are in accordance with their wishes. It should then make a diary note for further action to be taken if necessary. What that action will be depends upon the individual characteristics of the collection and more particularly upon the country on which it is drawn. The important thing is for the remitting bank to be aware at all times of the current status of the collection, and in this, of course, it must rely largely upon its correspondent. If it does not receive advice from the collecting bank within a reasonable time it should institute enquiries itself. These enquiries are usually referred to in the banking industry as "chasers", and are often copies of the original collection schedule which accompanied the documents. It has to be admitted that the value of these chasers is questionable in the extreme, since they seldom have the appearance of being important communications and tend to be either ignored completely or given very low priority. A formal letter, a telecommunication or e-mail, if it is considered that the additional expense is warranted, is far more likely to elicit a response than a routine chaser, and it is desirable that no more than one such be sent before resorting to other means of enquiry. Any advice received should be immediately passed on to the drawers, both to keep them informed of progress and to put them in a position to give any fresh instructions which they may consider appropriate.

The collecting bank

The collecting bank, when it receives the documents, should first ensure that they are complete in terms of the remitting bank's covering schedule, and should then carefully read the instructions which it has been given. If either of these operations reveals any cause for enquiry it should contact the remitting bank immediately. It should then check whether any of the documents requires its own endorsement to validate them and affix any stamps to the bill which may be required under the

COLLECTIONS

A Properly Completed Collection Order

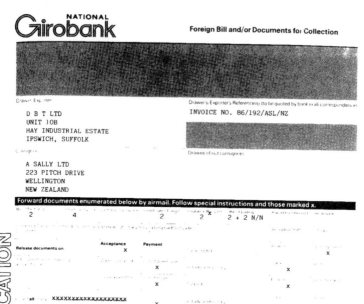

National Girobank

Foreign Bill and/or Documents for Collection

Drawer Exporter

D B T LTD
UNIT 10B
HAY INDUSTRIAL ESTATE
IPSWICH, SUFFOLK

Drawer's Exporter's References (to be quoted by bank in all correspondence)

INVOICE NO. 86/192/ASL/NZ

Consignee

A SALLY LTD
223 PITCH DRIVE
WELLINGTON
NEW ZEALAND

Drawee (if not consignee)

Forward documents enumerated below by airmail. Follow special instructions and those marked x.

| 2 | 4 | | 2 | X | 2 + 2 N/N | | |

Release documents on

Acceptance X   Payment

all XXXXXXXXXXXXXXXXXXX

Only

Special Instructions

PLEASE REQUEST COLLECTING BANK TO DISCOUNT ACCEPTED BILL AT OUR EXPENSE

In case of need refer to

3.10.86

90 D/S

Please collect the above mentioned Bill and/or Documents subject to the Uniform Rules for Collections (1978 Revision) International Chamber of Commerce, Publication No. 322 I/We agree that you shall not be liable for any loss, damage, or delay however caused which is not directly due to the negligence of your own officers or servants

Signature
for ...

date   6.10.86

XXXXXXXXX

£15,231.60

110

tax laws of its country. It is then faced with the problem of presentation of the collection to the drawees without prejudicing the interests of its principals, the drawers. There are a number of ways of achieving this, depending on local practice, on the standing of the drawees in the local community and their geographical location relative to the collecting bank.

Presentation

If the drawee's premises are nearby, it may be possible for their representative to call at the bank to inspect the documents, or for a bank messenger to take them to the drawee's premises for that purpose. If the documents are found to be in order, arrangements can then be made for payment, or a usance bill can be accepted and the documents released in exchange, unless of course the terms of the collection are D/P and the bill is at usance.

If, however, the drawees are at some distance from the bank, non-negotiable copy documents can be mailed for examination, the documents of title only being released when the drawing is honoured. This can be unsatisfactory, however, since often it is essential to have sight of the original bill of lading in particular before a decision can be made on the acceptability of the documents. An alternative, but more expensive and troublesome method, is to send photocopies of the documents, or to transmit copies by fax or e-mail, if available.

The collecting bank is in a much better position where the drawees are their own customers, since they then have the information necessary to make a decision on whether the documents may be sent or released on trust for examination. If distance is a problem, they may be able to use the services of their local branch to make physical presentation of the collection to the drawees. Since, however, the collecting bank has been entrusted with the drawing because of its correspondent relationship with the remitting bank rather than any connection with or proximity to the drawees, it is quite common for the drawees to be customers of a different bank as well as being too far distant for physical presentation to be a possibility. In these circumstances it is common for the collecting bank to ascertain the identity of the drawee's bankers and to forward the drawing to them with all relevant instructions for collection. The decision as to the trustworthiness of the drawees is thus delegated to those best placed to make it. The disadvantages of this method are that payment is likely to be made slower by the extra processing in the third bank, a further set of collection charges will be incurred, and the possibility of a fruitful marketing contact with another bank's customer is lost.

Large numbers of collections are on sight D/P terms and are paid without problems. In this situation, the only responsibility of the collecting bank is to remit the proceeds as quickly as possible in the manner laid down by the remitting bank in its instructions, under advice to that bank if necessary. It is entitled to deduct its charges from the amount sent, if they have not been collected from the drawees, and further charges may accrue where the payment is made through the collecting bank's correspondent to a nominated bank in a third country.

Payment "pipelines"

In some countries, a shortage of hard currency with which to pay for imports has led to a system whereby, provided the collection order so authorises, documents are released to the buyers against payment in local currency. The collecting bank then makes application to the authorities for an allocation of foreign exchange to enable it to remit proceeds to the remitting bank. If none is immediately available, the application is placed in what is known as a "pipeline", which means that it joins a queue and that payment will not reach the sellers until the application arrives at the head of that queue. Usually the sellers will have been aware of this factor at the time of entering into the contract, but it remains important that notification of payment in local currency is sent to the remitting bank so that all are aware that the buyers have fulfilled their obligations. Remitting banks should note that from this point on there is little to be gained by continuing to send monthly chasers, since there is nothing which the collecting bank can usually do to expedite payment — the matter is out of their hands. The waiting period for items in pipelines is normally a known factor and may be anything up to three years or beyond in some cases. In such cases, it may be advisable to obtain payment through a letter of credit instead.

Terms of payment

Where the terms are usance D/A, the acceptance on the bill should be checked for apparent correctness. It should be signed in the same name as is stated on the bill for the drawee and if the bill is payable at a given period after sight the acceptance must be dated in order that the maturity date may be ascertained. If the bill is domiciled for payment at the collecting bank by one of that bank's own customers, the acceptance amounts to an instruction to pay and should therefore be checked in accordance with the mandate held, and the signatures verified. There is no legislative requirement regarding the actual position of the acceptance, but the domestic regulations of many financial markets, including that of London, require the acceptance to be on the face of the bill and endorsements to be on the back.

What happens next will depend upon the instructions held. Sometimes it is requested that the bill be returned to the remitting bank after acceptance, and in these circumstances this should be done as soon as possible, any charges claimed and the item discharged. More often the instructions are to hold the bill until maturity and then to present it for payment, in which case it is essential to advise the remitting bank of acceptance and of the bill's maturity date as soon as possible. Particularly if a bill is to be protested for dishonour, it is vital that it is presented on its maturity date and so careful records must be kept in a diary specifically for that purpose. Although sight bills and unaccepted usance bills are virtually worthless, it should be remembered that an accepted usance bill is a promise of payment and a fully negotiable instrument. It is therefore potentially worth whatever amount is shown on its face. It should therefore be kept, unendorsed, in a secure place until the time comes for its presentation for payment. It must then be presented, after any necessary endorsement, to the place for payment stipulated, if the acceptance is a domiciled one, or to the drawee's address as shown on the bill if it is not. On payment, proceeds are dealt with as described above for a sight bill.

Where the terms of the collection are usance D/P, the bill should be presented for acceptance and its maturity noted in a diary in the same way as for a D/A bill. In this case, however, the documents must be kept with the bill and, furthermore, the collecting bank must ascertain from the shipping company's agents the expected arrival date of the carrying vessel (a diary note should be made of this). This is because the goods may well arrive and therefore need protective measures before the bill is presented for payment. In practice, many acceptors will want to take up the documents on arrival of the goods and will therefore pay the bill before its maturity, a process known as retiral. In some trades it is customary to allow a rebate on the amount of a retired bill to reflect the interest advantage to the drawers arising from early receipt of proceeds. This should be covered in the instructions received from the remaining bank.

Sometimes the drawees may state that they wish to defer payment or acceptance of a bill until arrival of the goods and in many countries this is accepted as standard practice. If this occurs, the collecting bank should again ascertain the expected arrival date of the vessel and immediately advise the remitting bank of the position, following which a diary note should be made for re-presentation and the documents kept securely until that time.

Procedure on dishonour

Similar considerations apply where a bill is dishonoured for any other reason, since the protection of the goods is of paramount importance. As previously stated, such action may be in accordance with specific instructions received, or may voluntarily be undertaken by the collecting bank to protect the interests of its principals. With this aspect taken care of, it should be clear from the instructions held as to what other actions are to be taken. In any case, the remitting bank must be informed immediately by telecommunication if possible, of the dishonour and of the reasons for it, if any have been given, the expected date of arrival of the carrying vessel and of what action has been or is being taken to obtain payment or acceptance of the bill.

If protest of the bill is required and it is an unaccepted usance bill payable at a stated period after sight, it must first be protested for non-acceptance. The only effect of this is to establish a date from which the bill's maturity can be calculated. When this date is reached it must be represented, this time for payment, and a fresh protest executed if payment is refused.

Where the remitting bank's instructions permit reference to a "case of need" where dishonour occurs, this must be done immediately, since any delay may make its intervention ineffective. Great care should be taken, however, to ensure that the case of need does not exceed its powers, and if those powers are stated to be advisory it must not be allowed to intervene in the goods themselves. If the extent of the case of need's powers is not clear from the instructions (and these instructions were not clarified on receipt, as they should have been), it must be assumed that its function is merely advisory. Where it is stated to have full powers, however, it would be in order for the collecting bank to release the documents to it against a simple receipt and possibly payment of any outstanding charges, and thereafter to discharge the item from its records. In these circumstances, of course, the remitting bank must be advised immediately of the action taken, and the receipt forwarded to it.

The drawees

It remains to consider the position of the drawees themselves, who of course are the strongest of any party involved in the collection process. When documents are presented for payment or acceptance it is essential that they be examined carefully to ensure that they are as called for in the contract, that they are in a form which will allow trouble-free import of the goods when they arrive, that those goods have not in fact already arrived and therefore are possibly incurring demurrage charges, that there is nothing in the documents to suggest that the goods are substandard or damaged in any way, and that the goods appear to be of the specification ordered.

In the absence of authority to inspect the goods or to take samples before paying or accepting the bill, there is little more that can be done to ensure that the merchandise will be in order and therefore much will rest upon the relationship between sellers and buyers, as has been said many times before. Should any dispute arise later it is outside the scope of the collection and must be settled under the contract itself. Where a bill has been accepted for payment at a future date, it is not unknown for buyers and sellers to notify the collecting bank, through the remitting bank, that a discount may be allowed when the bill is presented for payment to redress some discovered defect or shortage in the goods. It should be remembered, however, that this will not be possible if the bill has since been discounted and may be presented by a holder in due course who has no connection with and no knowledge of the underlying contract. For this reason, it is generally more satisfactory if such settlements are made outside the collection after the bill has been honoured.

CHAPTER 9

Uniform Rules for Collections

In keeping with its twin objectives of the standardisation and simplification of international trade procedures, the International Chambers of Commerce (ICC) published the first set of rules for voluntary adoptions by national banking associations or individual banks for the handling of collections, both clean and documentary. In keeping with the ICC policy of staying abreast of changes in international commerce, these rules were revised in 1968, 1979 and again in 1995. It is the latter version, which came into force on 1 January 1996, which form the current set of rules relating to collections under the title ICC Uniform Rules for Collections, publication No. 522 (URC522).

By comparison with the similar rules relating to documentary credits, the URC are a straightforward code, based largely upon common sense, reflecting established methods of handling international collections, technology and banking practices (both national and international) with the aim to assist in the resolution of any disputes. This is not to say that Uniform Customs and Practice for Documentary Credits (UCP500), to be discussed later in this book, are in any way not based on common sense principles, but collections by their nature are much simpler transactions than credits and this factor expresses itself in the relative simplicity of the rules required for their governance.

As with any set of rules, it is of paramount importance that all those who may be affected by them are fully aware of their contents. In countries where they have been adopted, all bank collection schedules will incorporate a clause stating that the collection is handled subject to the provisions of URC522. It therefore makes sense for exporters, forwarders, buyers and banks to familiarise themselves with the rules, since they will have a direct bearing on the way in which documents, and the monetary proceeds arising from them, are handled, and, as we have seen, may even extend to the treatment of the goods themselves.

Many of the processes and situations covered by URC522 have already been dealt with in the preceding chapters. The purpose of this one is to examine each rule with reference to how it relates to the collections as we have described it in Chapter 8, with such additional comment as may be necessary. The rules consist of 26 Articles, the first three being General Provisions and Definitions.

The URC522 Rules

ARTICLE 1 — Application of URC522

(a) The Uniform Rules for Collections, 1995 Revision, ICC Publication No. 522, shall apply to all collections as defined in Article 2 where such rules are incorporated into the text of the "collection instruction" referred to in Article 4 and are binding on all parties thereto unless otherwise expressly agreed of contrary to the provisions of a national, state or local law and/or regulations which cannot be departed from.

(b) Banks shall have no obligation to handle either a collection or any collection instruction or subsequent related instructions.

(c) If a bank elects, for any reason, not to handle a collection or any related instructions received by it, it must advise the party from whom it received the collection or the instructions by telecommunication or, if that is not possible, by other expeditious means, without delay.

Comment

Though adopted and recognised by most banks, the revised Rules for Collections still have not been as widely accepted as UCP500. This still leads to potential problems where one or the other banks involved in a collection does not recognise URC522. Under this article, it makes it a requirement for any bank electing not to handle the credit, for whatever reason, to notify the party initiating the collection. If the remitting bank states on its covering schedule that the terms of URC apply to the collection, and unless the collecting bank expressly rejects that stipulation in its acknowledgement of receipt it would be held to have accepted the condition along with all the other instructions contained in the schedule. In practice, therefore, even where one bank has not adopted the Rules they may be applied by the courts anyway, provided they do not contravene national, state or local law as stated in Article 1.

ARTICLE 2 — Definition of collection

For the purposes of these Articles:

2 (a) "Collection" means the handling by banks of documents as defined in sub-Article 2(b), in accordance with instructions received, in order to:

(i) obtain payment and/or acceptance, or

(ii) deliver documents against payment and/or against acceptance, or

(iii) deliver documents on other terms and conditions.

2 (b) "Documents" means financial documents and/or commercial documents:

(i) "Financial documents" means bills of exchange, promissory notes, cheques, or other similar instruments used for obtaining the payment of money

(ii) "Commercial documents" means invoices, transport documents, documents of title or other similar documents, or any other documents whatsoever, not being financial documents.

2 (c) "Clean collection" means collection of financial documents not accompanied by commercial documents.

2 (d) "Documentary collection" means collection of:

(i) Financial documents accompanied by commercial documents

(ii) Commercial documents not accompanied by financial documents.

Comment

2(a) sub-section (iii) relates to the situation which occasionally arises where documents are to be delivered free of payment against the provision of a simple receipt, or against the presentation of evidence that payment has been effected by other means, or against evidence of the issue of a standby letter of credit covering payment.

ARTICLE 3 — Parties to a collection

3 (a) For the purposes of these Articles the "parties thereto" are:

(i) the "principal" who is the party entrusting the handling of a collection to a bank

(ii) the "remitting bank" which is the bank to which the principal has entrusted the handling of a collection

(iii) the "collecting bank" which is any bank, other than the remitting bank, involved in processing the collection

(iv) the "presenting bank" which is the collecting bank making presentation to the drawee

3 (b) The "drawee" is the one to whom presentation is to be made in accordance with the collection instruction.

Comment

The use of the word "principal" (3a (i)) is interesting in that it is borrowed directly from the phraseology of the law of agency, of which much has been said in preceding chapters. It is important that principals in a collection procedure understand that they have the legal obligation to instruct all agents acting on their behalf (ie the banks). We now look at the article that covers the form and structure of collections and stresses the importance of Collection Instructions. Article 4 replaces a much shorter Article in URC 322 (Article 8) and reflects the problems and potential risks that were (and still are) encountered by banks when collection instructions are not give or are inadequate.

ARTICLE 4 — Collection instruction

4 (a)   (i)   All documents sent for collection must be accompanied by a collection instruction indicating that the collection is subject to URC 522 and giving complete and precise instructions. Banks are only permitted to act upon the instructions given in such collection instruction, and in accordance with these Rules.

        (ii)   Banks will not examine documents in order to obtain instructions.

        (iii)   Unless otherwise authorised in the collection instruction, banks will disregard any instructions from any party/bank other than the party/bank from whom they received the collection.

4 (b) A collection instruction should contain the following items of information, as appropriate.

        (i)   Details of the bank from which the collection was received including full name, postal and SWIFT addresses, telex, telephone, facsimile numbers and reference.

        (ii)   Details of the principal including full name, postal address, and if applicable telex, telephone and facsimile numbers

        (iii)   Details of the drawee including full name, postal address, or the domicile at which presentation is to be made and if applicable telex, telephone and facsimile numbers.

        (iv)   Details of the presenting bank, if any, including full name, postal address, and if applicable telex, telephone and facsimile numbers.

        (v)   Amount(s) and currency(ies) to be collected.

        (vi)   List of documents enclosed and the numerical count of each document.

(vii)   (a)   Terms and conditions upon which payment and/or acceptance is to be obtained.

      (b)   Terms of delivery of documents against:

          1.   payment and/or acceptance

          2.   other terms and conditions

It is the responsibility of the party preparing the collection instruction to ensure that the terms of the delivery of documents are clearly and unambiguously stated, otherwise banks will not be responsible for any consequences arising therefrom.

(viii) Charges to be collected, indicating whether they may be waived or not.

(ix)   Interest to be collected, if applicable, indicating whether it may be waived or not, including:

      (a)   rate of interest

      (b)   interest period

      (c)   basis of calculation (for example 360 or 365 days in a year) as applicable.

(x)   Method of payment and form of payment advice

(xi)   Instructions in case of non-payment, non-acceptance and/or non-compliance with other instructions.

4(c)   (i)   Collection instructions should bear the complete address of the drawee or of the domicile at which the presentation is to be made. If the address is incomplete or incorrect, the collecting bank may, without any liability and responsibility on its part, endeavour to ascertain the proper address.

      (ii)   The collecting bank will not be liable or responsible for any ensuing delay as a result of an incomplete/incorrect address being provided.

Comment

Incomplete or unclear instructions formed the majority of problems under the previous Rules (URC 322) hence the inclusion of this detailed Article in the new Rules. The onus is clearly on the principal or party preparing the collection instruction to issue clear, detailed and unambiguous instructions. Banks are not authorised to work without instructions and if instructions are missing or unclear banks are not responsible for any consequences arising therefrom. Unfortunately, poor instructions still cause problems. Many international banks have designed collection instructions to meet the provisions of sub-section (b) of this Article.

Sub-section (c) emphasises the importance of having the complete address of the drawee or of the domicile at which the presentation is to be made. This may sound obvious but Post Office Boxes are not sufficient for collection purposes. Though the collecting bank may endeavour to ascertain the proper address this will cause delays and may incur costs such as storage or demurrage on the goods. The banks, in such cases, are without any liability and responsibility for any ensuing delay as a result of an incomplete/incorrect address being provided.

The next section of the Rules (Section C) cover the "Form of Presentation".

ARTICLE 5 — Presentation

(a) For the purposes of these Articles, presentation is the procedure whereby the presenting bank makes the documents available to the drawee as instructed.

(b) The collection instruction should state the exact period of time within which any action is to be taken by the drawee.

Expressions such as "first", "prompt", "immediate", and the like should not be used in connection with presentation or with reference to any period of time within which documents have to be taken up or for any other action that is to be taken by the drawee. If such terms are used banks will disregard them.

(c) Documents are to be presented to the drawee in the form in which they are received, except that banks are authorised to affix any necessary stamps, at the expense of the party from whom they received the collection unless otherwise instructed, and to make any necessary endorsements or place any rubber stamps or other identifying marks or symbols customary to or required for the collection operation.

(d) For the purpose of giving effect to the instructions of the principal, the remitting bank will utilise the bank nominated by the principal as the collecting bank. In the absence of such nomination, the remitting bank will utilise any bank of its own, or another bank's choice in the country of payment or acceptance or in the country where other terms and conditions have to be complied with.

(e) The documents and collection instruction may be sent directly by the remitting bank to the collecting bank or through another bank as intermediary.

(f) If the remitting bank does not nominate a specific presenting bank, the collecting bank may utilise a presenting bank of its choice.

Comment
This new Article defines "presentation" and amalgamates Articles from the previous set of Rules indicating how, if instructions are unclear, a presenting bank may be nominated.

Sub-section (c) covers the authority to affix stamps. This is necessary because in countries where stamp duty is payable on bills of exchange such instruments would have no legal significance if duty were not paid and evidence on the bill. In some countries, similar conditions apply to other documents such as the bill of lading, insurance policies or certificates. The right to do this is probably also conferred later in Article 11(c) in its reference to foreign laws and usages. The addition of identifying marks refers to the practice of many banks of stamping their collection reference number on each document received to guard against the possibility of that document becoming detached from the rest and subsequently making it difficult or perhaps impossible to reunite the complete set, particularly the bank. Banks should not indelibly stamp accepted usance bills with the maturity date, if a mistake is made and an alteration become necessary, such a change would constitute a material alteration to the instrument, and as such, would require validation by all previous holders. It is therefore good practice to write the maturity date in pencil which can be erased if necessary.

The last 3 sub-sections of this Article are to prevent costly and irritating delays if unclear instructions are given with regard to nominating banks. To control the collection process it is advisable for the principal and/or remitting bank to nominate the collecting and presenting banks to be used but again, following the law of agency, sub-sections (d) and (e) allow banks to choose subsequent parties in the transaction while (f) extends the right of the collecting banks to utilise a presenting bank of its choice. Lack of control on behalf of the principal may lead to many banks being involved in the collection so invoking unexpected and costly banking charges.

ARTICLE 6 — Sight/acceptance

In the case of documents payable at sight the presenting bank must make presentation for payment without delay. In the case of documents payable at a tenor other than sight the presenting bank must, where acceptance is called for, make presentation for acceptance without delay, and where payment is called for, make presentation for payment not later than the appropriate maturity date.

ARTICLE 7 — Release of commercial documents

Documents Against Acceptance (D/A) v Documents Against Payment (D/P)

(a) Collections should not contain bills of exchange payable at a future date with instructions that commercial documents are to be delivered against payment.

(b) In the absence of such statement, commercial documents will be released only against payment and the collecting bank will not be responsible for any consequences arising out of any delay in the delivery of documents.

(c) If a collection contains a bill of exchange payable at a future date and the collection instruction indicates that commercial documents are to be released against payment, documents will be released only against such payment and the collecting bank will not be responsible for any consequences arising out of any delay in the delivery of documents.

Comment

Due to confusion of terms and contradictory instructions under collections procedures this Article was written specifically in order to clarify the terms D/A and D/P. Under the previous and current Rules, in the absence of proper instructions, the collecting bank will take the safest alternative open to it and retain documents until payment has been made for the goods. In practice, this places collecting banks in an extremely awkward situation when the drawees insisted the terms of their agreement with the sellers were D/A. This article does emphasis the point that the collecting bank is not responsible for any consequences arising out of any delay in the delivery of documents.

ARTICLE 8 — Creation of documents

Where the remitting bank instructs that either the collecting bank or the drawee is to create documents (bills of exchange, promissory notes, trust receipts, letters of undertaking or other documents) that were not included in the collection, the form and wording of such documents shall be provided by the remitting bank, otherwise the collecting bank shall not be liable or responsible for the form and wording of any such document provided by the collecting bank and/or the drawee.

Comment

A new Article for URC added to protect other parties against possible claims of liability where the remitting bank instructs them to raise or create documents without clear instructions. "Liabilities and Responsibilities" in detail make up the 4th section (D) of the Rules beginning with Article 9.

ARTICLE 9 — Good faith and reasonable care

Banks will act in good faith and exercise reasonable care.

Comment

Previously Article 1 of the Rules, it underlines the already established principle of the law of agency. It should be noted that past legal decisions have indicated that the judiciary expect a high standard in both these commodities from banks which are charging for professional services and are expected to provide staff with the necessary expertise to handle collections effectively and efficiently. Any bank which does not do so could be liable for breach of contract and bound to cover any losses to its principals which result from such breach.

ARTICLE 10 — Documents v goods/services/performances

(a) Goods should not be despatched directly to the address of a bank or consigned to or to the order of a bank without prior agreement on the part of that bank.

Nevertheless, in the event that goods are despatched directly to the address of a bank or consigned to or to the order of a bank for release to a drawee against payment or acceptance or upon other terms and conditions without prior agreement on the part of that bank, such bank shall have no obligation to take delivery of the goods, which remain at the risk and responsibility of the party despatching the goods.

(b) Banks have no obligation to take any action in respect of the goods to which a documentary collection relates, including storage and insurance of the goods even when specific instructions are given to do so. Banks will only take such action if, when, and to the extent that they agree to do so in each case. Notwithstanding the provisions of sub-Article 1(c), this rule applies even in the absence of any specific advice to this effect by the collecting bank.

(c) Nevertheless, in the case that banks take action for the protection of the goods, whether instructed or not, they assume no liability or responsibility with regard to the fate and/or condition of the goods and/or for any acts and/or omissions on the part of any third parties entrusted with the custody and/or protection of the goods. However, the collecting bank must advise without delay the bank from which the collection instruction was received of any such action taken.

(d) Any charges and/or expenses incurred by banks in connection with any action taken to protect the goods will be for the account of the party from whom they received the collection.

(e)

(i) Notwithstanding the provisions of sub-Article 10(a), where the goods are consigned to or to the order of the collecting bank and the drawee has honoured the collection by payment, acceptance or other terms and conditions, and the collecting bank arranges for the release of the goods, the remitting bank shall be deemed to have authorised the collecting bank to do so.

(ii) Where a collecting bank on the instructions of the remitting bank or in terms of sub-Article 10(e)(i), arranges for the release of the goods, the remitting bank shall indemnify such collecting bank for all damages and expenses incurred.

Comment

The justice of 10(a) provision should be apparent on two counts. Firstly, the handling of goods is not a service which the banks offer in the normal run of their business and is outside the scope of their usual activities. Although, as has been seen, they do quite frequently become involved with the goods, this takes place in specific circumstances and in no way obliges them to assume the duties of a mercantile agent. Secondly, no-one can be expected to assume the responsibility for a duty which they have not previously agreed to perform. This also includes the common use of the phrase "to the order of the bank" which many exporters use with the idea that this will give them some control over their goods prior to payment. Again, banks must have previously agreed to undertake responsibility of the goods before this phrase can be added to transport documents.

Though the statements under sub-sections (b), (c) and (d) clearly give banks no actual responsibility or liability it must be remembered that under Article 9 banks must act in good faith and exercise reasonable care. A good example of failure to exercise reasonable care might be arranging for the storage of perishable goods in unrefrigerated accommodation, so caution must be used by banks.

ARTICLE 11 — Disclaimer for acts of an instructed party

(a) Banks utilising the services of another bank or other banks for the purpose of giving effect to the instructions of the principal, do so for the account and at the risk of such principal.

(b) Banks assume no liability or responsibility should the instructions they transmit not be carried out, even if they have themselves taken the initiative in the choice of such other bank(s).

(c) A party instructing another party to perform services shall be bound by and liable to indemnify the instructed party against all obligations and responsibilities imposed by foreign laws and usages.

Comment
Again, this is following the principles of the law of agency.

ARTICLE 12 — Disclaimer on documents received

(a) Banks must determine that the documents received appear to be as listed in the collection instruction and must advise by telecommunication or, if that is not possible, by other expeditious means, without delay, the party from whom the collection instruction was received of any documents missing, or found to be other than listed.

Banks have no further obligation in this respect.

(b) If the documents do not appear to be listed, the remitting bank shall be precluded from disputing the type and number of documents received by the collecting bank.

(c) Subject to sub-Article 5(c) and sub-Articles 12(a) and 12(b) above, banks will present documents as received without further examination.

Comment
Despite the fact that banks have no obligation to examine the documents in detail, after verifying none is actually missing, there are in fact common sense reasons for at least a cursory examination of the documents, as outlined in Chapter 8, even though this is not a bank's responsibility. This Article again puts the onus on the principal to ensure that all documents are clearly listed and that they meet the requirements laid down in the order.

ARTICLE 13 — Disclaimer on effectiveness of documents

Banks assume no liability or responsibility for the form, sufficiency, accuracy, genuineness, falsification or legal effect of any document(s), or for the general and/or particular conditions stipulated in the document(s) or superimposed thereon; nor do they assume any liability or responsibility for the description, quantity, weight, quality, condition, packing, delivery, value or existence of the goods represented by any document(s), or for the good faith or acts and/or omissions, solvency, performance or standing of the consignors, the carriers, the forwarders, the consignees or the insurers of the goods, or any other person whomsoever.

ARTICLE 14 — Disclaimer on delays, loss in transit and translation

(a) Banks assume no liability or responsibility for the consequences arising out of delay and/or loss in transit of any message(s), letter(s) or document(s), or for delay, mutilation or other error(s) arising in transmission of any telecommunication or for error(s) in translation and/or interpretation of technical terms.

(b) Banks will not be liable or responsible for any delays resulting from the need to obtain clarification of any instructions received.

ARTICLE 15 — Force majeure

Banks assume no liability or responsibility for consequences arising out of the interruption of their business by Acts of God, riots, civil commotions, insurrections, wars, or any other causes beyond their control of by strikes or lockouts.

Comment

The above Articles (13, 14 and 15) emphasis the fact that the banks are only, repeat, only interested in documents. They do not have any legal responsibility to get involved with the actual transaction in any way, beyond accepting the documents. This Article gives banks even more protection than previously and should make the adoption of URC522 attractive to banks. Bearing in mind what has been said about their responsibilities under the law of agency, they have everything to gain and little to lose by the adoption of these Rules. It should be remembered though, that the protection afforded by these Articles does not absolve them from their responsibility to exercise reasonable care as required by Article 9.

The following 5th section of URC522 (E) deals with "Payment".

ARTICLE 16 — Payment without delay

(a) Amounts collected (less charges and/or disbursements and/or expenses where applicable) must be made available without delay to the party from whom the collection instruction was received in accordance with the terms and conditions of the collection instruction.

(b) Notwithstanding the provisions of sub-Article 1(c) and unless otherwise agreed, the collecting bank will effect payment of the amount collected in favour of the remitting bank only.

Comment

It should be remembered that the collecting bank is acting as the agent of the drawers and it follows that amounts collected in this capacity cannot be offset against debit balances of the remitting bank.

ARTICLE 17 — Payment in local currency

In the case of documents payable in the currency of the country of payment (local currency), the presenting bank must, unless otherwise instructed in the collection instruction, release the documents to the drawee against payment in local currency only if such currency is immediately available for disposal in the manner specified in the collection instruction.

Comment

In a number of countries, particularly those with exchange control regulations, money must be designated "external" before it may be credited to the account of a non-resident. Funds not so designated are likely to be of little use to the sellers and are therefore not acceptable as payment in exchange for the release of documents.

ARTICLE 18 — Payment in foreign currency

In the case of documents payable in a currency other than that of the country of payment (foreign currency), the presenting bank must, unless otherwise instructed in the collection instruction, release the documents to the drawee against payment in the designated foreign currency only if such foreign currency can immediately be remitted in accordance with the instructions given in the collection instruction.

ARTICLE 19 — Partial payments

(a) In respect of clean collections, partial payments may be accepted if and to the extent to which and on the conditions on which partial payments are authorised by the law in force in the place of payment. The financial document(s) will be released to the drawee only when full payment thereof has been received.

(b) In respect of documentary collections, partial payments will only be accepted if specifically authorised in the collection instruction. However, unless otherwise instructed, the presenting bank will release the documents to the drawee only after full payment has been received, and the presenting bank will not be responsible for any consequences arising out of any delay in the delivery of documents.

(c) In all cases partial payments will be accepted only subject to compliance with the provisions of either Article 17 or Article 18 as appropriate.

Partial payment, if accepted, will be dealt with in accordance with the provision of Article 16.

Comment

It should be remembered that the collecting bank is acting as the agent of the drawers and it follows that amounts collected in this capacity cannot be offset against debit balances of the remitting bank. The 6th section of URC522 (F) looks at Interest, Charges and Expenses.

ARTICLE 20 — Interest

(a) If the collection instruction specifies that interest is to be collected and the drawee refuses to pay such interest, the presenting bank may deliver the document(s) against payment or acceptance or on other terms and conditions as the case may be, without collecting such interest, unless sub-Article 20(c) applies.

(b) Where such interest is to be collected, the collection instruction must specify the rate of interest, interest period and basis of calculation.

(c) Where the collection instruction expressly states that interest may not be waived and the drawee refuses to pay such interest the presenting bank will not deliver documents and will not be responsible for any consequences arising out of any delay in the delivery of documents(s). When payment of interest has been refused, the presenting bank must inform by telecommunication or, if that is not possible, by other expeditious means without delay the bank from which the collection instruction was received.

Comment

As was seen in Chapter 7, if an interest clause on a bill of exchange is not unconditional and definitive, the document will very likely fail to qualify as a bill of exchange within the terms of the legal definition. The presenting bank will only insist on the payment of interest if it is clearly stated in the collection instruction that interest must not be waived. The delay this may cause in the release of goods could be costly and it should be clear in the original contract agreement between the buyer and seller that interest is to be paid and who is responsible for any charges incurred due to any delay in payment.

ARTICLE 21 — Charges and Expenses

(a) If the collection instructions specifies that collection charges and/or expenses are to be for account of the drawee and the drawee refuses to pay them, the presenting bank may deliver the document(s) against payment or acceptance or on other terms and conditions as the case may be, without collecting charges and/or expenses, unless sub-Article 21(b) applies.

(b) Where the collection instruction expressly states that charges and/or expenses may not be waived and the drawee refuses to pay such charges and/or expenses, the presenting bank will not deliver documents and will not be responsible for any consequences arising out of any delay in the delivery of the document(s). When payment of collection charges and/or expenses has been refused the presenting bank must inform by telecommunication of, if that is not possible, by other expeditious means without delay the bank from which the collection instruction was received.

(c) In all cases where in the express terms of a collection instruction or under these Rules, disbursements and/or expenses and/or collection charges are to be borne by the principal, the collecting bank(s) shall be entitled to recover promptly outlays in respect of disbursements, expenses and charges from the bank from which the collection instruction was received, and the remitting bank shall be entitled to recover promptly from the principal any amount so paid out by it, together with its own disbursements, expenses and charges, regardless of the fate of the collection.

(d) Banks reserve the right to demand payment of charges and/or expenses in advance from the party from whom the collection instruction was received, to cover costs in attempting to carry out any instructions, and pending receipt of such payment also reserve the right not to carry out such instructions.

Comment

Banks can only refuse to release documents on non-payment of charges (as with interest — Article 20) if it is expressly stated in the collection instruction that they cannot be waived. This again could lead to delays and incur costs; the banks shall not be made responsible if delays or costs are incurred. The only thing added to this under the new rules is that, if charges are refused by the drawee, the bank must notify the other party(ies) immediately.

Sub-sections (c) and (d) of Article 21, do mean that charges are payable by the drawers even though the banking system has failed to secure payment of the principal debt. Under the law of agency, this would in any case be the position, and justly so, since the time spent and expenses incurred by the banks have been at the instigation of the drawers, who are often not entirely blameless in the matter of the reasons for refusal of payment. In these circumstances, such charges are likely to be far higher than those which would have been incurred had the collection been paid on presentation, since factors such as the cost of fax, e-mail advices, storage of goods and protest of bills may well have been added to the normal collection charges. Also, many banks now make additional charges for irregular items, often based on the actual work performed. It, therefore, makes economic sense to take immediate action when a collection is first reported to the sellers as unpaid or unaccepted. The final section of URC522 (G) covers Other Provisions.

ARTICLE 22 — Acceptance

The presenting bank is responsible for seeing that the form of the acceptance of a bill of exchange appears to be complete and correct, but is not responsible for the genuineness of any signature or for the authority of any signatory to sign the acceptance.

ARTICLE 23 — Promissory notes and other instruments

The presenting bank is not responsible for the genuineness of any signature or for the authority of any signatory to sign a promissory note, receipt, or other instruments.

Comment

These two articles (22 and 23) make distinctions between bills accepted, and promissory notes made, by a bank's own customers and those accepted or made by the customers of other banks. In the former the bank has the means of checking on both the genuineness and the authority from the mandate it holds for operation of the account. In these circumstances it would be well-advised to check these aspects. In any case, if the acceptance or note is a domicile one, the checks will have to be made at some stage as the acceptance or note constitutes an authority to pay at maturity.

ARTICLE 24 — Protest

The collection instruction should give specific instructions regarding protest (or other legal process in lieu thereof), in the event of non-payment or non-acceptance.

In the absence of such specific instructions, the banks concerned with the collection have no obligation to have the document(s) protested (or subjected to other legal process in lieu thereof) for non-payment or non-acceptance.

Any charges and/or expenses incurred by banks in connection with such protest, or other legal process, will be for the account of the party from whom the collection instruction was received.

Comment

The article says that the collection order should give specific instructions. Where protest is not required a specific instruction would be the words "do not protest" or the like on the collection order, not an absence of reference of any kind to protest. Note that the collecting bank is not obliged to protest in the absence of specific instructions, but neither is it precluded from doing so if it sees fit. Most banks' pre-printed collection instructions have boxes to indicate whether the principal wishes an unpaid or unaccepted bill to be protested, and then room to indicate any special requirements and contact names. The principal may indicate that they would like to be contacted before the bill is protested — this can sometimes lead to a settlement of the bill as the drawee, on hearing from the principal that the bill is going to be protested, pays or accepts the bill before the protest can take place to prevent legal proceedings being taken against them. See also Article 25 — Case-of-need.

With regard to charges, as was stated in Chapter 7, the cost of the protest or noting of a bill is automatically added to its face amount and, therefore, if it is later paid these charges must be included in the payment made.

ARTICLE 25 — Case-of-need

If the principal nominates a representative to act as case-of-need in the event of non-payment and/or non-acceptance the collection instruction should clearly and fully indicate the powers of such case-of-need. In the absence of such indication banks will not accept any instructions from the case-of-need.

Comment

As with all instructions, the drawee or principal must be very specific. When nominating a case-of-need it should be clear to the bank up to what level this party can operate. If it is not clear they will be used purely as an advisor, ie they will be informed of the position and left to intercede with the drawees in an attempt to induce payment or acceptance but will be unable to instruct the bank.

ARTICLE 26 — Advices

Collecting banks are to advise fate in accordance with the following rules:
(a) Form of Advice
   All advices or information from the collecting bank to the bank from which the collection instruction was received, must bear

appropriate details including, in all cases, the latter bank's reference as stated in the collection instruction.

(b) Method of Advice

It shall be the responsibility of the remitting bank to instruct the collecting bank regarding the method by which the advices detailed in (c)i, (c)ii and (c)iii are to be given. In the absence of such instructions, the collecting bank will send the relative advices by the method of its choice at the expense of the bank from which the collection instruction as received.

(c)

    (i) Advice of Payment

        The collecting bank must send without delay advice of payment to the bank from which the collection instruction was received, detailing the amount or amounts collected, charges and/or disbursements and/or expenses deducted, where appropriate, and method of disposal of the funds.

    (ii) Advice of Acceptance

        The collecting bank must send without delay advice of acceptance to the bank from which the collection instruction was received.

    (iii) Advice of non-payment and/or non-acceptance

        The presenting bank should endeavour to ascertain the reason for non-payment and/or non-acceptance and advise accordingly, without delay, the bank from which it received the collection instructions.

        The presenting bank must send without delay advice of non-payment and/or advice of non-acceptance to the bank from which it received the collection instruction.

        On receipt of such advice the remitting bank must give appropriate instructions as to the further handling of the documents. If such instructions are not received by the presenting bank within 60 days after its advice of non-payment and/or non-acceptance, the documents may be returned to the bank from which the collection instruction was received without any further responsibility on the part of the presenting bank.

Comment

Banks should note that the mere acknowledgement of receipt of chasers, or the constant repetition of assurances that the principals have been advised of the position and their instructions are awaited, do not constitute instructions as to the further handling of the documents in the context of this article. The period of three months which is allowed for the remitting bank to initiate some positive action is in any case extremely generous and there can really be little excuse for a continued failure to do so. This being so, it is surprising that so many collections fall into this category.

CHAPTER 10

Documentary letters of credit

The basic principles of a documentary letter of credit were outlined in Chapter 1 of this book, along with a discussion of the advantages and disadvantages to sellers and buyers arising from the use of this method of settlement. Because the credit is frequently a dauntingly complicated document, at least in its general appearance if not in the actuality, attempts at defining it frequently lead to equally complex and verbose descriptions. In reality it is very simple: it is a promise by a bank that sellers will receive payment for goods provided that they comply with all the conditions laid down in the credit.

This promise is as solemn as that made by the issuing bank when it signs a bank draft. Just as the dishonour of such a draft when presented for payment would be damaging in the extreme to the bank's reputation, so the promise made in its letter of credit is one which it breaks at its peril. It is a great pity at the present time that some banks hedge the promise with so many conditions as to render it virtually worthless. The piece of paper issued by such banks may look like a letter of credit, may call itself such, but in reality carries with it no assurance to the sellers that they will receive payment if they carry out their duties under the contract. It is one of the prime objectives of this book to provide sellers with the ability to judge for themselves whether a particular instrument is truly a credit or not. If it is not, in that it does not guarantee payment, then buyers who have agreed in the contract to arrange for the issue of a letter of credit are in breach of that contract. The only way to purge the financial world of these undesirables is to reject them. True, this may lead to frustration of the contract, but it should be remembered that a sale of goods for which payment is not made is a loss.

Parties in a letter of credit transaction

Beneficiary	The person being paid, usually the exporter
Applicant	Party paying and/or raising the letter of credit, usually the buyer
Issuing Bank or Opening Bank	Bank in applicant's country which has "opened" the credit
Advising Bank	Bank in beneficiary's country which will act on behalf of the issuing bank
Confirming Bank	Bank in beneficiary's country which will pay on receipt of valid document
Negotiating Bank	Bank in beneficiary's country which will negotiate the L/C with the beneficiary and may pay on receipt of documents

Issue

When applying for a letter of credit, the chief concern of the buyers is, as far as possible, to ensure that they receive the goods they require and the correct documentation relating to those goods, at the right time. The advantages, discussed in Chapter 1, which accrue to the sellers from its use, while significant, are incidental to this objective. Most banks will not issue letters of credit other than under a pre-arranged facility and the agreed limit of such facilities will be treated by the bank in exactly the same way as an application to borrow money. In effect, this is what is happening, since although no money actually changes hands at the time of issue of the credit, the bank is committing itself to making payment to the sellers at a later date, and of course will look to the buyers for repayment. A request to a bank for letter of credit facilities will therefore only be granted when the bank has satisfied itself that its customers meet all the criteria which they would normally apply to a potential borrower. Several years' accounts will be required for analysis of trends in the customer's profitability; the bank will consider the type of goods to be dealt in and the experience and competence of the customer's management team in the markets in which they are engaged; security may well be asked for. Sometimes the latter may be in the form of the deposit with the bank of cash cover for a percentage of the amount of each credit issued.

The promise made by the issuing bank to the sellers, who from henceforward will be referred to as the *beneficiaries*, constitutes the core of the credit and theoretically no other parties need be involved. Even should the buyers, the *applicants*, go out of business, the core remains and the promise must be honoured.

Advising

In practical terms, however, other parties are brought into the process for various reasons, which will become apparent as we examine a typical transaction. Because of the distances, not to mention national frontiers, which separate sellers and buyers in international trade, the letter of credit on issue will not normally be sent direct to the beneficiaries. Although it is not unknown for this to happen, when it does the credit almost always turns out to be a forgery (see Chapter 17). The usual procedure is for the issuing bank to make use of its correspondent bank in the beneficiaries' country, and it will send the credit to that bank with the request that it advises the beneficiaries of its issue. The bank thus becomes the *advising bank* and it is by that title that it will be referred to in the remainder of this book.

The advising bank incurs no liability under the credit by acceding to its correspondent's request, but in advising the credit to the beneficiaries it does warrant to them, and to any other party who may become involved at a later stage, that it has taken all appropriate steps to check that the credit is genuine. Beneficiaries who may be unfamiliar with the issuing bank may therefore take reassurance regarding that bank's actual existence, and know that it is sufficiently highly regarded to have established a correspondent relationship with a bank in their own country with which they are familiar.

Confirmation

Very often beneficiaries desire more than this, however, and ask that the advising bank, or even a third bank, to join in the undertaking of the issuing bank. Where this occurs, and if the other bank is willing to comply, it adds its confirmation to the credit, which in effect means that it adds its own promise that payment will be made provided that the terms and conditions of the credit are complied with. It is often thought, mistakenly, that this is a guarantee that the confirming bank will make payment if the issuing bank does not. The promise of the confirming bank stands alone, however, with the beneficiaries looking to that bank to make payment irrespective of the status of the issuing bank. Hence the occasional reluctance of banks to provide confirmation, for the

The Documentary Credit Process

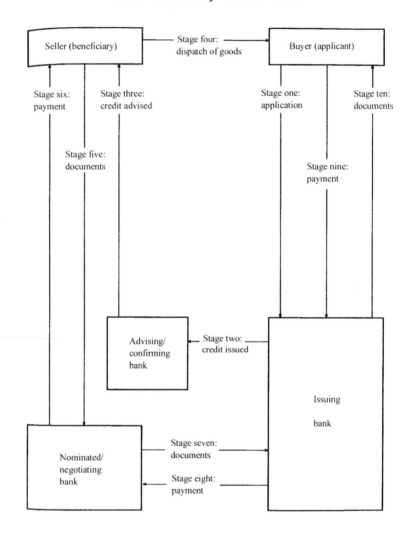

promise that they are required to make is every bit as binding as that of the issuing bank and since they are geographically closer to the beneficiaries theirs is the liability which will materialise first.

Presentation

When the beneficiaries are ready to present their documents for settlement, they do so to the bank, if any, nominated in the credit. What happens next depends upon the credit's terms. If the nominated bank is authorised to pay, or is the confirming bank of a sight credit, and does so, the transaction is complete so far as the beneficiaries are concerned. If, in a usance credit, it is authorised to accept the beneficiaries' bill of exchange (draft), or, where no draft is called for, to give an undertaking that payment will be made at a future date, the beneficiaries have that undertaking to rely on. If it is authorised to negotiate, the beneficiaries will receive reimbursement but the negotiating bank will retain a right of recourse to them in case of its not receiving payment from the issuing bank. If there is no nominated bank, then any bank is free to negotiate the drawing if it so wishes, although in practice such negotiation would normally be undertaken only by the advising bank or, perhaps, by the beneficiaries' own bank.

Reimbursement

One further bank may be involved in the transaction where the credit is expressed in a currency which is neither that of the applicants' nor the beneficiaries' countries, or where there is no account relationship between the nominated and issuing banks. Settlement will be made by the bank which will then look to obtain reimbursement for the amount it has paid from a paying agent named by the issuing bank in the credit. This is the *reimbursing bank*.

All this is the way in which the system should work. Sadly, the reality is often far removed from the ideal. Frequently, so-called confirmation of a credit is regarded by the bank which enters into it as more a source of income than a liability of honour, such as where it refuses to pay the beneficiaries until it has received covering funds from the issuing bank or the reimbursing bank. Many credits are issued, in this age of hyper-awareness of cost cutting possibilities, which are payable only upon receipt of documents by the issuing bank, or they are issued in a third country's currency without bearing any indication as to how a negotiating bank is to obtain reimbursement. Such instruments hardly deserve the title of credits at all, since they are tantamount to mere conditional guarantees of payment of collections.

It is, of course, the beneficiaries who are most concerned regarding the acceptability of a letter of credit. It is of vital importance, on receipt of a credit, to read it carefully without delay. The beneficiaries' concern is partly to ensure that the terms laid down for payment are acceptable to them in accordance with their own understanding of the commercial contract, and that unanticipated and onerous conditions have not been included, prices and specifications are as agreed, and so on. It is just as important, however, to examine the document from the point of view of how, where, when, and indeed, if, it will give rise to payment. Beneficiaries have the right to reject unworkable letters of credit, or if they are not in accordance with the contract terms. This will be looked at in more detail in Chapter 17.

Types of credit

Revocable/irrevocable

Credits may be revocable, in which case they may be amended or even cancelled without the beneficiaries' consent, or they may be irrevocable, in which case the beneficiaries have the right to refuse to accept any amendments. Since the greatest advantage to the sellers in utilising a letter of credit is security of payment, it might be thought that there would be no circumstances in which a revocable credit would be acceptable, but they do have one particular advantage over irrevocable credits: they are cheaper. This makes them attractive where the use of a credit is dictated not by commercial prudence but by government decree. This might be the case where trading partners have the kind of relationship which would normally foster an open account arrangement between them, but to satisfy local legislation they are compelled to utilise letters of credit.

The reason for the banks charging less for the issue of this type of credit is that where a bank is concerned about its customers, the applicants, and if it feels that it may not be able to obtain repayment of any drawings which may be made under the credit, it can cancel it unilaterally, without seeking the agreement of any other party. The degree of risk to which it is exposed is therefore considerably reduced and the commission it charges should reflect this.

Sight/usance

A credit may provide for payment at sight, or it may be a usance credit providing for payment to be deferred for a specified period. The credit thus caters for instances where the sellers have allowed a period of credit to the buyers. Usually a usance credit will call for the beneficiaries to accompany their documents with a bill of exchange drawn at the specified tenor and drawn on a named party. This drawee may be the nominated bank or the issuing bank. From the point of view of the beneficiaries the most advantageous drawee is undoubtedly the nominated bank, for they will then have a first-class acceptance which can be discounted at prime rates in the local bill market (for more information in discounting, see Chapter 18). Where the beneficiaries require to raise finance in this way and the bill is drawn on the issuing bank, they must request the bank to which they have presented the documents to negotiate the drawing, which will mean that, not only will they receive less money after allowance has been made for the transit times for documents and proceeds, but that the negotiating bank will retain recourse against them if it is unable to reimburse itself from the issuing bank.

Deferred payment

Not all credits which provide for payment other than at sight call for presentation of a bill of exchange. Where one or other of the countries involved applies heavy stamp duty to bills, they may be dispensed with by the replacement of the acceptance with an undertaking that payment will be made after expiry of the usance period. Such undertakings cannot be discounted, as can a bill, but the beneficiaries may be able to negotiate them, ie obtain an advance in anticipation of receipt of payment.

We have seen that a credit may be revocable or irrevocable, confirmed or unconfirmed, and provide for payment at sight or at usance. To further illustrate the flexibility of the letter of credit as a means of settlement, we will now look at various types of more specialised credits, designed to cater for specific circumstances affecting trade between the two parties to the commercial contract.

Revolving

Where buyers and sellers are trading with each other on a regular basis they may find it to their mutual advantage to utilise a revolving letter of credit. A normal non-revolving credit is issued for a specified amount and, provided it allows partial drawings, may be drawn against for fractions of that amount until it is exhausted, after which it is fully drawn and defunct. Furthermore, it will have an expiry date beyond which no further drawings may be made. Although a revolving credit will still have an expiry date, it is likely to be valid for a far longer period, being designed to cover the continuing trade between buyers and sellers.

There are two basic ways in which a revolving credit may operate, one relating to time and the other to payment. A time revolving credit will incorporate a clause providing for the reinstatement of the full amount of the credit at specified intervals, such as monthly. Thus, if it is estimated that the total annual value of imports from a particular supplier in US$600,000, with an average individual shipment worth US$10,000, this would either mean the issue over a year of about 60 letters of credit each covering a single consignment, or perhaps 12 credits allowing partial drawings and each covering one month's trade. Such a system would be wasteful of both time and money and, furthermore, would mean that the buyers' total outstanding liability under letters of credit issued on their behalf would be unnecessarily high. A revolving credit, however, would, say, allow the beneficiaries to draw up to US$50,000 in any one month, at the end of which the amount would be reinstated to cover the following month's shipments. In this instance, the issuing bank would probably regard its total liability under that credit as being US$100,000, since in theory the full value could be drawn on the last day of a month and again on the following day whilst the first set of documents were still in transit.

This consideration can be rendered unnecessary by the use of a revolving payment credit. Drawings can be made under this up to the amount of the credit and documents forwarded by the negotiating bank to the issuing bank in the normal way. As reimbursement for each drawing is obtained from the applicants the amount of that drawing is reinstated, by means of an advice by mail or telex from the issuing bank to the negotiating bank, and thus becomes available for further drawings. In this way the total outstanding liability never exceeds the value of the credit, though the credit is slightly less flexible as a result.

Whatever their format, revolving credits are extremely useful instruments where circumstances permit their use. Not only do they bring about a considerable saving in time and effort by replacing large numbers of applications and individual letters of credit with just one of each, but further time is saved by the familiarity of their terms to all parties concerned.

Packing/red clause

A packing or red clause credit is useful to sellers where the transport of goods is on FOB, ExWorks or FCA terms and payment is required before the goods are actually exported. This is especially true where the buyers instruct forwarders to consolidate consignments from a number of suppliers and only export goods, for example, every six weeks so they, the buyers, benefit from a cheaper price by having more freight travelling at one time. Under this arrangement if a normal letter of credit was used, sellers may have a frustrating time obtaining the required evidence of export and, in fact, the credit may expire before presentation can be made.

If buyers are prepared to assist, they may agree to have delivery to their nominated freight forwarder, or other such party, recognised as the accepted point for payment and instruct the bank to accept a warehouse receipt or a Forwarder's Certificate of Receipt (FCR) to claim payment before the goods are shipped.

Packing/Red Clause credits originated in the wool trade, where importers in England appointed buying agents in Australia whose task it was to travel round the outback farms at shearing time, or to the various official wool sales, to select and buy fleeces on behalf of their principals. They would then arrange with the local carrier for the fleeces to be transported to the nearest port for shipment. The problems which these agents faced was that the farmers with whom they were dealing had little use for a piece of paper issued by a bank in Bradford and much preferred to be paid in hard cash. To enable the agent to accommodate this preference, the letter of credit would carry a clause authorising the advising bank to advance a stated percentage of the credit's value to the beneficiary against presentation of a simple receipt and an undertaking to present full documentation as each consignment of wool was shipped. This clause was traditionally written in red ink to distinguish such credits from the normal kind. Red ink (and even red ribbons on typewriters) has disappeared into museums but the name remains with us (though amended slightly by the addition of "packing") to describe any credit which allows pre-shipment advances or full payment to be made to the beneficiary at the risk and expense of the applicant.

There has been an increased use of such credits in recent years because of the benefits to both sellers and buyers. The credit requires a third party, generally a forwarder, to assume control of the goods by accepting them into a warehouse in the exporter's country. Buyers must be satisfied that the forwarder they nominate is trustworthy and, will check that the goods do not appear damaged or short-shipped, will not issue receipts without goods being delivered into their control or unacceptably delay shipment.

Transferable

Similar considerations of finance for the purchase of goods by the party contracted to supply them brought about the introduction of another variant on the credit theme, the transferable letter of credit. In this case the beneficiaries may be buying agents but in many cases are merchants, whose task is to act as intermediaries between original suppliers and ultimate buyers of goods. They rely on commission or profit for their livelihood but never enter into physical possession of the goods. Their problem is the matching of a contract to supply goods with the natural reluctance of suppliers to relinquish control of those goods without the assurance of being paid for them.

The answer is to request the issue of a transferable credit in their favour. They can then ask the advising bank to transfer all or part of the value of that credit to a third party, the suppliers of the goods, who thus have the advantage of a promise by a bank that they will receive payment for their wares. The suppliers can then safely arrange for shipment of those goods to their ultimate destination, claiming payment under the transferred credit. The first beneficiaries can then exchange their own invoices for those of the suppliers and draw under the original credit for the balance, if any, between the amount of their invoices and the amount paid by the bank to the second beneficiaries. This amount represents their profit on the transaction, and the bank now has a full set of documents conforming to the terms of the original credit and can claim reimbursement from the issuing bank. Thus, again a particular set of circumstances has been met by the flexibility of the letter of credit as an instrument of settlement.

A word of warning to buyers at this point. It is not unusual to develop blind spots to such words as transferable, particularly when they are all but concealed in a string of adjectives, as in the phrase "settlement by means of a confirmed, irrevocable, transferable letter of credit" which might appear on the proforma invoice. The request for a transferable credit should always put buyers on notice that they are not dealing with the actual manufacturers of the goods. This has two major implications. One is that a strong possibility exists that the buyers could obtain the goods more cheaply by dealing directly with the manufacturers; the other is that, whatever enquiries they have made about the sellers, they have no means of knowing the status of the party who will ship the goods and must rely upon the judgment of the merchant with whom they are dealing.

The transferable credit is dealt with by *Uniform Customs and Practice for Documentary Credits* (Section F, Article 48) and will be looked at again in that context in Chapter 13. The circumstances under which it is used can be similar to those giving rise to the back-to-back credit but this will be dealt with in its proper place in the chapter on bank finance for international trade.

Standby

A standby letter of credit can be regarded as a "link" between a normal credit and trading with open account or bills of exchange, though this versatile financial document can act as a guarantee in many circumstances, see below. The basic "Direct Pay Standby" may be opened, for example, for 12 months validity, and is used as a method of trade debt guarantee, held as a "backup" to open account terms of payment or bills of exchange for collection, and invoked when payments are overdue. It remains dormant as a security for the seller, unless invoked in a case of need arising but could affect the buyers' finance facilities.

All standbys are issued to support payment, when due or after default, of obligations based on money loaned or advanced, or upon the occurrence or non-occurrence of another contingency. A standby credit need not be a complex document tied into strict compliance of documents, unlike the normal documentary letters of credit procedure. Indeed, the only document that is really necessary is a statement by the beneficiary that the obligations of the other party have not been met, eg payment has been claimed but not received within the agreed timescale.

Standby L/C are now governed by their own set of banking rules known as International Standby Practices — ISP98 (UCP500 being deemed inappropriate for the differing activities covered by standby credits). While the standby is associated with the United States where it originated and where it is most widely used, it is truly an international product being used increasingly throughout the world. The formulation of separate rules for governing standby credit evidences the maturity and importance of this financial product. According to the ICC in the Preface to ISP98, the amounts outstanding of standbys greatly exceed the outstanding amounts of commercial letters of credit.

For convenience, standbys are commonly classified descriptively based on their function in the underlying transaction or other factors not necessarily related to the terms and conditions of the standby itself. For example:

- A "Direct Pay Standby" (as mentioned earlier) supports payment when due of an underlying payment obligation typically in connection with a financial standby without regard to a default.
- An "Advance Payment Standby" supports an obligation to account for an advance payment made by the beneficiary to the applicant.
- A "Bid Bond/Tender Bond Standby" supports an obligation of the applicant to execute a contract if the applicant is awarded a bid.
- A "Commercial Standby" supports the obligations of an applicant to pay for goods or services in the event of non-payment by other methods.
- A "Counter Standby" supports the issuance of separate standby or other undertaking by a beneficiary of the counter standby.
- A "Financial Standby" supports an obligation to pay money, including any instrument evidencing an obligation to repay borrowed money.
- An "Insurance Standby" supports an insurance or reinsurance obligation of the applicant.
- A "Performance Standby" supports an obligation to perform other than to pay money including for the purpose of covering losses arising from a default of the applicant in completion of the under lying transactions.

The rules governing standby credits (ISP98), like UCP 500 for commercial letters of credit, simplifies, standardises and streamlines the drafting of standbys, and provides clear and widely accepted answers to common problems. There are basic similarities with the UCP because standby and commercial practices are fundamentally the same. Even where the rules overlap, however, the ISP is more precise, stating the intent implied in the UCP rules, in order to make the standby more dependable when a drawing or honour is questioned. Since standbys infrequently require presentation of negotiable documents, standby practice is currently more conducive to electronic presentations, and the ISP provides definitions and rules encouraging such presentations.

Standby credits are similar to both documentary commercial credit and other forms of bonds and guarantees which both have their own rules (UCP500 and URDG respectively). If a credit (or guarantee) is to be subject to the rules relating to standby credits, then it should clearly be indicated that it is issued subject to ISP98.

The format of a letter of credit

Having examined the variety of forms which the letter of credit may take, and the above list is by no means exhaustive, we will now return to the ordinary, everyday credit covering the sale of goods under a single contract. We are seeing the gradual adoption as a standard format of the design brought into being by the International Chamber of Commerce. This process is far from complete, as is the situation regarding the introduction of a standard form of bill of lading, but slowly banks are recognising the advantages of abandoning their own distinctive, but often defective designs, and adopting the ICC format which groups particular aspects of the credit in the same position on the form, regardless of which bank has issued the credit. Since application forms are similarly designed, this greatly facilitates the transfer of the information from application to credit, and is also of enormous assistance to those banks which advise credits by transferring the data from the original instrument on to their own paper. Also, with the increased use of electronic messaging a standard computer version of a letter of credit is replacing the old-fashioned formats.

At the top of the form appear three important pieces of information: the name and address of the issuing bank; the title of the document indicating that it is either a revocable or an irrevocable letter of credit; and the credit number, usually accompanied by a statement that it must appear on all bills of exchange drawn under the credit. Although the vast majority of credits are irrevocable, it is worth checking it is not revocable when a credit is received, if it does not state it is revocable under the UCP rules it is automatically irrevocable.

Issue and expiry

Next, on the right hand side of the form, appear the date and place of issue and the date and place of expiry of the credit. The place of expiry is important, as has already been mentioned, since if the beneficiaries are to enjoy the full advantages of a letter of credit it should expire in their own country.

Applicant and beneficiary

Below this comes a series of boxes, the top two of which contain the applicant's name on the left and the beneficiary's name and address on the right. It is particularly important that the name and address of the beneficiaries is given accurately and in full, since without this information the advising bank may be unable to fulfil its function.

Amount

The next two boxes contain the name of the advising bank on the left and the amount of the credit in words and figures on the right. Obviously, the latter should agree with each other. If the amount is stated as "approximately", UCP (Article 39) states that it may be reduced or exceeded by up to ten per cent. This will be discussed further both later in this chapter and in Chapter 13.

Shipment

The lower box on the left-hand side is subdivided to accommodate the credit's requirements regarding the shipment of the goods. Separate sections state whether partial shipments are allowed, whether transhipment is permitted, and whether insurance will be covered by the applicants. The credit then gives details of the journey which is to be evidenced by the transport document and the latest date on which the goods may be shipped or taken in charge.

Drawings

The corresponding space on the right gives the name of the bank which is nominated to honour drawings and whether that honour is to be by way of payment, negotiation, acceptance or deferred payment undertaking. Details of the required bill of exchange, if any, are also given, including its tenor and on whom it is to be drawn.

Documents

What follows may vary according to which bank has issued the credit. The extremes are represented by a completely blank area, in which any documentary and other requirements may be inserted in precise terms, or preprinted requirements with boxes to be marked to show which documents are actually required and blank spaces left to allow for special requirements relating to those documents. It is the author's opinion that the former is the preferable option, since any attempt to

International Chamber of Commerce Standard Format Letter of Credit

NAME OF ISSUING BANK - NOM DE LA BANQUE EMETTRICE

Irrevocable Documentary Credit
Crédit documentaire irrévocable

Number - Numéro

Place and date of issue - Lieu et date d'émission

Date and place of expiry - Date et lieu de validité

Applicant - Donneur d'ordre

Beneficiary - Bénéficiaire

Advising Bank - Banque notificatrice   Ref. nr. - No. Réf.

Amount - Montant

Credit available with - Crédit réalisable auprès de

- [ ] by sight payment / par paiement à vue
- [ ] by acceptance / par acceptation
- [ ] by negotiation / par négociation
- [ ] by deferred payment at / par paiement différé à

against the documents detailed herein
contre les documents précisés ci-après

- [ ] and beneficiary's draft at / et la traite du bénéficiaire au

Partial shipments
Expéditions partielles
- [ ] allowed / autorisées
- [ ] not allowed / non autorisées

Transhipment
Transbordement
- [ ] allowed / autorisé
- [ ] not allowed / non autorisé

Loading on board/dispatch/taking in charge at/from
Mise à bord/expédition/prise en charge à/de

for transportation to:
à destination de:

on
sur

Advice for the Beneficiary - Avis pour le bénéficiaire

Documents to be presented within
Documents à présenter dans les [ ] days after the date of issuance of the transport document(s) but within the validity of the credit.
jours après la date d'émission du/des document(s) de transport mais dans la période de validité du crédit.

We hereby issue the Documentary Credit in your favour. It is subject to the Uniform Customs and Practice for Documentary Credits (1983 Revision, International Chamber of Commerce, Paris, France, Publication No. 400) and engages us in accordance with the terms thereof. The number and the date of the credit and the name of our bank must be quoted on all drafts required. If the credit is available by negotiation, each presentation must be noted on the reverse of this advice by the bank where the credit is available.

Nous émettons par la présente ce crédit documentaire en votre faveur. Il est soumis aux Règles et Usances Uniformes relatives aux Crédits Documentaires (Révision 1983, Publication No. 400 de la Chambre de Commerce Internationale, Paris, France) et nous engage selon leurs termes. Le numéro et la date du crédit ainsi que le nom de notre banque devront être mentionnés sur toute traite requise. Si le crédit est utilisable par négociation chaque présentation devra être inscrite au verso de cet avis par la banque où le crédit est utilisable.

This document consists of
Ce document consiste en [ ] signed page(s)
page(s) signée(s)

© Copyright 1985, International Chamber of Commerce / Chambre de Commerce Internationale standardise documentary requirements inevitably omits essential items and clutters the credit with irrelevant sections which only serve to confuse the reader. Furthermore, special requirements for a particular transaction must be squeezed into any unoccupied space on the credit, resulting in extensive use of continuation marks such as single, double and even triple asterisks, daggers and the like. The result is usually an incomprehensible mess.

The customary order in which the documents which are required under the credit are listed commences with the invoices and the packing list, stating how many copies of each are required, what information should appear on each and, in respect of the invoice, usually repeating the contract terms. The required transport document is customarily described next and if this is to be a bill of lading the number of originals which are needed will be stated. The credit will specify whether or not the transport document should or should not indicate prepayment of freight and whatever is stated should be compatible with the terms of the contract as evidenced elsewhere in the credit.

There follows reference to the requirements regarding insurance, which, depending on the contract, will be either details of the document required or a statement that insurance will be attended to by the applicants.

Goods

Any further documents which may be required will then be listed and there follows a description of the goods. Banks only require a description sufficiently detailed to enable them to ascertain that the correct goods have been shipped, there is nothing to be gained by the inclusion of excessive detail. Applicants should not, as sometimes happens, attach a copy of the purchase order to the application as itemised descriptions are just not necessary in the Credit procedure. A brief description such as: *"Aircraft instrument parts as detailed on purchase order number XYZ dated 20.4.2000"*, supported by a separate certificate from the exporter (beneficiary) that the goods comply with that relative order or contract is preferable.

The description of goods, as stated on the letter of credit, must be repeated, exactly (no differences in spelling, no change of punctuation or other marks, no abbreviations) on the invoice. In all other documents — unless the letter of credit expressly states that a full description must appear — the goods may be described in general terms not inconsistent with the description of the goods in the Credit. Exporters should be wary of using "general terms" though as a shortened description on, say, the transport document, may lead banks to say it is not consistent with the Credit description and reject the presentation.

Also shown in this section are the contract terms applicable to the transaction. From this information can be determined whether or not the transport document should evidence that freight has been prepaid, and whether or not an insurance document should be called for. Special circumstances may occasionally give rise to an apparent discrepancy here, but any such variation from the norm should at least give grounds for query, as when an FOB contract is stated for an air freight shipment or call for a transport document to show that freight has been paid by the shipper.

Presentation

The credit now states the number of days after the date of issue of the transport document which are allowed for presentation of documents by the beneficiaries. If no stipulation is made, UCP specifies that 21 days will be the maximum period allowed. Where the voyage is sufficiently long, and it is essential that documents of title are received by a certain time in order to avoid demurrage or other extra charges being incurred, it may be possible by manipulation of this period to minimise the chances of late receipt. By estimating the period required for processing the documents in the banks and adding the time required for transit, then deducting the total from the estimated duration of the voyage of the carrying vessel, a figure will be reached which is a rough indication of the maximum period which may safely be allowed between the date of shipment and the date of presentation. This figure should, however, be realistic in being of sufficient length to allow the beneficiaries to meet it.

It is an encouraging sign, indicating that the credit has been prepared by professionals, when the number of days so allowed corresponds with the period between the latest date for shipment and the expiry date of the credit. To illustrate this, if a credit states that shipment must be not later than September 30, and expires on October 15, but allows only ten days for presentation of documents, then where goods are shipped on the last possible date the effective expiry of the credit falls on October 10, not October 15 as stated therein, because the ten-day rule must be complied with. Beneficiaries who fall into this trap are understandably annoyed, but there is absolutely nothing which the nominated or negotiating bank can do to help.

Miscellaneous provisions

The credit will normally then state for whose account the bank charges are and give any instructions intended for the negotiating bank, such as those relating to disposal of documents and the obtaining of reimbursement for amounts paid or negotiated under the credit.

Finally, there will be a statement that the credit is subject to Uniform Customs and Practice for Documentary Credits, identifying the appropriate revision of those rules which is applicable, probably an undertaking that payment will be made against conforming documents (although in view of the allusion to UCP this is not strictly necessary) and the signature(s) on behalf of the issuing bank.

Such, then, is the usual content of the documentary letter of credit. As stated, many banks have yet to adopt the ICC recommended format, but nonetheless all the above information should appear on the credit, however it is laid out. Further consideration of the detailed aspects of the credit will be given in the following chapters on UCP and in those with particular relevance to the various parties involved.

CHAPTER 11

Uniform Customs and Practice for Documentary Credits 1

Like the Uniform Rules for Collections, dealt with in Chapter 9, the UCP were drawn up by the International Chamber of Commerce (ICC) in order to regulate the practices and procedures relating to documentary credits as adopted by banks worldwide. The UCP are considerably senior to the URC, having been first formulated in 1933, and the current edition, is the sixth, its official title being the 1993 Revision and published by the ICC in their Publication No. 500. They are also far more widely adopted than URC, and therefore the likelihood of encountering a credit which is not subject to their provisions is remote.

It is perhaps even more important than was the case with URC that all parties involved in the documentary credit should have at least a working knowledge of the content of UCP, since its provisions are far more comprehensive than that of its younger cousin and may have a profound effect upon the rights and duties of each of those parties. Furthermore, from time to time the apparent effects of the rules are modified by decisions taken by the ICC's Banking Commission, which attempts to arbitrate in cases of dispute arising from differing interpretations. All concerned, particularly banks, are urged to keep themselves up to date with such decisions, which are published periodically by the ICC. These publications make interesting reading, since they illustrate the ways in which disputes can arise and perhaps point the way to the means of their future avoidance.

It should be mentioned here that the ICC is placed in a very difficult situation when doubts arise as to the correct interpretation of the rules as published. Amendment and republication in revised form is a lengthy and costly procedure, involving as it does obtaining a consensus of opinion from the ICC's worldwide membership, and where its assistance is sought in cases of dispute the ICC can only give its considered opinion on the facts of the case before it. Whether or not the disputants choose to accept that opinion is their own affair, and in any case the decision is not binding upon any parties who may later be in dispute from the same cause. Each time a new revision is published, it is the aim of the ICC to attain the greatest possible simplification of the rules in order to remove, or at least minimise, the causes of such disputes.

Original documents

Since UCP500 came into effect in 1993 there has been a many queries raised on the interpretation of the Articles but none as significant as the issue raised by the question: *"What constitutes an original document?"*

Documents presented for payment against a letter of credit must be originals unless the credit says that copies are acceptable. Article 20(b), which is detailed later in this section, says that documents will be accepted as *original* if they are marked as original and where necessary appear to be signed but where a document is labelled copy or *not marked original* it will be accepted by the bank as a *copy document*.

This point was crucial in a British court case settled in autumn 1995 and upheld by the Court of Appeal in 1996. In *Bayerische Vereinbank and Glencore International AG v Bank of China*, the judge accepted the defendant bank's refusal to accept a certificate which was produced from another by alteration and photocopying and hand-signed but was not marked "ORIGINAL". The certificate was merely a declaration that specified documents had been sent to the beneficiary, and the bank had accepted similarly-produced certificates before but with the judge upholding the bank's decision it set a precedent in British law.

In practice it means documents will only be accepted by banks as original if they are clearly marked original. Many companies have purchased rubber stamps saying "original" for this purpose. Advising banks, in their covering letter to the beneficiary, usually make reference to this ruling as a clear warning to companies presenting documents for payment. A typical warning reads: *"Following a court of appeal judgment there has been a need for the banking community to re-examine their interpretation of what constitutes an"original" document under UCP500.*

To avoid any unnecessary delays or problems in receiving payment under this credit can you please ensure that all documents, except where copies are acceptable for negotiation, are clearly marked on their face as"original" subject always to Article 20(c)ii of UCP500..."

The UCP500 rules are examined below.

A: General provisions and definitions

ARTICLE 1 — Application of UCP

The *Uniform Customs and Practice for Documentary Credits*, 1993 Revision, ICC Publication No. 500, shall apply to all documentary credits (including, to the extent to which they may be applicable, standby letter(s) of credit) where they are incorporated into the text of the credit. They are binding on all parties thereto, unless otherwise expressly stipulated in the credit.

Comment

It is worthy of note that a credit is not automatically subject to UCP, but must include a clause specifically incorporating the rules. If any Article is intended not to be applicable to a specific credit, this must also be specifically stated. In the case of a credit transmitted by SWIFT message, UCP automatically apply unless the message states otherwise. The advising bank must, however, make a specific reference to this inclusion when transmitting the credit on to the beneficiaries.

ARTICLE 2 — Meaning of credit

For the purposes of these articles, the expressions "documentary credit(s)" and "standby letter(s) of credit" (hereinafter referred to as "credit(s)"), mean any arrangement, however named or described, whereby a bank (the "issuing bank") acting at the request and on the instructions of a customer (the "applicant") or on its own behalf,

   (i) is to make payment to or to the order of a third party (the "beneficiary"), or is to accept and pay bills of exchange (drafts) drawn by the beneficiary, or

  (ii) authorises another bank to effect such payment, or to accept and pay such bills of exchange (draft(s)), or

 (iii) authorises another bank to negotiate,

against stipulated document(s), provided that the terms and conditions of the credit are complied with.

For the purposes of these articles, branches of a bank in different countries are considered another bank.

Comment

Note that an instrument does not have to call itself a documentary credit in order for the rules to apply. It must merely comply with the requirements and specifically incorporate the UCP as stated in Article 1. Presentation of documents in order to secure payment is an essential feature, though presentation of a bill of exchange is not. Generally speaking, a sight bill of exchange under a letter of credit is completely unnecessary, and issuing banks should consider seriously the question of deleting this requirement from their letter of credit forms.

Specific instruments which have been considered to qualify for incorporation of UCP in their terms have been the "documentary payment orders" commonly issued by banks in Greece, which in fact differ from the common concept of a documentary credit only in their title; and letters of guarantee which, although they are similar in effect to a credit, the ICC would prefer were styled "standby letters of credit" in order to avoid any possible confusion.

This article includes the placing on the accepting bank in a usance credit transaction the obligation of payment of the accepted bill of exchange at maturity, and the extension of the definition of "another bank" to include foreign branches of the issuing bank. The latter removes possible grounds for contention where the same bank acts in both issuing and negotiating capacities (using the word "negotiating" in its older, broad, sense) and also establishes the right of a foreign branch of the issuing bank to make charges for advising or confirming what was previously regarded as its own paper.

ARTICLE 3 — Credits v contracts

(a) Credits, by their nature, are separate transactions from the sales or other contract(s) on which they may be based and banks are in no way concerned with or bound by such contract(s), even if any reference whatsoever to such contract(s) is included in the credit. Consequently, the undertaking of a bank to pay, accept and pay draft(s) or negotiate and/or to fulfil any other obligation under the credit, is not subject to claims or defences by the applicant resulting from his relationships with the issuing bank or the beneficiary.

(b) A beneficiary can in no case avail himself of the contractual relationships existing between the banks or between the applicant and the issuing bank.

Comment

In practical terms, this article is one which cannot be repeated frequently enough. Banks are not party to the commercial contract between buyer and seller, have no wish to be, and formulate their charges accordingly. It is the buyer's responsibility to ensure that all relevant conditions of the contract are incorporated in the credit, and the seller's responsibility upon receipt of that credit to ensure that such conditions have been so incorporated. Where the credit is irrevocable, the buyer's task is the more onerous, since if a mistake is made the credit is binding in its issued form unless the seller agrees to its amendment.

ARTICLE 4 — Documents v goods/services/performances

In credit operations all parties concerned deal with documents, and not with goods, services and/or other performances to which the documents may relate.

Comment

This is another article which should be etched deep into the consciousness of all concerned with credits. Suspicion that the goods are defective, or even non-existent, cannot be used as grounds to prevent an issuing or confirming bank from discharging its solemn obligations under a credit, such matters being the concern solely of the buyers and sellers under the appropriate law of contract. It also emphasises the fact that backs can only accept documents that strictly comply to the terms of the credit.

ARTICLE 5 — Instructions to issue/amend credits

(a) Instructions for the issuance of a credit, the credit itself, instructions for an amendment thereto, and the amendment itself must be complete and precise.

In order to guard against confusion and misunderstanding, banks should discourage any attempt:

    (i) to include excessive detail in the credit or in any amendment thereto

    (ii) to give instruction to issue, advise or confirm a credit by reference to a credit previously issued (similar credit) where such previous credit has been subject to accepted amendment(s), and/or unaccepted amendment(s).

(b) All instructions for the issue of a credit and the credit itself and, where applicable, all instructions for an amendment thereto and the amendment itself, must state precisely the document(s) against which payment, acceptance or negotiation is to be made.

Comment

It was stated in Chapter 10 that the preferable alternative to the inclusion of excessive detail is to call for a signed declaration from the beneficiaries to the effect that they have supplied goods which conform with the requirements of the relative contract, which can be identified by reference to a proforma invoice and/or order number. Generally speaking, the more complex a credit is, the more chance there is that something will go wrong with it, but such is the mystique of the subject that many issuing banks seem to feel that the credit gains in stature in line with the increase in the number of pages required to express its terms and conditions. In pursuance of this mistaken belief they will blithely accept pages of detailed specification of the goods, lifted straight from the contract, as appendages to form part of the terms of the credit. As a result, all concerned are occasioned much unnecessary work in checking all this superfluous detail, the chances of a mistake being made are greatly increased, and, most significantly, the applicants gain no additional security in the process.

(a) Two interesting decisions have been made by the Banking Commission with relevance to this article. The first concerns the frequent stipulation in the credit that the packages containing the goods be marked in a specific fashion. The Commission has ruled that unless the credit stipulates otherwise, banks will accept shipping documents showing the required marks as a minimum, and will not reject those showing additional markings.

(b) The second decision relates to the equally frequent requirement that the letter of credit or export licence number appears on all documents. For legal reasons in certain countries it is undesirable from the point of view of the carriers for such detail to be included in the bill of lading, and the ICC have indicated that such conditions in credits should be discouraged.

B: Form and notification of credits

ARTICLE 6 — Revocable v irrevocable credits

(a) A credit may be either:
  (i) revocable, or
  (ii) irrevocable.

(b) The credit, therefore, should clearly indicate whether it is revocable or irrevocable.

(c) In the absence of such indication the credit shall be deemed to be irrevocable.

Comment

Particular note should be taken of this article, which completely reverses the position previously taken. From the inception of UCP until the adoption of the present revision, a credit was deemed revocable unless it said otherwise, a situation potentially dangerous for beneficiaries. The risk now passes to the applicants and the issuing bank, on whom the responsibility for eliminating errors at the issue stage rests heavily. In practice, however, the use of revocable credits has dwindled to such an extent that there should be little trouble with this change.

ARTICLE 7 — Advising bank's liability

(a) A credit may be advised to a beneficiary through another bank (the "advising bank") without engagement on the part of the advising bank, but that bank, if it elects to advise the credit, shall take reasonable care to check the apparent authenticity of the credit which it advises. If the bank elects not to advise the credit, it must so inform the issuing bank without delay.

(b) If the advising bank cannot establish such apparent authenticity it must inform, without delay, the bank from which the instructions appear to have been received that it has been unable to establish the authenticity of the credit, and if it elects nonetheless to advise the credit it must inform the beneficiary that it has not been able to establish the authenticity of the credit.

Comment

This topic was mentioned in Chapter 10, and will be looked at again in the sections dealing with the advising bank and with fraud and forgery. From the beneficiaries' point of view, and from that of the negotiating bank if that bank is different from the advising bank, the article gives some relief from the worry about whether or not a credit is forged, since the responsibility of verification is placed squarely upon the advising bank. The latter should note that, in certain circumstances, "reasonable care" may mean more than the mere verification of signatures from specimens held.

The article has been considerably expanded in the current revision, and, in particular, gives guidance to the advising bank which is being pressed by the beneficiaries to advise a credit which it has received but cannot authenticate. Beneficiaries would, however, be extremely foolish to act in reliance on a credit in the face of such a warning.

ARTICLE 8 — Revocation of a credit

(a) A revocable credit may be amended or cancelled by the issuing bank at any moment and without prior notice to the beneficiary.

(b) However, the issuing bank must:

(i) reimburse another bank with which a revocable credit has been made available for sight payment, acceptance or negotiation — for any payment, acceptance or negotiation made by such bank — prior to receipt by it of notice of amendment or cancellation, against documents which appear on their face to be in compliance with the terms and conditions of the credit

(ii) reimburse another bank with which a revocable credit has been made available for deferred payment, if such a bank has, prior to receipt by it of notice of amendment or cancellation, taken up documents which appear on their face to be in compliance with the terms and conditions of the credit.

Comment

For security reasons it would be unwise for a bank to negotiate documents under a revocable credit which it has not advised, since that credit may have been subsequently amended or cancelled and such a bank would have no knowledge of this. Whether it would be able to claim protection under this article is questionable, since normal banking prudence ought to dictate that it should not negotiate. The ICC has in the past expressed the opinion that all revocable credits should nominate a bank to which documents must be presented for negotiation, but this apparently useful suggestion has not so far been adopted into UCP itself.

ARTICLE 9(a) — Liability of issuing and confirming banks

An irrevocable credit constitutes a definite undertaking of the issuing bank, provided that the stipulated documents are presented to the nominated bank or to the issuing bank and that the terms and conditions of the credit are complied with:

(i) if the credit provides for sight payment — to pay at sight

(ii) if the credit provides for deferred payment — to pay, on the maturity date(s) determinable in accordance with the stipulations of the credit

    (iii) if the credit provides for acceptance:
        (a) by the issuing bank — to accept draft(s) drawn by the beneficiary on the issuing bank and pay them at maturity
        (b) by another drawee bank — to accept and pay at maturity draft(s) drawn by the beneficiary on the issuing bank in the event the drawee bank stipulated in the credit does not accept draft(s) drawn on it, or to pay drafts accepted but not paid by such drawee bank at maturity
    (iv) if the credit provides for negotiation — to pay without recourse to drawers and/or bona fide holders, draft(s) drawn by the beneficiary and/or document(s) presented under the credit. A credit should not be issued available by draft(s) on the applicant. If the credit nevertheless calls for draft(s) on the applicant, banks will consider such draft(s) as an additional document(s).

Comment

This article, of course, defines the very heart of the principle of the irrevocable credit — the absolute liability of the issuing bank to honour its obligations thereunder provided that the beneficiaries have honoured theirs.

Much confusion tends to arise as to the difference between payment and negotiation under a credit. With a sight credit the situation is really quite simple. If the credit nominates a bank in the sellers' country which is authorised to pay drawings, and documents are presented to that bank in order, then payment takes place at that point, without recourse and with no question of interest being charged for any period for which the paying bank may be out of funds. If they are presented to any other bank, negotiation takes place. If the negotiating bank has confirmed the credit its position is the same as a paying bank except that it is entitled to charge interest. If it has not confirmed the credit the negotiating bank retains recourse against the drawer (beneficiary) until it is reimbursed. Where the credit calls for drafts on the issuing bank, only negotiation can take place in the beneficiaries' country, payment being made by the issuing bank, without recourse in both cases, in view of its obligations under the credit.

A major change to this article which was implemented in the 1993 Revision is the prohibition of drafts on the applicant, which has too often in the past been used by banks as a means of postponing, if not evading, their liabilities under credits. The justification put forward was that, since drafts were on the applicants, issuing banks had no responsibility for checking documents presented under the credit and merely acted as collection agents. Perhaps in the knowledge that some banks will not give this practice up lightly, sub-article (iv) gives other banks the power to ignore such stipulations if included in the credit. The ICC is to be greatly applauded for its courage in tackling this problem, which has done a great deal to undermine confidence in the documentary credit as a means of payment.

Another welcome change is the clarification of the right of the beneficiaries to present documents direct to the issuing bank, which also serves to underline the absolute liability of that bank to honour its own undertaking.

ARTICLE 9(b)

A confirmation of an irrevocable credit by another bank (the "confirming bank") upon the authorisation or request of the issuing bank, constitutes a definite undertaking of the confirming bank, in addition to that of the issuing bank, provided that the stipulated documents are presented to the confirming bank or to any other nominated bank and that the terms and conditions of the credit are complied with:

(i) if the credit provides for sight payment — to pay at sight

(ii) if the credit provides for deferred payment — to pay on the maturity date(s) determinable in accordance with the stipulations of the credit

(iii) if the credit provides for acceptance:

(a) by the confirming bank — to accept draft(s) drawn by the beneficiary on the confirming bank and pay them at maturity,

(b) by another drawee bank — to accept and pay at maturity draft(s) drawn by the beneficiary on the confirming bank, in the event the drawee bank stipulated in the credit does not accept draft(s) drawn on it, or to pay draft(s) accepted but not paid by such drawee bank at maturity

(iv) if the credit provides for negotiation — to negotiate without recourse to drawers and/or bona fide holders, draft(s) drawn by the beneficiary and/or documents presented under the credit. A credit should not be issued available by draft(s) on the applicant. If the credit nevertheless calls for draft(s) on the applicant, banks will consider such draft(s) as an additional document(s).

Comment

This section (b) of Article 9 effectively places exactly the same burden of responsibility on the confirming bank as the preceding section did on the issuing bank, ie where documents are in order its liability is absolute and without recourse.

ARTICLE 9(c)

(i) If a bank is authorised or requested by the issuing bank to add its confirmation to a credit but is not prepared to do so, it must so inform the issuing bank without delay.

(ii) Unless the issuing bank specifies otherwise in its confirmation authorisation or request to add confirmation, the advising bank may advise the credit to the beneficiary without adding its confirmation.

Comment

Circumstances under which a bank might be unwilling to confirm another bank's credit include the following:

(i) where it is not the correspondent of the issuing bank

(ii) where it is not happy with the terms of the credit, or with the arrangements for reimbursement

(iii) where its commitments on behalf of the issuing bank are already at the limit of what it is prepared to undertake

(iv) where its commitments on behalf of the issuing bank's country have already reached a similar limit.

ARTICLE 9(d)

(i) Except as otherwise provided by Article 48, an irrevocable credit can neither be amended nor cancelled without the agreement of the issuing bank, the confirming bank, if any, and the beneficiary.

(ii) The issuing bank shall be irrevocably bound by an amendment(s) issued by it from the time of the issuance of such amendment(s). A confirming bank may extend its confirmation to an amendment and shall be irrevocably bound as of the time of its advice of the amendment. A confirming bank may, however, choose to advise an amendment to the beneficiary without extending its confirmation and if so, must inform the issuing bank and the beneficiary without delay.

Comment

We have seen under Article 9(c) above that there are circumstances in which a bank might be unwilling to confirm a credit. An amendment, of course, changes the terms of the credit, and it is proper that the confirming bank should have the right to refuse to associate itself with the amendment. This right, however, has no effect upon its original commitment.

ARTICLE 9(d)(iii)

The terms of the original credit (or a credit incorporating previously accepted amendment(s)) will remain in force for the beneficiary until the beneficiary communicates his acceptance of the amendment to the bank that advised such amendment. The beneficiary should give notification of acceptance or rejection of amendment(s). If the beneficiary fails to give such notification, the tender of documents to the nominated or issuing bank, that conform to the credit and to not yet accepted amendment(s), will be deemed to be notification of acceptance by the beneficiary of such amendment(s) and as of that moment the credit will be amended.

Comment

This sub-article was newly introduced in the 1993 Revision, and is an important change from the previous position. Formerly, the beneficiaries' role was, by default since UCP was silent on the subject, entirely passive in the matter of amendments. They could elect to accept or reject such amendments, but were required to give no formal notification to any other party in either case. Now, although they may take a passive role if they agree to the amendment, no such dispensation is allowed in the case of rejection, and notification must be given if such is intended.

ARTICLE 9(d)(iv)

Partial acceptance of amendments contained in one and the same advice of amendment is not allowed and consequently will not be given any effect.

ARTICLE 10 — Types of credit

(a) All credits must clearly indicate whether they are available by sight payment, by deferred payment, by acceptance or by negotiation.

(b)

    (i) Unless the credit stipulates that it is available only with the issuing bank, all credits must nominate the bank (the "nominated bank") which is authorised to pay, incur a deferred payment undertaking, accept draft(s) or to negotiate. In a freely negotiable credit, any bank is a nominated bank.

    (ii) Negotiation means the giving of value for draft(s) and/or document(s) by the bank authorised to negotiate. Mere examination of the documents without giving of value does not constitute a negotiation.

Comment

Sub-section (ii), introduced in the 1993 Revision, gives an overdue and valuable definition of the hitherto loosely-defined term "negotiation". The term "freely negotiable credit", although self-explanatory, has only been introduced to UCP in this Revision, and applies to any credit which does not nominate the bank to which documents must be presented.

ARTICLE 10(c)

Unless the nominated bank is the confirming bank, nomination by the issuing bank does not constitute any undertaking by the nominated bank to pay, to incur a deferred payment undertaking, to accept draft(s), or to negotiate. Except where expressly agreed to by the nominated bank and so communicated to the beneficiary, the nominated bank's receipt of and/or examination and/or forwarding of the documents does not make that bank liable to pay, to incur a deferred payment undertaking, to accept draft(s), or to negotiate.

Comment

Where the nominated bank has confirmed the credit, this section has no relevance. Where this is not the case, beneficiaries should note that, however the credit is worded in respect of the bank nominated, unless that bank gives its written agreement before presentation of documents, whether or not it chooses to carry out the function for which it has been nominated by the issuing bank is entirely at its discretion. When the nominated bank does give such agreement, it should be remembered that, if negotiation is the nominated function, such negotiation will, in the absence of confirmation of the credit, be with recourse.

ARTICLE 10(d)

By nominating another bank, or by allowing for negotiation by any bank, or by authorising or requesting another bank to add its confirmation, the issuing bank authorises such bank to pay, accept draft(s), or negotiate as the case may be, against documents which appear on their face to be in compliance with the terms and conditions of the credit and undertakes to reimburse such bank in accordance with the provisions of these articles.

Comment

A frequent problem is where a credit restricts negotiation to a particular nominated bank and drawings are in fact negotiated by a third bank. Here, the ICC has given the opinion that the issuing bank is obliged to pay against documents presented to it which are in all other respects in compliance with the terms of the credit, regardless of how or from whom those documents were received. This is, of course, very much in the spirit of the provisions of Article 9 with regard to the obligations of the issuing bank.

ARTICLE 11 — Teletransmitted and pre-advised credits

(a)

    (i) When an issuing bank instructs an advising bank by an authenticated teletransmission to advise a credit or an amendment to a credit, the teletransmission will be deemed to be the operative credit instrument or the operative amendment, and no mail confirmation should be sent. Should a mail confirmation nevertheless be sent, it will have no effect and the advising bank will have no obligation to check such mail confirmation against the operative credit instrument or the operative amendment received by teletransmission.

    (ii) If the teletransmission states "full details to follow" (or words of similar effect), or states that the mail confirmation will be the operative credit instrument or the operative amendment, then the teletransmission will not be deemed to be the operative credit instrument or the operative amendment. The issuing bank must forward the operative credit instrument or the operative amendment to such advising bank without delay.

(b) If a bank uses the services of an advising bank to have the credit advised to the beneficiary, it must also use the services of the same bank for advising an amendment(s).

(c) A preliminary advice of the issuance or amendment of an irrevocable credit (pre-advice) shall only be given by an issuing bank if such bank is prepared to issue the operative credit instrument or the operative amendment thereto. Unless otherwise stated in such preliminary advice by the issuing bank, an issuing bank having given such pre-advice shall be irrevocably committed to issue or amend the credit, in terms not inconsistent with the pre-advice, without delay.

Comment

The provisions of Article 11 regarding the use of teletransmitted credits or amendments, section (c) in particular, go a long way towards solving problems which formerly arose from potential conflicts between the rules of SWIFT (Society for Worldwide Interbank Financial Telecommunications) and the UCP. Until the adoption of the 1993 Revision there was no obligation in UCP for the issuing bank to follow a pre-advice of the issue of a credit or amendment with the instrument itself, although such an obligation was incorporated into the SWIFT rules under which the majority of telecommunicated credits are transmitted. There remains, however, the danger that a pre-advice is sent which fails to make it clear that it is such, and contains sufficient details to enable it to be mistaken for the operative instrument and advised as such to the beneficiary. However, this is unlikely to happen where a SWIFT message is used, since the message format for a pre-advice is completely different from that for an operative credit or amendment.

ARTICLE 12 — Incomplete or unclear instructions

If incomplete or unclear instructions are received to advise, confirm or amend a credit, the bank requested to act on such instructions may give preliminary notification to the beneficiary for information only and without responsibility. This preliminary notification should state clearly that the notification is provided for information only and without the responsibility of the advising bank. In any event, the advising bank must inform the issuing bank of the action taken and request it to provide the necessary information.

The issuing bank must provide the necessary information without delay. The credit will be advised, confirmed, or amended, only when complete and clear instructions have been received and if the advising bank is then prepared to act on the instructions.

C: Liabilities and responsibilities

ARTICLE 13 — Standard for examination of documents

(a) Banks must examine all documents stipulated in the credit with reasonable care, to ascertain whether or not they appear, on their face, to be in compliance with the terms and conditions of the credit. Compliance of the stipulated documents on their face with the terms and conditions of the credit, shall be determined by international standard banking practice as reflected in these articles. Documents which appear on their face to be inconsistent with one another will be considered as not appearing on their face to be in compliance with the terms and conditions of the credit.

Documents not stipulated in the credit will not be examined by banks. If they receive such documents, they shall return them to the presenter or pass them on without responsibility.

Comment
A section with a disproportionately high degree of significance. It really constitutes three articles, since the constituent parts have little connection with each other. The first refers to "reasonable care", and this catch-all expression will mean totally different things depending on whether it is being interpreted by the prosecution or the defence. What constitutes reasonable care will vary according to the circumstances of the case. In one example, a bank was held not to have applied reasonable care when it accepted a certificate of origin which although on an official form and properly signed, failed to state from where the goods had come. On the other hand, the ICC has ruled that the requirement does not extend to the detailed checking of arithmetical calculations on documents, unless the error is an obvious one; it does not suggest, however, what should be considered as obvious and what should not.

In 1996 the IFSA issued a booklet entitled "*Standard Banking Practice for the Examination of Letter of Credit Practice*". The booklet, which has received highly favourable comment, was written as a practice guide to sub-Article 13(a). The ICC is currently (May 2000) considering whether to adapt this IFSA book into an ICC document and to bring it out under the auspices of the Commission. The booklet is, in effect, a checklist for key documents that may be presented under the Credit summarising key-points, common errors, country differences and banking decisions made under the guidance of relevant UCP500 Article. The documents looked at are the:

- letter of credit
- draft (or bill of exchange)
- commercial invoice
- ocean/marine/port to port bill of lading
- non-negotiable sea waybill
- charter party bill of lading
- multi-modal transport documents.

The second sentence of the first paragraph, covering inconsistencies, gives a requirement which provides a dangerous trap for beneficiaries who are unfamiliar with the rules. As we shall see when we come to discuss the checking of documents under credits, there are a number of checks which must be made other than the obvious one against the terms of the credit, and this is one of them.

In fact, since the introduction of UCP the second most common reason for the banks' rejection of documents has been that they are "inconsistent" with each other. Inconsistencies can be as simple as having a total shipment weight of 387.5 kg on the invoice and the air waybill showing 388kg, or the value being £121,876.97 and another document rounding the value up to £121,877 and even a typing mistake when keying in a part number. The bank examining the documents has a duty to ensure that information appearing on more than one document is reproduced in a consistent manner; this duty extends beyond the information required by the letter of credit document itself.

The second paragraph is a provision introduced by the 1993 Revision, and gives the answer to a long-standing dilemma as to whether banks should or should not take into account documents presented which are not called for in the credit, in reaching their decision as to whether or not the credit's terms have been complied with. The answer, emphatically, is that they should not.

ARTICLE 13(b)

The issuing bank, the confirming bank, if any, or a nominated bank acting on their behalf, shall each have a reasonable time, not to exceed seven banking days following the day of receipt of the documents, to examine the documents and determine whether to take up or refuse the documents and to inform the party from which it received the documents accordingly.

Comment
The content of this section, introduced in the 1993 Revision, is really quite revolutionary. The previous position merely imposed the "reasonable time" requirement on the issuing bank only, with no indication of what length of time might be considered "reasonable". We now have a transformed situation where an absolute limit of seven banking days is set upon *all* banks involved in the credit procedure.

ARTICLE 13(c)

If a credit contains conditions without stating the document(s) to be presented in compliance therewith, banks will deem such conditions as not stated and will disregard them.

Comment
This section is also new in the 1993 Revision and removes another longstanding problem in dealing with documentary credits. An example would be where a credit states that shipment must be by conference line vessel; this formerly imposed upon the bank the responsibility of

ensuring that such shipment had actually occurred. Now, unless such a credit actually calls for a certificate to this effect to be presented, the requirement will be totally ignored.

ARTICLE 14 — Discrepant documents and notice

(a) When the issuing bank authorises another bank to pay, incur a deferred payment undertaking, accept draft(s), or negotiate against documents which appear on their face to be in compliance with the terms and conditions of the credit, the issuing bank and the confirming bank, if any, are bound:
>
> (i) to reimburse the nominated bank which has paid, incurred a deferred payment undertaking, accepted draft(s), or negotiated
>
> (ii) to take up the documents.

Comment
Effectively, this is restating the liability of the issuing bank laid down in Article 9.

ARTICLE 14(b)

Upon receipt of the documents the issuing bank and/or confirming bank, if any, or a nominated bank acting on their behalf, must determine on the basis of the documents alone whether or not they appear on their face to be in compliance with the terms and conditions of the credit. If the documents appear on their face not to be in compliance with the terms and conditions of the credit, such banks may refuse to take up the documents.

Comment
An important article, much of its significance lying in the words "on the basis of the documents alone". Where goods are sent by air or are otherwise available for inspection before documents have arrived, and are found to be substandard, issuing banks frequently come under pressure from the applicants to find some pretext for the rejection of the documents when they are received. Such a course would obviously be contrary to the spirit of this article.

ARTICLE 14(c)

If the issuing bank determines that the documents appear on their face not to be in compliance with the terms and conditions of the credit, it may in its sole judgment approach the applicant for a waiver of the discrepancy(ies). This does not, however, extend the period mentioned in sub-Article 13(b).

Comment

This was a new provision introduced by the 1993 Revision, and serves to give recognition to, and to bring under control, what in fact has been common practice among issuing banks for some time.

ARTICLE 14(d)

(i) If the issuing bank and/or confirming bank, if any, or a nominated bank acting on their behalf, decides to refuse the documents, it must give notice to that effect by telecommunication or, if that is not possible, by other expeditious means, without delay but in any case no later than the close of the seventh banking day following the day of receipt of the documents. Such notice shall be given to the bank from which it received the documents, or to the beneficiary, if it received the documents directly from him.

(ii) Such notice must state the discrepancies in respect of which the bank refuses the documents and must also state whether it is holding the documents at the disposal of, or is returning them to, the presenter.

(iii) The issuing bank and/or confirming bank, if any, shall then be entitled to claim from the remitting bank refund, with interest, of any reimbursement which may have been made to that bank.

Comment

Issuing banks will no doubt have welcomed the inclusion of the two words "with interest" in this sub-Article in the 1993 Revision, which usually arises where the credit is expressed in a third currency and the nominated bank has been authorised to reimburse itself for drawings by claiming from a bank holding an account in the name of the issuing bank in the currency of the credit. Where it has done so, the issuing bank would normally charge the resulting interest to the applicants, but where documents are discrepant it is of course unable to do so, and although it may claim interest from the remitting bank, has hitherto had no means of enforcing such a claim.

ARTICLE 14(e)

If the issuing bank and/or confirming bank, if any, fails to act in accordance with the provisions of this article and/or fails to hold the documents at the disposal of, or return them to the presenter, the issuing bank and/or confirming bank, if any, shall be precluded from claiming that the documents are not in compliance with the terms and conditions of the credit.

ARTICLE 14(f)

If the remitting bank draws the attention of the issuing bank and/or confirming bank, if any, to any discrepancy(ies) in the document(s) or advises such banks that it has paid, incurred a deferred payment undertaking, accepted draft(s) or negotiated under reserve or against an indemnity in respect of such discrepancy(ies), the issuing bank and/or confirming bank, if any, shall not be thereby relieved from any of their obligations under any provision of this article. Such reserve or indemnity concerns only the relations between the remitting bank and the party towards whom the reserve was made, or from whom, or on whose behalf, the indemnity was obtained.

Comment

What frequently happens in practice in these circumstances is that the remitting bank extends its own guarantee to the issuing bank in respect of the discrepancies, in which case the issuing bank does become involved. In most cases, the issuing bank will still seek instructions from its principals, but in doing so must nevertheless notify the remitting bank of its actions if it wishes to preserve its right to later reject the documents. If the applicants agree to take up the documents in reliance on the indemnity, it is vital that when advising the remitting bank of payment the issuing bank makes it absolutely clear that payment is being made under the protection of the indemnity offered. Such indemnities are normally valid for a restricted period only, traditionally six months but often less, to allow the buyers time to inspect the goods on arrival and to then decide whether or not they are acceptable. If they are accepted, the remitting bank should be released from its indemnity or reserve immediately in order that it may in turn release the beneficiaries, since they will, if proper records are being kept, be showing the indemnity or reserve in their books as a contingent liability.

ARTICLE 15 — Disclaimer on effectiveness of documents

Banks assume no liability or responsibility for the form, sufficiency, accuracy, genuineness, falsification or legal effect of any document(s), or for the general and/or particular conditions stipulated in the document(s) or superimposed thereon; nor do they assume any liability or responsibility for the description, quantity, weight, quality, condition, packing, delivery, value or existence of the goods represented by any document(s), or for the good faith or acts and/or omissions, solvency, performance or standing of the consignors, the carriers, the forwarders, the consignees or the insurers of the goods, or any other person whomsoever.

Comment

This article emphasises and expands upon what has already been said in relation to Articles 4 and 13(a).

ARTICLE 16 — Disclaimer on the transmission of messages

Banks assume no liability or responsibility for the consequences arising out of delay and/or loss in transit of any message(s), letter(s) or document(s), or for delay, mutilation or other error(s) arising in the transmission of any telecommunication. Banks assume no liability or responsibility for errors in translation and/or interpretation of technical terms, and reserve the right to transmit credit terms without translating them.

Comment

With regard to translation, except in the relatively rare cases where staff in both the advising bank and the beneficiaries are bilingual, the credit will have to be translated at some stage in order that documents may be checked when presented for negotiation. It is therefore a good idea if at an early stage both the beneficiaries and the prospective negotiating bank are working from the same translation. It is suggested, therefore, that even though the advising bank has no duty to provide a translation, it does so and requests the beneficiaries to confirm that their own translation agrees with the bank's. If exporters receive an untranslated credit, they should take the initiative and provide the advising bank with their own translation accompanied by a similar request.

It is unwise to attempt any translation of technical terms, particularly in the description of the goods, since not only an absolute fluency in both languages but an intimate knowledge of the particular product and its manufacture is required in order to do so. Even given this unlikely combination (particularly in a bank), some terms simply do not readily translate from one language into another, and the result may be shipment of the wrong goods.

ARTICLE 17 — Force majeure

Banks assume no liability or responsibility for the consequences arising out of the interruption of their business by Acts of God, riots, civil commotions, insurrections, wars or any other causes beyond their control, or by any strikes or lockouts. Unless specifically authorised, banks will not, upon resumption of their business, pay, incur a deferred payment undertaking, accept draft(s) or negotiate under credits which expired during such interruption of their business.

ARTICLE 18 — Disclaimer for acts of an instructed party

(a) Banks utilising the services of another bank or other banks for the purpose of giving effect to the instructions of the applicant for the credit do so for the account and at the risk of such applicant.

(b) Banks assume no liability or responsibility should the instructions they transmit not be carried out, even if they have themselves taken the initiative in the choice of such other bank(s).

(c)

   (i) A party instructing another party to perform services is liable for any charges, including commissions, fees, costs or expenses incurred by the instructed party in connection with its instructions

   (ii) Where a credit stipulates that such charges are for the account of a party other than the instructed party, and charges cannot be collected, the instructing party remains ultimately liable for the payment thereof.

(d) The applicant shall be bound by and liable to indemnify the banks against all obligations and responsibilities imposed by foreign laws and usages.

Comment

This article applies the principles of agency, which we have already discussed in some detail in relation to collections, to letters of credit. The difference, of course, is that here the chain of agency runs in the opposite direction to that of a collection, since in the case of the latter all banks are acting on behalf of the sellers whereas with a credit they act on behalf of the buyers. Sub-Article (c) was introduced by the 1993 Revision, UCP previously making no specific provision for charges and expenses. However, it merely brings into the scope of the rules that which was previously imposed by the law of agency.

ARTICLE 19 — Bank to bank reimbursement arrangements

(a) If an issuing bank intends that the reimbursement to which a paying, accepting or negotiating bank is entitled shall be obtained by such bank (the "claiming bank") claiming on another party (the "reimbursing bank") it shall provide such reimbursing bank in good time with the proper instructions or authorisation to honour such reimbursement claims.

(b) Issuing banks shall not require a claiming bank to supply a certificate of compliance with the terms and conditions of the credit to the reimbursing bank.

Comment

Despite the provisions of this article, some banks persist in calling for a certificate that the terms of the credit have been complied with to be included with any reimbursement claim made under that credit. This does not, of course, affect the beneficiary or the applicant, but it is a problem which must be sorted out between the banks concerned. Since the advising bank is under no obligation to advise the credit unless it is satisfied with its terms, including the arrangements for reimbursement, it would be perfectly justified in refusing to advise until the offending requirement had been deleted. The reimbursing bank is acting merely as a paying agent and is in no way concerned with the credit itself, and therefore has no interest in whether or not the terms have been complied with. This is solely a matter between the negotiating and issuing banks.

ARTICLE 19(c) and (d)

Article 19(c) An issuing bank shall not be relieved from any of its obligations to provide reimbursement if and when reimbursement is not received by the claiming bank from the reimbursing bank.

Article 19(d) The issuing bank shall be responsible to the claiming bank for any loss of interest if reimbursement is not provided by the reimbursing bank on first demand, or as otherwise specified in the credit, or mutually agreed, as the case may be.

Comment

The question of interest accrued on delayed payment of claims for reimbursement continues to be a problem. Sometimes it is the beneficiaries who must bear the cost of this (where their drawing is presented for negotiation), and sometimes the negotiating bank (where they are acting as a paying bank), but whoever has lost, the article puts the responsibility for payment of interest squarely on the shoulders of the issuing bank. Prevarication over such claims is rife, but in reality the dispute should be between the issuing bank and its paying agent, and, if they are frequent, then perhaps it is time for the issuing bank to seek a new paying agent.

ARTICLE 19(e)

The reimbursing bank's charges should be for the account of the issuing bank. However, in cases where the charges are for the account of another party, it is the responsibility of the issuing bank to so indicate in the original credit and in the reimbursement authorisation. In cases where the reimbursing bank's charges are for the account of another party they shall be collected from the claiming bank when the credit is drawn under. In cases where the credit is not drawn under, the reimbursing bank's charges remain the obligation of the issuing bank.

Comment

By introduction of this sub-Article in the 1993 Revision, the ICC has codified another long-standing problem. Reimbursing bank's charges have often in the past only affected the beneficiaries' consciousness when they have been deducted from the amount of their drawing under the credit. Now they will receive due warning of them in the credit itself, and if this does not happen the responsibility will be the issuing bank's. In practice, of course, the issuing bank will normally pass any such charges on to its customers, the applicants.

CHAPTER 12

Uniform Customs and Practice for Documentary Credits 2

D: Documents

ARTICLE 20 — Ambiguity as to the issuers of documents

(a) Terms such as "first class", "well known", "qualified", "independent", "official", "competent", "local" and the like shall not be used to describe the issuers of any document(s) to be presented under a credit. If such terms are incorporated in the credit, banks will accept the relative document(s) as presented, provided that it appears on its face to be in compliance with the other terms and conditions of the credit and not to have been issued by the beneficiary.

(b) Unless otherwise stipulated in the credit, banks will also accept as an original document(s), a document(s) produced or appearing to have been produced:

(i) by reprographic, automated or computerised systems,

(ii) as carbon copies,

provided that it is marked as an original(s), and, where necessary, appears to be signed.

A document may be signed by handwriting, by facsimile signature, by perforated signature, by stamp, by symbol, or by any other mechanical or electronic method of authentication.

Comment

The relevance of section (a) is fairly evident. It is unfair to leave the negotiating bank to judge whether the issuer of a document is first class (a term often encountered in credits in connection with the insurers of the goods) and impractical to demand evidence of an issuer's qualifications (a veterinary surgeon, for instance). It is the responsibility of the applicants to identify the party who should issue each document and to nominate them in the credit having made prior arrangements for them to carry out the required work or service.

Section (b) sets out the basic position of the banks and is intended to accommodate modern cost-saving methods of production of documents. Many countries will not accept such short cuts, and insist, for example, on at least one originally-typed and signed (sometimes black ink is frowned upon as being indistinguishable from a photocopy!) invoice being presented. What extra security they imagine accrues from a human typist or a hand-written signature is difficult to comprehend, but where this is the case, the applicants and the issuing bank should be aware of the requirement and ensure that the credit makes it clear that Article 20 is not to apply in its entirety.

It is unfortunate that the Article states that these documents must be marked as originals, since this is not the normal practice with such documents as commercial invoices. Beneficiaries should note that where they are using one of these systems of production of documents they should be so marked to avoid any possibility of rejection of the drawing on these grounds.

ARTICLE 20(c)(i)

Unless otherwise stipulated in the credit, banks will accept as a copy(ies), a document(s) either labelled copy or not marked as an original — a copy(ies) need not be signed.

Comment

This is the Article that lead to that crucial British court case (*Bayerische Vereinbank and Glencore International AG v Bank of China*) mentioned prior to this section covering the UCP Rules where a judge (and a Court of Appeal) upheld the defendant bank's refusal to a accept a certificate which hand-signed but not marked "ORIGINAL". It cannot be emphasised too often — all documents that you present which are required in original (see Article 20(c)(ii) below) must be clearly marked original. If it does not say it is original it is a copy. Never forget this — it is one of the main discrepancies, and a very frustrating one.

ARTICLE 20(c)(ii)

Credits that require multiple document(s) such as "duplicate", "two fold", "two copies" and the like, will be satisfied by the presentation of one original and the remaining number in copies except where the document itself indicates otherwise.

Comment

This needs clarifying as it is important in the light of the ruling made on original documents. The banks will be satisfied by the following when multiple documents are required under the following examples of wording:

- insurance certificate in duplicate — 2 marked original or 1 marked original and 1 copy
- commercial invoice (6) — 6 originals or 1 marked original and 5 copies
- two copies of a certificate of origin — 2 marked original or 1 marked original and 1 copy
- bills of lading (2/2) — must have two originals and two copies (the full set being the 2 originals)
- a copy of a letter sent to applicant — 1 copy either marked copy or unmarked in any way.

ARTICLE 20(d)

Unless otherwise stipulated in the Credit, a condition under a Credit calling for a document to be authenticated, validated, legalised, visaed, certified or indicating a similar requirement, will be satisfied by any signature, mark, stamp or label on such document that on its face appears to satisfy the above condition.

Comment

Again, this reiterates the fact seen in other Articles, that the bank does not have to validate the authenticity of the party issuing the documents, they only have to be satisfied that the documents "appear" to satisfy the conditions.

ARTICLE 21 — Unspecified issuers or contents of documents

When documents other than transport documents, insurance documents and commercial invoices are called for, the credit should stipulate by whom such documents are to be issued and their wording or data content. If the credit does not so stipulate, banks will accept such documents as presented, provided that their data content is not inconsistent with any other stipulated document presented.

Comment

As with Article 20 (a), the responsibility of ensuring that the credit's requirements are clearly and unambiguously stated lies with the applicants. An example might be a requirement for presentation of a certificate of origin, where, in the absence of any further stipulation the beneficiaries' own certificate would be perfectly acceptable, and the applicants could not refuse the drawing because they had actually needed a certificate issued by a chamber of commerce.

ARTICLE 22 — Issuance date of document v credit date

Unless otherwise stipulated in the credit, banks will accept a document bearing a date of issuance prior to that of the credit, subject to such document being presented within the time limits set out in the credit and in these articles.

Comment

Some countries will not accept such documents as bills of lading which are dated prior to the issue of the credit or, alternatively, the relative import licence. Again, where this is the case the applicants and the issuing bank are expected to be aware of the situation and must clause the credit accordingly.

ARTICLE 23 — Marine/ocean bills of lading

(a) If a credit calls for a bill of lading covering a port-to-port shipment, banks will, unless otherwise stipulated in the credit, accept a document, however named, which:

(i) appears on its face to indicate the name of the carrier and to have been signed or otherwise authenticated by:

- the carrier or a named agent for and on behalf of the carrier, or
- the master or a named agent for and on behalf of the master.

Any signature or authentication of the carrier or master must be identified as carrier or master, as the case may be. An agent signing or authenticating for the carrier or master must also indicate the name and the capacity of the party, ie carrier or master, on whose behalf that agent is acting, and

(i) indicates that the goods have been loaded on board, or shipped on a named vessel.

Loading on board or shipment on a named vessel may be indicated by preprinted wording on the bill of lading that the goods have been loaded on board a named vessel or shipped on a named vessel, in which case the date of issuance of the bill of lading will be deemed to be the date of loading on board and the date of shipment.

In all other cases loading on board a named vessel must be

evidenced by a notation on the bill of lading which gives the date on which the goods have been loaded on board, in which case the date of the on board notation will be deemed to be the date of shipment. If the bill of lading contains the indication "intended vessel", or similar qualification in relation to the vessel, loading on board a named vessel must be evidenced by an on board notation on the bill of lading which, in addition to the date on which the goods have been loaded on board, also indicates the name of the vessel on which the goods have been loaded, even if they have been loaded on the vessel named as the "intended vessel".

If the bill of lading indicates a place of receipt or taking in charge different from the port of loading, the on board notation must also include the port of loading stipulated in the credit and the name of the vessel on which the goods have been loaded, even if they have been loaded on the vessel named in the bill of lading. This provision also applies whenever loading on board the vessel is indicated by preprinted wording on the bill of lading, and

(ii) indicates the port of loading and the port of discharge stipulated in the credit, notwithstanding that it:
   - indicates a place of taking in charge different from the port of loading, and/or a place of final destination different from the port of discharge, and/or
   - contains the indication "intended" or similar qualification in relation to the port of loading an/or port of discharge, as long as the document also states the ports of loading and/or discharge stipulated in the credit, and

(iii) consists of a sole original bill of lading or, if issued in more than one original, the full set as so issued, and

(iv) appears to contain all of the terms and conditions of carriage, or some of such terms and conditions by reference to a source or document other than the bill of lading (short form/blank back bill of lading); banks will not examine the contents of such terms and conditions, and

(v) contains no indication that it is subject to a charter party and/or no indication that the carrying vessel is propelled by sail only, and

(vi) in all other respects meets the stipulations of the credit.

Comment

Over the years the article(s) dealing with transport documents have grown steadily more complex and lengthy as the ICC struggles to find wording which leaves no loopholes and is capable of providing a reliable tool for the operation of documentary credits, and this sub-Article, together with the remainder of Article 23 and the following ten articles, represent their latest efforts. No blame attaches to the ICC for the complexity of the current rules: rather such blame lies with the people, and it must be said that the principal culprits have been the banks, who in the past have procrastinated over interpretation of the rules, often to the benefit of no-one in particular but merely for the sake of argument itself. It has been argued that Article 23(a) only applies if the credit actually contains the words "port-to-port shipment", whereas that is, of course, not the case. If a credit calls for shipment from a UK port to Singapore, then it is calling for port-to-port shipment. If it seems far-fetched that such a misleading argument could be put forward in order to avoid payment under a credit, consider Article 32(c), which is in the UCP because banks interpreted the two separate adjectives in the expression "clean on board bill of lading" as requiring those words to appear on the bill, rather than considering what the words actually meant.

The requirements can be summarised by saying that, to be acceptable under a credit calling for a marine or ocean bill of lading, the document presented must be signed by or on behalf of the carriers or the master, must indicate actual shipment on a named vessel at the port specified in the credit for carriage to the port specified in the credit, must not indicate that it is subject to a charter party or that the carrying vessel is a sailing vessel, and must consist of the full set of originals to the number stated on the bill to have been issued. The remainder of the wording of the sub-Article is there because disputes have arisen in the past which have made them necessary in order to prevent recurrence of such disputes. It is worth noting that in almost all cases the ICC, following the path of common sense, has over-ridden objections put forward by banks to various aspects of the bill of lading.

The first requirement deals with the vexed matter of the signature to the bill of lading. It is now necessary that the status of the signatory is clearly shown, and the bill of lading illustrated in Chapter 3 provides a perfect example of how things should be done. Where disputes may now be expected is where, using the same bill of lading as an example, the document is signed "for OJ Africa Line Ltd" without using the word "carriers". There are occasions when this can be important, particularly when the bill is issued by a forwarding agent, but in the example given we would have another case of an argument generated for the benefit of no-one.

It is interesting that in the present version of UCP the position of freight forwarders in modern transportation has finally been recognised, and provided that it complies with the requirements of Article 23 there is nothing to prevent a house bill of lading being presented as an ocean bill of lading under a credit.

The second requirement deals with the question of actual shipment. Regrettably, some banks are unable to cope with the idea that if a bill of lading states in its printed preamble that the goods have been shipped, rather than "received for shipment" or merely "accepted" then no further notation is required. The expressions "shipped", "loaded" and "on board" are synonymous from the point of view of UCP, and are freely interchangeable.

The requirements of this Article, and similar requirements in those which follow, cannot be deviated from, as has been made clear in repeated opinions given by the ICC where dispute has arisen. In many cases, the words "shipped on board" or "clean on board" are typed on the bill of lading by the shippers before the document is lodged with the carriers for signature. Where the printed preamble to the bill of lading states that the goods are "received for shipment" the "on board" clause still requires to be added and dated by the carriers, even though the words were present at the time when the bill was signed. In this respect, these rules, which are international in nature and application, are at variance with English law, since in what must rank as one of the most questionable decisions they have ever made, the Judicial Committee of the Privy Council, the final court of appeal in England, recently ruled that a bill of lading which bore the words "clean on board" at the time it was signed could not be rejected by a bank under a letter of credit. Apart from making the law of England divergent from that of the rest of the world and from the requirements of UCP, this decision fails to take into account the underlying reason for the existence of the Article, which is that a bank can have no means of verifying when and by whom the words were placed on the bill. With all due respects to their Lordships, therefore, banks have no choice but to disregard this ruling.

Requirement (iii) relates to modern methods of cargo-handling whereby goods are accepted by the carriers at places which may be remote from the actual port of loading, usually container bases, and their similar delivery at destination. Such methods are essential in order that valuable space at the dockside may be kept free from goods other than those currently being loaded or discharged from vessels alongside, thus ensuring the speedy turn-round of those vessels.

It is to be anticipated that some difficulty will be experienced arising from the apparent contradiction between the last sentence of requirement (ii) and the provisions of requirement (iii). A "shipped" bill of lading only requires an "on board" endorsement when the name of the carrying vessel is qualified by the word "intended", and when this happens and the goods have been taken in charge by the carriers elsewhere than the port of loading (eg a container base), the "on board" notation must include the date of loading, the name of the vessel, and the port of loading. Where the name of the carrying vessel on a "shipped" bill of lading is unqualified, the bill may indicate that goods have been taken in charge at a place different from the port of loading as stated in requirement (iii). In other words, the last paragraph of requirement (ii) is to be read as subsidiary to the paragraph immediately preceding it, and not as a self-contained requirement.

Note that it is no longer a requirement of UCP that the "on board" notation be separately signed by the carriers.

The essence of requirement (v) has been in UCP for many years now, yet still some banks incorporate in their preprinted credit forms a stipulation that short-form bills of lading are not acceptable, this without any legal justification whatever. Whether through laziness or ignorance on the part of those banks, this practice, like that previously mentioned of asking for certificates of compliance, should be discouraged, and refusal on the part of advising banks and beneficiaries to accept such anachronistic restrictions would be greatly beneficial in furtherance of this aim.

With regard to requirement (vi), the defects of charter party bills of lading were discussed in Chapter 3. To sum up these defects, charter party bills do not necessarily indicate the true conditions of carriage since they are issued subject to the provisions of another document, the charter party itself; they do not cover liner voyages which means that the date of arrival of the goods cannot be accurately forecast; the status of the issuers is sometimes in doubt; they often cover shipment by substandard vessels; and they often feature in cases of fraud, either maritime or documentary. They must therefore be specifically permitted under a credit, and applicants should bear this in mind when applying for the issue of the credit if it is known that, because of the nature of the goods or voyage, or because of specific arrangements with the sellers under the contract, the goods will or may be shipped on a chartered vessel. From the above, they will also be aware of the dangers inherent in allowing their presentation. A positive development, however, is that charter party bills of lading are now specifically provided for in Article 25.

Many of the problems encountered in the application of UCP result from the habit of banks of including in their credit forms, and in the relative application forms, a preprinted requirement for presentation of a marine or ocean bill of lading. Too often this is allowed to stand without any consideration being given to the method of transport which will actually be used.

Both the buyers, when completing their application, and the sellers, on receipt of the credit, should give careful consideration to this question in the light of these articles and ensure that the wording of the credit is adequate to the situation.

ARTICLE 23 (continued)

(a) For the purpose of this article, transhipment means unloading and reloading from one vessel to another vessel during the course of ocean carriage from the port of loading to the port of discharge stipulated in the credit.

(b) Unless transhipment is prohibited by the terms of the credit, banks will accept a bill of lading which indicates that the goods will be transhipped, provided that the entire ocean carriage is covered by one and the same bill of lading.

(c) Even if the credit prohibits transhipment, banks will accept a bill of lading which:

    (i) indicates that transhipment will take place as long as the relevant cargo is shipped in container(s), trailer(s) and/or "LASH" barge(s) as evidenced by the bill of lading, provided that the entire ocean voyage is covered by one and the same bill of lading, and/or

    (ii) incorporates clauses stating that the carrier reserves the right to tranship.

Comment

These sub-Articles recognise the integrity of a container, trailer, or LASH barge as a means of conveyance of goods and, in effect, accords to them the status of a carrying vessel. This concept caused some concern when it was first introduced in the 1983 Revision, since it has the effect of nullifying any prohibition of transhipment in the credit. At that time, the intention of the ICC was to provide for the necessary transhipment of containers, etc in their transfer between the carrying vessel and the container depot at each end of the ocean voyage, but it naturally follows that if a container can be considered secure in such circumstances there is no reason to suppose that it is any less secure during a transhipment between different carrying vessels. Much of the benefit of containerised transportation would be lost if the carriers were deprived of the freedom to move containers in the most efficient way possible, and this has been recognised and the necessary freedom accorded.

The reasons for the unpopularity of transhipment are the dangers which threaten goods during the period between discharge and reloading at the port of transhipment, including exposure to the weather, inappropriate storage facilities being available, pilferage, accidental damage, and undue delay. Most of these considerations do not apply if the goods are in a container. Where this is not the case, all the objections given above continue to apply, and UCP in no way seeks to interfere with the wishes of the parties concerned regarding transhipment, provided that it is specifically mentioned in the credit.

For those who are in any doubt, a "LASH" barge is a floating container, either towed by a tug or proceeding under its own power to a port where it is either loaded on board the ocean vessel or is accommodated between the hulls of a catamaran type of vessel.

Where non-containerised cargo is concerned, careful consideration should be given by applicants to the facts of each case before asking that transhipment be prohibited in a credit, and this aspect should be checked by beneficiaries on receipt of the credit. Some voyages are simply not possible, or are rarely possible, without transhipment taking place. On the other hand, some commodities (live animals provide an excellent example) would be put at great risk should transhipment take place.

ARTICLE 24 — Non-negotiable sea waybill

(a) If a credit calls for a non-negotiable sea waybill covering a port-to-port shipment, banks will, unless otherwise stipulated in the credit, accept a document, however named, which:

    (i) appears on its face to indicate the name of the carrier, and to have been signed or otherwise authenticated by:

        – the carrier or a named agent for and on behalf of the carrier, or

        – the master or a named agent and on behalf of the master.

    Any signature or authentication of the carrier or master must be identified as carrier or master, as the case may be. An agent signing or authenticating for the carrier or master must also indicate the name and the capacity of the party, ie carrier or master, on whose behalf that agent is acting, and

(ii) indicates that the goods have been loaded on board, or shipped on a named vessel.

Loading on board or shipment on a named vessel may be indicated by preprinted wording on the non-negotiable sea waybill that the goods have been loaded on board a named vessel or shipped on a named vessel, in which case the date of issuance of the non-negotiable sea waybill will be deemed to be the date of loading on board and the date of shipment.

In all other cases loading on board a named vessel must be evidenced by a notation on the non-negotiable sea waybill which gives the date on which the goods have been loaded on board, in which case the date of the on board notation will be deemed to be the date of shipment.

If the non-negotiable sea waybill contains the indication "intended vessel", or similar qualification in relation to the vessel, loading on board a named vessel must be evidenced by an on board notation on the non-negotiable sea waybill which, in addition to the date on which the goods have been loaded on board, includes the name of the vessel on which the goods have been loaded, even if they have been loaded on the vessel named as the "intended vessel".

If the non-negotiable sea waybill indicates a place of receipt or taking in charge different from the port of loading, the on board notation must also include the port of loading stipulated in the credit and the name of the vessel on which the goods have been loaded, even if they have been loaded on a vessel named in the non-negotiable sea waybill. This provision also applies whenever loading on board the vessel is indicated by preprinted wording on the non-negotiable sea waybill, and

(iii) indicates the port of loading and the port of discharge stipulated in the credit, notwithstanding that it:

– indicates a place of taking in charge different from the port of loading, and/or a place of final destination different from the port of discharge, and/or

– contains the indication "intended" or similar qualification in relation to the port of loading and/or port of discharge, as long as the document also states the ports of loading and/or discharge stipulated in the credit, and

(iv) consists of a sole original non-negotiable sea waybill or, if issued in more than one original, the full set as so issued, and

(v) appears to contain all of the terms and conditions of carriage, or some of such terms and conditions by reference to a source or document other than the non-negotiable sea waybill (short form/blank back non-negotiable sea waybill); banks will not examine the contents of such terms and conditions, and

(vi) contains no indication that it is subject to a charter party and/or no indication that the carrying vessel is propelled by sail only, and

(vii) in all other respects meets the stipulations of the credit.

(b) For the purpose of this article, transhipment means unloading and reloading from one vessel to another vessel during the course of ocean carriage from the port of loading to the port of discharge stipulated in the credit.

(c) Unless transhipment is prohibited by the terms of the credit, banks will accept a non-negotiable sea waybill which indicates that the goods will be transhipped, provided that the entire ocean carriage is covered by one and the same non-negotiable sea waybill.

(d) Even if the credit prohibits transhipment, banks will accept a non-negotiable sea waybill which:

(i) indicates that transhipment will take place as long as the relevant cargo is shipped in container(s), trailer(s) and/or "LASH" barge(s) as evidenced by the non-negotiable sea waybill, provided that the entire ocean voyage is covered by one and the same non-negotiable sea waybill, and/or

(ii) incorporates clauses stating that the carrier reserves the right to tranship.

Comment

It will readily be seen that the wording of this Article is practically identical to that of Article 23, and in many ways this is a pity. This article dealing specifically with the non-negotiable sea waybill appeared for the first time in the 1993 Revision, but in according the document the same treatment as for a marine bill of lading some of its usefulness is lost. The essence of a waybill is that it is non-negotiable, and therefore is not a document of title to the goods which it covers. For this reason, its presentation is not necessary in order for the consignee to obtain delivery of the goods, mere proof of identity being all that is normally required. There is therefore no possibility of demurrage charges being incurred because of non-arrival of the bill of lading, or conversely no costs incurred for the issue of a bank indemnity in order to secure delivery. Therefore such requirements as presentation of the full set of originals where more than one has been issued are completely superfluous, since only one is necessary to evidence despatch of the goods.

The problem lies with the banks, which continue to regard the underlying goods as part of their security when issuing letters of credit on behalf of their customers. Since the contract of carriage is between the shippers and the carriers, the carriers will act in accordance with the shippers' instructions, and if instructed to change the name of the consignee or otherwise vary the instructions received, will have no reason to refuse if the change is not to their own disadvantage — they are, after all, merely carrying out the wishes of the prima-facie owners of the goods.

Some (but not all) carriers incorporate a clause in their waybills to the effect that, following presentation of the waybill to a bank under a credit, the shippers' right to vary the contract is forfeited, but unless presentation of the waybill is insisted on before changed instructions will be accepted, this clause has no practical value. Insistence on such presentation would be detrimental to shipments which are not the subject of letters of credit. Another possibility is that the waybill may be claused to the effect that delivery can only take place on written authority from the bank, but this is a procedure even more cumbersome than the negotiable bill of lading which the waybill is designed to replace.

The only effective way in which the waybill can be used so as to take full advantages of its merits is for the banks to abandon goods as security for credits, and instead to rely on their normal lending criteria to ensure that, as far as possible, they do not issue credits on behalf of untrustworthy or insolvent applicants.

ARTICLE 25 — Charter party bill of lading

(a) If a credit calls for or permits a charter party bill of lading, banks will, unless otherwise stipulated in the credit, accept a document, however named, which:

    (i) contains any indication that it is subject to a charter party, and

    (ii) appears on its face to have been signed or otherwise authenticated by:

        – the master or a named agent for and on behalf of the master, or

        – the owner or a named agent for and on behalf of the owner.

    Any signature or authentication of the master or owner must be identified as master or owner as the case may be. An agent signing or authenticating for the master or owner must also indicate the name and the capacity of the party, ie master or owner, on whose behalf the agent is acting, and

(iii) does or does not indicate the name of the carrier, and

(iv) indicates that the goods have been loaded on board or shipped on a named vessel.

Loading on board or shipment on a named vessel may be indicated by preprinted wording on the bill of lading that the goods have been loaded on board a named vessel or shipped on a named vessel, in which case the date of issuance of the bill of lading will be deemed to be the date of loading on board and the date of shipment.

In all other cases loading on board a named vessel must be evidence by a notation on the bill of lading which gives the date on which the goods have been loaded on board, in which case the date of the on board notation will be deemed to be the date of shipment, and

(v) indicates the port of loading and the port of discharge stipulated in the credit, and

(vi) consists of a sole original bill of lading or, if issued in more than one original, the full set as so issued, and

(vii) contains no indication that the carrying vessel is propelled by sail only, and

(viii) in all other respects meets the stipulations of the credit.

(b) Even if the credit requires the presentation of a charter party contract in connection with a charter party bill of lading, banks will not examine such charter party contract, but will pass it on without responsibility on their part.

Comment

This Article was newly introduced in the 1993 Revision, and is to be welcomed in that, whereas before the charter party bill of lading had been a vaguely undesirable document, it is now recognised as an essential one in certain trades, where the use of credits has been inhibited by the absence of rules to cover the documentation. However, because the field was new (to UCP) and a vast one, when credits are used in conjunction with charter parties, unforeseen problems may arise which the ICC will have to attempt to provide for in future amendments to the rules. It is also possible that banks would have difficulty in enforcing sub-Article (b) in the face of specific instructions from their customers regarding the contents of a charter party, even if only to the extent of verifying the parties which have signed the agreement. The IFSA *"Standard Banking Practice for the Examination of Letter of Credit Practice"* has 15 checkpoints to guide banks in their acceptance of such bills.

ARTICLE 26 — Multi-modal transport document

(a) If a credit calls for a transport document covering at least two different modes of transport (multi-modal transport document), banks will, unless otherwise stipulated in the credit, accept a document, however named, which:

   (i) appears on its face to indicate the name of the carrier or multi-modal transport operator and to have been signed or otherwise authenticated by:

   – the carrier or multi-modal transport operator or a named agent for and on behalf of the carrier or multi-modal transport operator, or

   – the master or a named agent for and on behalf of the master.

   Any signature or authentication of the carrier, multi-modal transport operator or master must be identified as carrier, multi-modal transport operator or master, as the case may be. An agent signing or authenticating for the carrier, multi-modal transport operator or master must also indicate the name and the capacity of the party, ie carrier, multi-modal transport operator or master, on whose behalf that agent is acting, and

   (ii) indicates that the goods have been dispatched, taken in charge or loaded on board, a named vessel.

   Dispatch, taking in charge or loading on board may be indicated by wording to that effect on the multi-modal transport document and the date of issuance will be deemed to be the date of dispatch, taking in charge or loading on board and the date of shipment. However, if the document indicates, by stamp or otherwise, a date of dispatch, taking in charge or loading on board, such date will be deemed to be the date of shipment, and

   (iii)

   – indicates the place of taking in charge stipulated in the credit which may be different from the port, airport or place of loading, and the place of final destination stipulated in the credit which may be different from the port, airport or place of discharge, and/or

   – contains the indication "intended", or similar qualification in relation to the vessel and/or port of loading and/or port of discharge, and

     (iv) consists of a sole original multi-modal transport document or, if issued in more than one original, the full set as so issued, and

     (v) appears to contain all of the terms and conditions of carriage, or some of such terms and conditions by reference to a source or document other than the multi-modal transport document (short form/blank back multi-modal transport document); banks will not examine the contents of such terms and conditions, and

     (vi) contains no indication that it is subject to a charter party and/or no indication that the carrying vessel is propelled by sail only, and

     (vii) in all other respects meets the stipulations of the credit.

  (b) Even if the credit prohibits transhipment, banks will accept a multi-modal transport document which indicates that transhipment will or may take place, provided that the entire carriage is covered by one and the same multi-modal transport document.

Comment

This was another new article introduced by the 1993 Revision and represents the first attempt to deal with the multi-modal transport document in a separate article. In many respects it follows the format of Articles 23 and 24 and comments made under those Articles should be looked at also in connection with this one, where applicable. Multi-modal transport documents are seldom specifically called for in credits, but more often may be implied from the stipulated places of dispatch and delivery in the credit, as for instance where one or both are inland. Regarding sub-Article (b), it is obvious that where more than one mode of transport is used, then transhipment must take place, and any prohibition of transhipment in a credit deserves to be ignored. The IFSA *"Standard Banking Practice for the Examination of Letter of Credit Practice"* has 19 check points to guide banks in their acceptance of multi-modal transport documents.

ARTICLE 27 — Air transport document

  (a) If a credit calls for an air transport document, banks will, unless otherwise stipulated in the credit, accept a document, however named, which:

     (i) appears on its face to indicate the name of the carrier and to have been signed or otherwise authenticated by:
      – the carrier, or
      – a named agent for or on behalf of the carrier.

Any signature or authentication of the carrier must be identified as carrier. An agent signing or authenticating for the carrier must also indicate the name and capacity of the party, ie carrier, on whose behalf that agent is acting, and

(ii) indicates that the goods have been accepted for carriage, and

(iii) where the credit calls for an actual date of dispatch, indicates a specific notation of such date, the date of dispatch so indicated on the air transport document will be deemed to be the date of shipment.

For the purpose of this Article, the information appearing in the box on the air transport document (marked "For Carrier Use Only" or similar expression) relative to the flight number and date will not be considered as a specific notation of such date of dispatch.

In all other cases, the date of issuance of the air transport document will be deemed to be the date of shipment, and

(iv) indicates the airport of departure and the airport of destination stipulated in the credit, and

(v) appears to be the original for consignor/shipper even if the credit stipulates a full set of originals, or similar expressions, and

(vi) appears to contain all of the terms and conditions of carriage, or some of such terms and conditions, by reference to a source or document other than the air transport document; banks will not examine the content of such terms and conditions, and

(vii) in all other respects meets the stipulations of the credit.

(b) For the purpose of this Article, transhipment means unloading and reloading from one aircraft to another aircraft during the course of carriage from the airport of departure to the airport of destination stipulated in the credit.

(c) Even if the credit prohibits transhipment, banks will accept an air transport document which indicates that transhipment will or may take place, provided that the entire carriage is covered by one and the same air transport document.

Comment

The article dealing specifically with an air transport document returned to UCP in 1993 after a 10 year absence, and is to be welcomed as such. It has been criticised for imposing too strict requirements upon a document which is, after all, not a document of title and can be regarded merely as evidence of dispatch of the goods. For instance, requirement (i) which lays down how the document must be signed calls for the status of the party on whose behalf an air transport document is signed to be stated. Reference to the example in Chapter 4 will show that although the document is signed by Panalpina for and on behalf of British Caledonian Airways, which seems perfectly reasonable in the author's opinion, because it does not state that British Caledonian are the carriers it will be rejected. Such requirements of a not-very-important document are an open invitation to banks to reject documents which represent no risk to their customers, and such rejections achieve nothing other than reducing confidence in the documentary credit as a means of settlement.

The significance of requirement (iii) is that unless the credit calls for a "certification of flight details" to appear on the air transport document, its date of issue will be taken as the date of shipment in assessing whether or not the credit's terms have been complied with. Unfortunately, if the credit does not call for such evidence, the date of issue of the document will take precedence over the factual information contained in the flight stamp. In other words, your presentation days begin ticking away from the date the air waybill was raised ("cut") not from the date the goods flew.

It is a sad reflection on the expertise exhibited by banks when issuing letters of credit that requirement (v) is still considered necessary, but credits are still issued from time to time which call for a "full set of original air waybills", suggesting that the issuing bank cannot distinguish between a negotiable and a non-negotiable document.

Sub-Article (c) is interesting in that it takes away from the applicants and the issuing bank the power to prohibit transhipment where goods are to be shipped by air. As was the case with containerised sea cargo, this is merely recognition of the realities of air transport, where it is often difficult to ascertain from the transport document whether or not goods are to be transhipped.

Air waybills, and to a lesser extent air consignment notes, have long been difficult documents to which to apply UCP. Co-operation from the airlines is not always forthcoming since, owing to the superior speed of air transportation, by the time documents are presented under a letter of credit the transaction is, to them, history, and the contract is closed.

ARTICLE 28 — Road, rail or inland waterway transport documents

(a) If a credit calls for a road, rail or inland waterway transport document, banks will, unless otherwise stipulated in the credit, accept a document of the type called for, however named, which:
   (i) appears on its face to indicate the name of the carrier and to have been signed or otherwise authenticated by the carrier or a named

agent for and on behalf of the carrier and/or to bear a reception stamp or other indication of receipt by the carrier or a named agent for and on behalf of the carrier.

Any signature, authentication, reception stamp or other indication of receipt of the carrier, must be identified on its face as that of the carrier. An agent signing or authenticating for the carrier, must also indicate the name and the capacity of the party, ie carrier, on whose behalf that agent is acting, and

(ii) indicates that the goods have been received for shipment, dispatch or carriage or wording to this effect. The date of issuance will be deemed to be the date of shipment unless the transport document contains a reception stamp, in which case the date of the reception stamp will be deemed to be the date of shipment, and

(iii) indicates the place of shipment and the place of destination stipulated in the credit, and

(iv) in all other respects meets the stipulations of the credit.

(b) In the absence of any indication on the transport document as to the numbers issued, banks will accept the transport document(s) presented as constituting a full set. Banks will accept as original(s) the transport document(s) whether marked as originals or not.

(c) For the purpose of this article, transhipment means unloading and reloading from one means of conveyance to another means of conveyance, in different modes of transport, during the course of carriage from the place of shipment to the place of destination stipulated in the credit.

(d) Even if the credit prohibits transhipment, banks will accept a road, rail or inland waterway transport document which indicates that transhipment will or may take place, provided that the entire carriage is covered by one and the same transport document and within the same mode of transport.

Comment

Little further may be added in respect of this article which has not already been said in relation to the air transport document. The usual documents for road, rail or inland waterway transport are the CMR, CIM, and water-way bill of lading, none of which are negotiable documents. Accordingly, none warrants detailed treatment in UCP, and it may be thought that they already have more than their due in this new (1993) article. In respect of sub-Article (b), it is very rare for any of these documents to be issued in a set of originals — there is simply no point. The ruthless pursuit of transhipment as a discrepancy is continued in this Article, transhipment only being regarded as having taken place where goods are transferred from road to rail or inland waterway, or any other combination of these three. In practice, of course, containers are frequently transferred from road to rail where longer journeys are involved, but the transport document usually makes no mention of this occurrence, and so long as this remains the case there should be no problems with this article. Without such a rule, we could well have had documents being rejected, for instance, where although the goods were completing the entire journey by rail, transhipment had to take place where there was a break in the gauge of the rails, as between France and Spain, or between Poland and Russia. This cannot now happen.

ARTICLE 29 — Courier and post receipts

(a) If a credit calls for a post receipt or certificate of posting, banks will, unless otherwise stipulated in the credit, accept a post receipt or certificate of posting which:

    (i) appears to have been stamped or otherwise authenticated and dated in the place from which the credit stipulates the goods are to be shipped or dispatched and such date will be deemed to be the date of shipment or dispatch, and

    (ii) in all other respects meets the stipulations of the credit.

(b) If a credit calls for a document issued by a courier or expedited delivery service evidencing receipt of the goods for delivery, banks will, unless otherwise stipulated in the credit, accept a document, however named, which:

    (i) appears on its face to indicate the name of the courier/service, and to have been stamped, signed or otherwise authenticated by such named courier/service (unless the credit specifically calls for a document issued by a named courier/service, banks will accept a document issued by any courier/service), and

    (ii) indicates a date of pick-up or of receipt or wording to this effect, such date being deemed to be the date of shipment or dispatch, and

    (iii) in all other respects meets the stipulations of the credit.

Comment

Sub-Article (b) was introduced in the 1993 Revision, and serves to bring within the scope of UCP the increasing proportion of goods which would formerly have travelled by parcel post or by air freight which are now carried by courier companies. The transport document is of little value in itself, since it is completed by the consignors themselves and its verification usually consists of the scribbled signature of the individual who calls to collect the parcel. The Article is another step towards completeness of coverage in UCP, and precludes any attempt by banks to relate the shipment date stipulated in the credit to the date on which the goods actually leave the exporting country.

ARTICLE 30 — Transport documents issued by freight forwarders

Unless otherwise authorised in the credit, banks will only accept a transport document issued by a freight forwarder if it appears on its face to indicate:

  (i) the name of the freight forwarder as a carrier or multi-modal transport operator and to have been signed or otherwise authenticated by the freight forwarder as carrier or multi-modal transport operator,

   or

  (ii) the name of the carrier or multi-modal transport operator and to have been signed or otherwise authenticated by the freight forwarder as a named agent for or on behalf of the carrier or multi-modal transport operator.

Comment

Note that the article does not commence with the words: "Where the credit calls for presentation of a document issued by a freight forwarder...." which implies a welcome departure from the pre-1993 position whereby most forwarders' documents were rejected out of hand unless specifically authorised in the credit. In order for their documents to be accepted by banks under credits, forwarders now have a straight choice — they either sign as authorised agents for the carriers, or they take upon themselves the responsibilities of the carriers. This acceptance of the position in international transportation of the NVOCC (non-vessel-owning common carrier) must be welcomed by all who have encountered this problem with credits in the past.

ARTICLE 31 — "On deck", "shipper's load and count", name of consignor

Unless otherwise stipulated in the credit, banks will accept a transport document which:

  (i) does not indicate, in the case of carriage by sea or by more than one means of conveyance including carriage by sea, that the goods are or will be loaded on deck. Nevertheless, banks will accept a transport document which contains a provision that the goods may be carried on deck, provided that it does not specifically state that they are or will be loaded on deck, and/or

(ii) bears a clause on the face thereof such as "shipper's load and count" or "said by shipper to contain" or words of similar effect, and/or

(iii) indicates as the consignor of the goods a party other than the beneficiary of the credit.

Comment

It is generally undesirable that goods be loaded on the deck of a ship rather than in the hold for two main reasons. Obviously goods stowed on deck are more liable to damage from the elements or from being washed overboard in a storm, but also such goods are likely to be the first to go when it becomes necessary to jettison cargo in order to lighten the ship and save it from foundering. When the goods are of a nature which indicates that they will probably be stowed on deck, such as where they are hazardous or inflammable, or where they are too bulky for hold stowage, due provision should be made in the credit for acceptance of bills of lading indicating stowage on deck.

Regarding provision (iii) it is incumbent upon the applicants and the issuing bank to ensure that, if the laws of their country prohibit the name of a third party from being shown on the bill of lading as shipper, the credit so states. This particularly applies where it is known that the beneficiary is not the supplier of the goods, or that the bill of lading is likely to be a carrier's bill issued to a forwarding agent.

ARTICLE 32 — Clean transport documents

(a) A clean transport document is one which bears no clause or notation which expressly declares a defective condition of the goods and/or the packaging.

(b) Banks will not accept transport documents bearing such clauses or notations unless the credit expressly stipulates the clauses or notations which may be accepted.

(c) Banks will regard a requirement in a credit for a transport document to bear the clause "clean on board" as complied with if such transport document meets the requirements of this article and of Articles 23, 24, 25, 26, 27, 28 or 30.

Comment

Though ostensibly among the simpler articles in UCP, this one seems to be one of the most regularly misunderstood or disregarded. If the bill is a "shipped" one and bears nothing which indicates that there is anything wrong with the goods or the packing, then whatever it says in the credit the words "clean on board" are completely superfluous and, in fact, can cause more problems than they solve.

Disputes also arise as to what constitutes a clause indicating a defect in the goods and/or the packing, and the attitude of banks varies wildly in this respect. Banks have been known to reject a bill of lading as dirty when it bears a clause stating that surcharges may be payable at destination if the ship is delayed in entering harbour by factors beyond the captain's control, a matter which is not even covered by this article but by Article 33(d). "Wrapping on bales torn and stained" should undoubtedly be regarded as detrimental, and the document be rejected, but "In the opinion of the carrier the packing of these goods is insufficient, etc" should not. Where it is felt that because of the nature of the cargo a claused bill of lading may well be issued but the clause will be acceptable to the buyers, it is as well to provide for its acceptance in the credit. As always, it is also in the beneficiaries' interest if they consider this aspect when the credit is received and if necessary call for an amendment. The alternative may well be a severe delay in payment or worse.

ARTICLE 33 — Freight payable/prepaid transport documents

(a) Unless otherwise stipulated in the credit, or inconsistent with any of the documents presented under the credit, banks will accept transport documents stating that freight or transportation charges (hereafter referred to as "freight") have still to be paid.

(b) If a credit stipulates that transport document has to indicate that freight has been paid or prepaid, banks will accept a transport document on which words clearly indicating payment or prepayment or freight appear by stamp or otherwise, or on which payment of prepayment of freight is indicated by other means. If the credit requires courier charges to be paid or prepaid banks will also accept a transport document issued by a courier or expedited delivery service evidencing that courier charges are for the account of a party other than the consignee.

(c) The words "freight prepayable" or "freight to be prepaid" or words of similar effect, if appearing on transport documents, will not be accepted as constituting evidence of the payment of freight.

(d) Banks will accept transport documents bearing reference by stamp or otherwise to costs additional to the freight, such as costs of, or disbursements incurred in connection with, loading, unloading or similar operations, unless the conditions of the credit specifically prohibit such reference.

Comment

In practice, carriers do not normally release bills of lading to the shippers until freight has been paid, or unless they operate an open account system for payment of freight by those shippers.

ARTICLE 34 — Insurance documents

(a) Insurance documents must appear on their face to be issued and signed by insurance companies or underwriters or their agents.

(b) If the insurance document indicates that it has been issued in more than one original, all the originals must be presented unless otherwise stipulated in the credit.

(c) Cover notes issued by brokers will not be accepted, unless specifically authorised in the credit.

Comment

The drawbacks of brokers' cover notes were dealt with in Chapter 5. Sellers should note that if they intend obtaining insurance cover from the continent of Europe, a brokers' cover note may well be the document provided, since it is well-established in that insurance market. They should therefore either request that the credit be framed so as to authorise presentation of such a document, or specifically request the brokers to provide the insurers' own policy or certificate.

All concerned, but especially the banks, should remember that a document is not always what it seems to be at first glance, and it has been known for an insurance document bearing the letterhead of a broker to transpire to be the actual document signed by the various syndicates of underwriters which have subscribed to the cover provided.

ARTICLE 34(d)

Unless otherwise stipulated in the credit, banks will accept an insurance certificate or a declaration under an open cover pre-signed by insurance companies, underwriters or their agents. If a credit specifically calls for an insurance certificate or a declaration under an open cover, banks will accept, in lieu thereof, an insurance policy.

Comment

This is a common sense rule, bearing in mind that underlying every insurance certificate or declaration under open cover there must be either an agreement to issue a policy or the policy itself. No legal rights attach to the certificate or declaration, the right to claim under the to-be-issued or existing policy lying in the law of contract rather than insurance legislation.

ARTICLE 34(e)

Unless otherwise stipulated in the credit, or unless it appears from the insurance document that the cover is effective at the latest from the date of loading on board or dispatch or taking in charge of the goods, banks will refuse insurance documents presented which bear a date later than the date of loading on board or dispatch or taking in charge of the goods as indicated by the transport document(s).

Comment

Broadly speaking, this means that where the insurance document is a policy it must not be dated later than the relevant transport document. However, where it is a certificate issued under an open or a floating policy, the agreement between the insurers and the insured is that all shipments will be held covered, and the cover is therefore in force from the time the goods leave the sellers' warehouse, even though the certificate is not issued until a later date.

ARTICLE 34(f)

(i) Unless otherwise stipulated in the credit, the insurance document must be expressed in the same currency as the credit.

(ii) Unless otherwise stipulated in the credit, the minimum amount for which the insurance document must indicate the insurance cover to have been effected is the CIF (cost, insurance and freight (…"named port of destination")) or CIP (freight/carriage and insurance paid to ("named place of destination")) value of the goods, as the case may be plus 10%, but only when the CIF or CIP value can be determined from the documents on their face. Otherwise banks will accept as such minimum amount 110% of the amount for which payment, acceptance or negotiation is requested under the credit, or 110% of the gross amount of the invoice, whichever is the greater.

Comment

Surprisingly, the ICC has given the opinion that where a credit specifies that insurance cover be effected for, say, CIF value plus 10%, where this percentage is exceeded even by a small amount the document should be rejected. It would seem, bearing in mind the low cost of insurance premiums relative to the value of the goods, and the fact that the total amount of drawings will in any case be restricted by the amount of the credit, that this is taking too rigid a view of the kind which, if strictly enforced, gets banks a bad name among exporters. However, this is a personal view, and the ICC's opinion must be respected.

ARTICLE 35 — Type of insurance cover

(a) Credits should stipulate the type of insurance required and, if any, the additional risks which are to be covered. Imprecise terms such as "usual risks" or "customary risks" shall not be used; if they are used, banks will accept insurance documents as presented, without responsibility for any risks not being covered.

(b) Failing specific stipulations in the credit, banks will accept insurance documents as presented, without responsibility for any risks not being covered.

(c) Unless otherwise stipulated in the credit, banks will accept an insurance document which indicates that the cover is subject to a franchise or an excess (deductible).

Comment

Although a common practice in other areas of insurance, it is unusual for a percentage to be applied to marine cargo insurance, requiring the claimant to bear a stated percentage of any loss.

ARTICLE 36 — All risks insurance cover

Where a credit stipulates "insurance against all risks", banks will accept an insurance document which contains any "all risks" notation or clause, whether or not bearing the heading "all risks", even if the insurance document indicates that certain risks are excluded, without responsibility for any risk(s) not being covered.

Comment

As mentioned in Chapter 5, the old "all risks" clauses drawn up by the Institute of London Underwriters have been superseded by a new set, simply designated "Clauses A". The purpose of this article is to cater for the surprising number of banks which have not yet realised this and continue to call for cover as per the Institute's "all risks" clauses in their credits.

ARTICLE 37 — Commercial invoices

(a) Unless otherwise stipulated in the credit, commercial invoices:
  (i) must appear on their face to be issued by the beneficiary named in the credit (except as provided in Article 48), and
  (ii) must be made out in the name of the applicant (except as provided in sub-Article 48 (h)),
    and
  (iii) need not be signed.

(b) Unless otherwise stipulated in the credit, banks may refuse commercial invoices issued for amounts in excess of the amount permitted by the credit. Nevertheless, if a bank authorised to pay, incur a deferred payment undertaking, accept draft(s), or negotiate under a credit accepts such invoices, its decision will be binding upon all parties, provided that such bank has not paid, incurred a deferred payment undertaking, accepted draft(s) or negotiated for an amount in excess of that permitted by the credit.

(c) The description of the goods in the commercial invoice must correspond with the description in the credit. In all other documents, the goods may be described in general terms not inconsistent with the description of the goods in the credit.

Comment

Sub-Articles (a) (i) and (ii), whilst appearing straightforward, contain traps for unwary beneficiaries. This is one of the areas where spelling mistakes, usually in the credit, can mean that the issuing bank can deny that the invoice is acceptable under the terms of this Article. The attitude of banks in this situation varies enormously — some apply common sense, others do not. The answer, from the point of view of beneficiaries, is to check such things upon receipt of the credit, and, if spelling mistakes are found, to request an amendment to the credit. When doing so, remember to stipulate that amendment charges, as with any other amendment brought about by an error on the part of the applicants or the issuing bank, are not for the beneficiaries' account.

Sub-Article (b) covers the situation where, because of unforeseen increases in costs, or because of a miscalculation of the amount of freight payable, the sellers invoice the full cost to the buyers, but draw under the credit only for the amount payable thereunder. The negotiating bank is given the option of accepting or rejecting such invoices. Often there is no danger in doing this, and the bank may be prepared to treat the difference between the amounts of the draft and the invoice as a separate clean collection. Sometimes, however, the bank will know from its experience that the discrepancy in amount will cause problems in the buyers' country; this frequently applies where that country exercises strict exchange control, and in these circumstances the bank may well exercise its option to refuse the invoice.

Sub-Article (c) is one of the instances where UCP must be obeyed quite literally to the letter. Even if the credit description of the goods includes a spelling mistake this should be faithfully reproduced in the invoice description, or an amendment obtained at the applicant's expense. This is because the detailed description is likely to be of a technical nature and banks cannot be expected to make judgments on whether or not a discrepancy is crucial. For example, a Swiss bank rejected a drawing negotiated through a bank in New York because the invoice included the word "polyethilene" in the goods description, whereas the credit gave the word as "polyethylene". These are respectively the American and English spellings of the same word, but it would have been unfair to expect the Swiss bank to make a judgment on this. One-letter differences can be crucial, as in "bisulphate" and "bisulphite", which indicate entirely different chemicals.

Unless specifically required by the credit or by the regulations of the importing country, a detailed description on the bill of lading is unnecessary, and is discouraged by most carriers. There is a tendency among shippers, however, to describe the goods in such a way as to attract the lowest possible freight rate without (it is to be hoped) resorting to actual deception. This is a matter concerning only the contract of carriage, but where the saving on the freight may possibly be vastly exceeded by the loss when payment under a credit is refused this becomes a false economy.

ARTICLE 38 — Other documents

If a credit calls for an attestation or certification of weight in the case of transport other than by sea, banks will accept a weight stamp or declaration of weight which appears to have been superimposed on the transport document by the carrier or his agent unless the credit specifically stipulates that the attestation or certification of weight must be by means of a separate document.

Comment

It is worth repeating that this Article does NOT apply to goods dispatched by sea.

CHAPTER 13

Uniform Customs and Practice for Documentary Credits 3

E: Miscellaneous Provisions

ARTICLE 39 — Allowances in credit amount, quantity and unit price

(a) The words "about", "approximately", "circa" or similar expressions used in connection with the amount of the credit or the quantity or the unit price stated in the credit are to be construed as allowing a difference not to exceed 10% more or 10% less than the amount or the quantity or the unit price to which they refer.

(b) Unless a credit stipulates that the quantity of the goods specified must not be exceeded or reduced, a tolerance of 5% more or 5% less will be permissible, always provided that the amount of the drawings does not exceed the amount of the credit. This tolerance does not apply when the credit stipulates the quantity in terms of a stated number of packing units or individual items.

(c) Unless a credit which prohibits partial shipments stipulates otherwise, or unless sub-Article (b) above is applicable, a tolerance of 5% less in the amount of the drawing will be permissible, provided that if the credit stipulates the quantity of goods, such quantity of goods is shipped in full, and if the credit stipulates a unit price, such price is not reduced. This provision does not apply when expressions referred to in sub-Article (a) above are used in the credit.

Comment

Sub-Article (a) is fairly clear in its meaning. The difficulty arises when the words "about" or "approximately" are used in relation to the quantity or the unit price without being also applied to the credit amount. The resulting contradiction inevitably means that the beneficiary cannot be paid under the credit, and all concerned should be alert for examples of this trap.

Sub-Article (b) is intended to apply to bulk cargoes, allowing for such potential sources of discrepancy as absorption of moisture, residue in tanks, etc. Note that the tolerance applies to the quantity only.

Sub-Article (c) was newly introduced in the 1993 Revision, and removes the temptation which formerly existed to stretch the application of sub-Article (b). Where no unit price is given in the credit and the credit is short-drawn, the immediate assumption by the banks used to be that inferior goods had been supplied. The result was rejection of the documents, even though the real cause was usually the freight amount differing from that estimated in the proforma invoice. It will be remembered from Chapter 2 that the usual basis for commercial quotations is the FOB price, since this is a constant. In estimating other costs, such as freight and insurance, sellers naturally tend to err on the high side in order that they are not left with a shortfall which cannot be drawn under the credit, but where those costs are less than estimated and they are honest enough to pass the saving on to their customers it is manifestly apparent that they should not be penalised by having their documents rejected as described above.

ARTICLE 40 — Partial shipments/drawings

(a) Partial drawings and/or shipments are allowed, unless the credit stipulates otherwise.

(b) Transport documents which appear on their face to indicate that shipment has been made on the same means of conveyance and for the same journey, provided they indicate the same destination, will not be regarded as covering partial shipments, even if the transport documents indicate different dates of shipment and/or different ports of loading, taking in charge, or dispatch.

(c) Shipments made by post or by courier will not be regarded as partial shipments if the post receipts or certificates of posting or courier's receipts or dispatch notes appear to have been stamped, signed or otherwise authenticated in the place from which the credit stipulates the goods are to be dispatched, and on the same date.

Comment

Sub-Article (b) is designed to cover situations such as where part only of a consignment is ready for shipment by the advertised dates for the vessel receiving cargo at a particular port, but the balance is able to be shipped on the same vessel when it calls at another port. Reason suggests that provided that all the goods arrive together on the same vessel it is of little relevance that they may have been shipped at different ports on different dates.

ARTICLE 41 — Instalment shipments/drawings

If drawings and/or shipments by instalments within given periods are stipulated in the credit and any instalment is not drawn and/or shipped within the period allowed for that instalment, the credit ceases to be available for that or any subsequent instalments, unless otherwise stipulated in the credit.

Comment

This article provides a dangerous trap of which all exporters should be aware. It is designed to protect buyers who have planned their business on the basis of receiving consignments of imports at certain times, an example being a contractor ordering raw materials for delivery at the appropriate stage of a construction project. If a particular shipment is late, the contract may be lost, or the contractors may wish to seek alternative and more reliable sources of supply, and so Article 41 automatically cancels the credit where any instalment is shipped or any drawing made later than the date specified in the credit. Normal procedure when this happens is for the bank handling the discrepant drawing to seek confirmation from the issuing bank that the credit will continue to be valid. The issuing bank will refer to its customer and either reinstate or confirm the cancellation of the credit. This is the only case where the irrevocability of a credit is threatened by UCP, and beneficiaries should take great care when they are shipping goods under such a credit, first that bills of lading are dated in accordance with the shipment dates specified for each instalment, and second that documents for each shipment are presented within the specified time after shipment.

ARTICLE 42 — Expiry date and place for presentation of documents

(a) All credits must stipulate an expiry date and a place for presentation of documents for payment, acceptance or with the exception of freely negotiable credits, a place for presentation of documents for negotiation. An expiry date stipulated for payment, acceptance or negotiation will be construed to express an expiry date for presentation of documents.

(b) Except as provided in sub-Article 44 (a), documents must be presented on or before such expiry date.

(c) If an issuing bank states that a credit is to be available "for one month", "for six months" or the like, but does not specify the date from which the time is to run, the date of issuance of the credit by the issuing bank will be deemed to be the first day from which such time is to run. Banks should discourage indication of the expiry date of the credit in this manner.

ARTICLE 43 — Limitation on the expiry date

In addition to stipulating an expiry date for presentation of documents, every credit which calls for a transport document(s) should also stipulate a specified period of time after the date of shipment during which presentation must be made in compliance with the terms and conditions of the credit. If no such period of time is stipulated, banks will not accept documents presented to them later than 21 days after the date of shipment. In any event, documents must be presented not later than the expiry date of the credit.

Comment

The 21-day rule should be deeply embedded in the consciousness of anyone involved with credits at the negotiation stage, whether they be the beneficiaries or the negotiating bank. The rule was introduced in the 1973 Revision of UCP to take the question of stale bills of lading out of the documentary credits field completely. Up until that time it was the duty of the negotiating bank to determine in each case whether the bill of lading had been presented in sufficient time for it to be able to reach the destination of the goods before their arrival, and in many cases the only way in which they could do this was to institute enquiries of the shipowners as to the arrival date of the carrying vessel.

This troublesome duty is no longer necessary, and it is left to the applicants to calculate how long they can afford to allow the beneficiaries for presentation of documents without running the risk of receiving stale bills of lading. This appears in the credit as the number of days after shipment within which the documents must be presented, and in some cases this can be impractically short. Beneficiaries are advised to consider this point when the credit is received and to request an amendment if it is considered that they will be unable to comply with the requirements. Such an amendment may not be forthcoming, of course, if the applicants have done their calculations correctly. The greatest danger arises when the credit is silent on the topic and Article 47 (a) is applied, or when negotiation is delayed because of other discrepancies to the point where the crucial date is passed.

ARTICLE 43(b)

In cases in which sub-Article 40(b) applies, the date of shipment will be considered to be the latest shipment date on any of the transport documents presented.

ARTICLE 44 — Extension of expiry date

If the expiry date of the credit and / or the last day of the period of time for presentation of documents stipulated by the credit or applicable by virtue of Article 43 falls on a day on which the bank to which presentation has to be made is closed for reasons other than those referred to in Article 17, the stipulated expiry date and / or the last day of the period of time after the date of shipment for presentation of documents, as the case may be, shall be extended to the first following day on which such bank is open.

Comment

Article 17 covered closure of banks for reasons outside their control, and stated that the dates referred to were not extended as a result of that closure. This article covers the weekend and public holiday types of closure, and effectively applies the same rules to letters of credit as apply to maturing bills of exchange.

ARTICLE 44(b)

The latest date for shipment shall not be extended by reason of the extension of the expiry date and / or the period of time after the date of shipment for presentation of documents in accordance with sub-Article (a) above. If no such latest date for shipment is stipulated in the credit or amendments thereto, banks will not accept transport documents indicating a date of shipment later than the expiry date stipulated in the credit or amendments thereto.

Comment

It should be stressed that in the final sentence the expiry date referred to is the stated expiry date in the credit, not the extended one.

ARTICLE 44(c)

The bank to which presentation is made on such first following business day must provide a statement that the documents were presented within the time limits extended in accordance with sub-Article 44(a) of the *Uniform Customs and Practice for Documentary Credits*, 1993 Revision, ICC Publication No. 500.

Comment

This certification is necessary because of the unlikelihood of the issuing bank being aware of the dates of weekends and public holidays in every country where beneficiaries of its credits may reside.

ARTICLE 45 — Hours of presentation

Banks are under no obligation to accept presentation of documents outside their banking hours.

Comment

But they are not precluded from doing so.

ARTICLE 46 — General expressions as to dates for shipment

(a) Unless otherwise stipulated in the credit, the expression "shipment" used in stipulating an earliest and/or a latest date for shipment will be understood to include expressions such as "loading on board", "dispatch", "accepted for carriage", "date of post receipt", "date of pick-up", and the like, and in the case of a credit calling for a multi-modal transport document the expression "taking in charge".

(b) Expressions such as "prompt", "immediately", "as soon as possible", and the like should not be used. If they are used, banks will disregard them.

(c) If the expression "on or about" or similar expressions are used, banks will interpret them as a stipulation that shipment is to be made during the period from five days before to five days after the specified date, both end days included.

Comment

Sub-Article (a) removes the possibility of petty arguments developing over what constitutes shipment where, for instance, a combined transport document is called for.

It is a great pity that sub-Article (b) appears here and not in a more general context, since its wording makes it clear that it relates only to the shipment of the goods. The greatest problems arising from words such as "immediately" occur when the credit uses them in connection with such requirements as the sending of a set of non-negotiable documents to the applicants, or the faxing or telexing of details of the shipment to an insurance company "immediately after shipment". Given that such details as reference numbers of transport documents, definitive shipping marks, and details of freight charges, are not known until the transport document is received, and that until such time it is impossible to draw up the commercial invoice and other documents which require such information to be incorporated in them; and also given that it can very often take a week or more for the shipping company to process all the bills of lading relating to a particular sailing, the use of such words in a credit often creates an instant recipe for rejection of the drawing. When asked for help with this problem, the Banking Commission of the ICC were able to do no more than to look up the definition of the word "immediately" in *The Concise Oxford Dictionary*. Beneficiaries are therefore recommended to be on the alert for such requirements and to reject credits which include them, on the grounds that they incorporate a "built-in discrepancy".

ARTICLE 47 — Date terminology for periods of shipment

(a) The words "to", "until", "till", "from", and words of similar import applying to any date term or period in the credit referring to shipment will be understood to include the date mentioned.

(b) The word "after" will be understood to exclude the date mentioned.

(c) The terms "first half", "second half" of a month shall be construed respectively as from the 1st to the 15th, and the 16th to the last day of such month, all dates inclusive.

(d) The terms "beginning", "middle", or "end" of a month shall be construed respectively as from the 1st to the 10th, the 11th to the 20th, and the 21st to the last day of such month, all dates inclusive.

F: Transferable credit

ARTICLE 48 — Transferable credit

A transferable credit is a credit under which the beneficiary (first beneficiary) may request the bank authorised to pay, incur a deferred payment undertaking, accept or negotiate (the "transferring bank"), or in the case of a freely negotiable credit, the bank specifically authorised in the credit as a transferring bank, to make the credit available in whole or in part to one or more other beneficiary(ies) (second beneficiary(ies)).

Comment
Note that the beneficiary has the right to request, not to compel, and there might be circumstances, such as where the bank suspects fraud, where it would decline to transfer the credit. The facility to transfer to more than one second beneficiary is later qualified in sub-Article (g). It is important to note that transfer can only be effected by a bank which is authorised to pay, accept or negotiate drawings under the original credit, and that this is not invariably the advising bank. Where a credit is freely negotiable, issuing banks should note that the credit is required to nominate the bank which is authorised to effect transfer, and banks which are requested by the beneficiary of a freely negotiable transferable credit to effect transfer should note that they may only do so if they are so nominated in the credit.

ARTICLE 48(b)

A credit can be transferred only if it is expressly designated as "transferable" by the issuing bank. Terms such as "divisible", "fractionable", "assignable", and "transmissible" do not render the credit transferable. If such terms are used they shall be disregarded.

Comment
As was stated in Chapter 10, when asked for a transferable credit, the applicants should immediately be aware that they are not dealing with the suppliers of the goods, and this sub-Article ensures that this fact cannot be concealed from them.

ARTICLE 48(c)

The transferring bank shall be under no obligation to effect such transfer except to the extent and in the manner expressly consented to by such bank.

Comment
Sub-Article (a) gave the transferring bank the right to stand aside from the transaction if it was in any way unhappy with it: this sub-Article extends that protection to allow the bank to strictly control the manner of the transfer even when it has agreed to put it into effect. The reason for such delicacy on the part of the banks is that, although the vast majority of users of transferable credits are perfectly legitimate, the first beneficiaries are in fact obtaining goods not on their own creditworthiness but on that of the applicants for the credit. This factor

can attract the casual trader, the undercapitalised, and even the criminal element into this aspect of documentary credits, and the higher risks to which they are thereby exposed can make the transfer of a credit an unattractive proposition to a bank.

ARTICLE 48(d)

At the time of making a request for transfer and prior to transfer of the credit, the first beneficiary must irrevocably instruct the transferring bank whether or not he retains the right to refuse to allow the transferring bank to advise amendments to the second beneficiary(ies). If the transferring bank consents to the transfer under these conditions, it must, at the time of transfer, advise the second beneficiary(ies) of the first beneficiary's instructions regarding amendments.

Comment

It seems that if the transferring bank is agreeable, the first beneficiaries may elect to "retain the right" to refuse to allow advice of subsequent amendments to the second beneficiaries. Furthermore, the first beneficiaries must "irrevocably instruct" the transferring bank in this matter (the difficulties which banks encounter when receiving instructions from parties which are not their own customers, and when attempting to enforce the irrevocability of such instructions, are very real and will be discussed again in the comments on Article 49).

It is difficult to see how irrevocable instructions can be given concerning a matter which, from the way in which the sub-Article is worded, will remain a matter of choice for the first beneficiaries. If they state that the right to refuse to permit onward advice of amendments is retained, this does not preclude them from requesting such onward advice if it suits their purposes; furthermore, they may apparently request onward advice to one or some second beneficiaries but not to all. If they state that they do not retain the right, they can still effectively prevent onward advice by refusing to accept the amendment on their own behalf under the provisions of sub-Article 9(d)(iii).

It is possible that, with the co-operation of the applicants, first beneficiaries may be tempted to use this sub-Article as a means of circumventing the provisions of sub-article 48(h), which severely limits the scope of changes which are permitted to be made between the credit in its original and transferred forms. By persuading the applicants to omit unwelcome requirements until the credit has been transferred and then installing them in the original credit by amendment, the second beneficiaries may be able to prevent such requirements becoming part of the transferred credit.

The reactions of transferring banks and of second beneficiaries to the first beneficiaries' refusal to allow amendments to be passed on will be interesting, with suspicion being the most likely feeling in both parties.

ARTICLE 48(e)

If a credit is transferred to more than one second beneficiary(ies), refusal of an amendment by one or more second beneficiary(ies) does not invalidate the acceptance(s) by the other second beneficiary(ies) with respect to whom the credit will be amended accordingly. With respect to the second beneficiary(ies) who rejected the amendment, the credit will remain unamended.

Comment

This sub-Article is a new addition to the 1993 Revision, but it merely codifies the situation as it existed previously. Under the provisions of Article 9, any beneficiary has the right to reject an amendment to an irrevocable credit. What is interesting is the effect on the first beneficiaries' presentation under the original credit where some second beneficiaries have accepted an amendment and some have not. The answer, of course, is that since the applicants have knowingly requested the issue of a transferable credit subject to UCP, with the terms of which they must be presumed to be familiar, they are bound to accept the documents if they conform with the terms of the credit in either its amended or unamended forms. Since Article 9 now requires specific notification of rejection of an amendment, all parties will be aware in advance of the possible discrepancies between different presentations under the same transferable credit. It remains a matter for conjecture whether, having rejected an amendment, any beneficiary, whether covered by Article 9 or Article 48, can rescind that rejection in respect of later presentations under the same credit — the word "irrevocable" is not used in this connection. Acceptance, of course, must be regarded as irrevocable.

ARTICLE 48(f) and (g)

Transferring bank charges in respect of transfers including commissions, fees, costs or expenses are payable by the first beneficiary unless otherwise agreed. If the transferring bank agrees to transfer the credit it shall be under no obligation to effect the transfer until such charges are paid.

Unless otherwise stated in the credit, a transferable credit can be transferred once only. Consequently, the credit cannot be transferred at the request of the second beneficiary to any subsequent third beneficiary. For the purpose of this Article, a retransfer to the first beneficiary does not constitute a prohibited transfer.

Fractions of a transferable credit (not exceeding in the aggregate the amount of the credit) can be transferred separately, provided partial shipments are not prohibited, and the aggregate of such transfers will be considered as constituting only one transfer of credit.

Comment

Before the adoption of the 1993 Revision of UCP the rules were quite clear — a transferable credit could be transferred once only. Now they are qualified by the words "unless otherwise stated in the credit". In the author's view, this is unfortunate. There can rarely be any commercial justification requiring an order for goods to be passed through more than one merchant before reaching the actual supplier of the goods. It is far more usual for the reason to be political; in other words, it is desired to conceal from the suppliers, and from the authorities in their country, the ultimate destination of the goods, or conversely to conceal from the importing country's authorities the true origin of those goods. Since the following sub-Article states that, except for certain matters of which this is not one, a credit can only be transferred on the terms and conditions contained in the original credit, this presumably would include any negation of sub-Article 48 (g), and therefore the chain of transferees could in theory be limitless. Certainly any buyers who are asked to arrange for the issue of a credit which is transferable more than once should, unless they have special reasons for concurring, refuse. The reasons will be apparent from the comments on sub-Article 48 (h), below.

Retransfer back to the original beneficiary does take place from time to time, such as when the first transferees find themselves unable to supply the goods but the first beneficiaries are able to identify alternative suppliers. In these circumstances the credit may be transferred back, enabling the first beneficiaries to again have the credit transferred to new second beneficiaries.

Regarding the second paragraph of this sub-Article, it is evident that where the goods are to emanate from more than one supplier, and the credit is therefore transferred to more than one second beneficiary, separate shipments will be made and separate sets of documents presented, so it is essential that the original credit permits partial shipments/drawings.

ARTICLE 48 (h)

(a) The credit can be transferred only on the terms and conditions specified in the original credit, with the exception of:
- the amount of the credit
- any unit prices stated therein
- the expiry date
- the last date for presentation of documents in accordance with Article 43
- the period for shipment,

any or all of which may be reduced or curtailed.

The percentage for which insurance cover must be effected may be increased in such a way as to provide the amount of cover stipulated in the original credit, or these Articles.

In addition, the name of the first beneficiary can be substituted for that of the applicant, but if the name of the applicant is specifically required by the original credit to appear in any document(s) other than the invoice, such requirement must be fulfilled.

Comment

The restrictions upon the aspects of a credit which may be varied on transfer reflect once again the reluctance of the banks to deal with certain elements of the trading community in respect of transferable credits. It is often of major concern to the first beneficiaries that the identity of the second beneficiaries is not revealed to the applicants, and vice versa, thereby making it possible for them to be eliminated from future transactions. Consequently, first beneficiaries will often bring pressure upon the transferring bank to omit any requirements of the original credit which might bring about this undesirable result. Banks would do well to resist such requests, since they are afforded considerable protection by Article 48, and by setting it aside in part may well find that they have lost that protection altogether.

The amount of the credit and the unit prices must be alterable to allow for the first beneficiaries' profit margin. The dates of shipment and negotiation, and the period allowed for presentation of documents, often need to be brought forward in order to protect the applicants against receiving stale documents. This will be discussed further under sub-Article (j). The insurance percentage must be alterable, because the cover taken out by the second beneficiary will be based on a lower CIF value than that quoted in the original contract. The name of the first beneficiaries will appear as the applicants, but it should always be made clear that the credit is a transferred one, since by remaining silent on this point the credit would give a false impression of their creditworthiness to the second beneficiaries.

It has also been ruled by the ICC that the place of payment may be changed, to accommodate negotiation in the second beneficiaries' country where it is different from that of the first beneficiaries. All other terms of the credit must remain unaltered.

ARTICLE 48(i)

The first beneficiary has the right to substitute his own invoice(s) (and draft(s)) for those of the second beneficiary(ies), for amounts not in excess of the original amount stipulated in the credit and for the original unit prices if stipulated in the credit, and upon such substitution of invoice(s) (and draft(s)) the first beneficiary can draw under the credit for the differences, if any, between his invoice(s) and the second beneficiary's(ies) invoice(s).

When a credit has been transferred and the first beneficiary is to supply his own invoice(s) (and draft(s)) in exchange for the second beneficiary's(ies) invoice(s) (and draft(s)) but fails to do so on first demand, the transferring bank has the right to deliver to the issuing bank the documents received under the transferred credit, including the second beneficiary's(ies) invoice(s) (and draft(s)) without further responsibility to the first beneficiary.

Comment

This sub-Article affords a considerable degree of protection to the transferring bank. Where the first beneficiaries do not produce their substitute invoices the transferring bank is left with a set of documents against which it has paid in accordance with its obligations under the transferred credit, but which are not in conformity with the original credit. By invocation of this article, it can obtain reimbursement from the issuing bank of the amount which it has paid. It will become clear, however, why emphasis was placed in the comments on sub-Article (h) on the inadvisability of allowing any variations in the transferred credit other than those specifically authorised by this article, since in such circumstances it would be impossible to present a conforming set of documents to the issuing bank and therefore impossible to claim reimbursement.

ARTICLE 48(j)

The first beneficiary may request that payment or negotiation be effected to the second beneficiary(ies) at the place to which the credit has been transferred, up to and including the expiry date of the credit, unless the original credit expressly states that it may not be made available for payment or negotiation at a place other than that stipulated in the credit. This is without prejudice to the first beneficiary's right to substitute subsequently his own invoice(s) (and draft(s)) for those of the second beneficiary and to claim any difference due to him.

Comment

The implications of this sub-Article can be far-reaching for the applicants for the original credit. First, although ordering goods in a particular country of their choosing, they may find that the goods supplied emanate from a completely different country with which they might not wish to deal in normal circumstances. Second, because the dates may be transferred with the rest of the credit which then becomes available within those dates in the second country, by the time that documents have been processed by the negotiating bank, sent to the transferring bank, processed by them including the substitution of invoices and then sent to the issuing bank, there is a very strong possibility that the documents will be stale on receipt. In one extreme case, where a transferable credit was issued in Jersey on behalf of English applicants in favour of a first beneficiary in France and then transferred to a second beneficiary in Taiwan, the demurrage charges which were payable in order to obtain delivery of the goods exceeded the value of the goods themselves, which were in any case substandard. When asked to issue a transferable credit it is a good idea for the issuing bank to draw the attention of the applicants to this danger and to suggest suitable restrictions which may be incorporated in the credit to reduce it. The sub-Article itself suggests one obvious way in which this may be achieved — specify in the credit that it cannot be made available for payment or negotiation at any place other than that stated. In this way, although the credit may still be transferred to a different country, the first beneficiaries are forced to so alter the dates for presentation of documents by the second beneficiaries (as permitted by sub-Article 48(h) as to ensure that negotiation under the original credit can take place before expiry. The risk of the applicants receiving stale documents thus becomes no greater than in any non-transferable credit.

G: Assignment of proceeds

ARTICLE 49 — Assignment of proceeds

The fact that a credit is not stated to be transferable shall not affect the beneficiary's right to assign any proceeds to which he may be, or may become, entitled under such credit, in accordance with the provisions of the applicable law. This Article relates only to the assignment of proceeds and not to the assignment of the right to perform under the credit itself.

Comment

Very much the sting in the tail of UCP, this is one of the shortest articles and at the same time one of those which can cause the most trouble, and many believe that UCP should not mention it at all but leave disputes to be settled under the applicable law to which it refers.

The usual circumstances where an assignment is made are where merchants are the beneficiaries of a credit which they have not asked to be transferable because they do not wish their buyers to be aware that they are not the source suppliers of the goods. They do not themselves have the wherewithal to buy the goods from the source suppliers, however, and those suppliers will not release the goods without some guarantee that they will receive payment. A credit is not possible, because the merchants do not have the requisite standing to persuade a bank to issue one on their behalf. The letter of assignment is the answer. It usually takes the form of an "irrevocable" instruction to the bank requesting that it pay the suppliers out of the proceeds which will become due when documents are presented in compliance with the terms of the credit.

Understandably, banks do not like this type of transaction. It is fraught with danger for them, for a number of reasons. First, there is the inescapable fact that they are dealing with people who have little substance, or they would have access to facilities from their own bankers; second, there is the difficulty of authenticating such instructions, since even verification of signatures by the beneficiaries' bankers would not necessarily mean that the signatories had authority to sign this type of document, and would in any case be enforceable only in respect of the bank account to which the mandate relates; third, there is the difficulty in enforcing the "irrevocability" of the assignment when faced with subsequent countermanding instructions, such as where the beneficiaries elect for whatever reason to change the supplier; fourth, there is the possibility that documents will never be presented under the credit, but will be sent on a collection basis through another bank; fifth, though probably not the last, there is the fact that such assignments do not dovetail easily into the bank's normal methods of operation. To make matters worse, it is dubious whether the banks can legitimately charge for acceptance of such assignments. They are therefore expected to provide what is intended to be the equivalent of a letter of credit on behalf of persons who they would not normally consider worthy of such a service, and to shoulder all the risks that that entails, for little or no reward.

It cannot be overstated that these instruments are dangerous, both for the party receiving the benefit of them (the assignees) and for the bank accepting them. The only effective answer is for each of these parties to refuse to have anything to do with them. In the case of the banks, this may mean denying to someone what is a basic legal right, and there is a very slight risk that legal action may follow; but this risk really is very slight, for an organisation which is forced to resort to this type of instrument in order to carry out its business is unlikely to possess the means to take on expensive litigation merely to prove a point, however much they may threaten to do so.

CHAPTER 14

The avoidance of loss: the applicants

From the foregoing chapters, readers should have a thorough basic understanding of the way in which credits work and the rules which govern their use. It is time to put that knowledge to use by applying it, in turn, to the differing interests of the four main parties involved: the applicants, the issuing bank, the advising/confirming bank and the beneficiaries. Where the documentary credit is used properly, those interests, while differing, need not necessarily be conflicting and, given good faith coupled with the controls built into the system, the number of disputes should be minimal.

From the applicants' point of view, the chief benefits to be derived from the use of a documentary credit are that it answers any doubts their suppliers may have about their ability to pay, thus enabling the transaction to take place, whilst providing themselves with the means of ensuring that they receive both the goods (by stipulation of the latest date for shipment) and the correct documents (where possible, by stipulation of the period after the date of the relative transport document within which documents must be presented) at the right time. In order that this may be achieved, great care must be taken when making out the application form for the issue of the credit, since where it is irrevocable it cannot later be changed without the agreement of the beneficiaries.

As has been said many times in this book, it is of vital importance that before reaching this stage, the applicants have done all in their power to establish the *bona fides* of the suppliers, by means of bank enquiries, credit rating agencies and any other sources which may be available.

This is because the credit will convey no assurance that the goods shipped will be in accordance with their description in the documents which relate to them. At the other extreme, government regulations aside, there is little point in using the more expensive letter of credit where a cheaper form of payment system would be acceptable to both parties and, as confidence builds up, suppliers may well be prepared to reconsider their payment terms.

It is advisable to give prior notification to the sellers of all requirements relating to the goods or the documents by including mention of them in the order. As we have seen, this forms part of the contract on which the credit will be based and if that credit, when it is issued, contains requirements of which the suppliers were formerly unaware and which they consider onerous, and which may, had they had foreknowledge, have affected their quotation, they may well be able to avoid the contract altogether. In fact, the more consultation which takes place between buyers and sellers prior to the issue of the credit, the less chance there is of misunderstandings and disputes at a later stage. To reduce these chances still further, it is a good idea to agree that the appropriate Incoterms will govern the contract. This brings the advantage of both parties knowing exactly what their responsibilities are and the costs for which they are liable under the contract. One thing which will not be covered by Incoterms is responsibility for payment of bank charges, which in the absence of any agreement are the applicants' responsibility as principals even though the credit may have been opened at the insistence of the sellers; prior agreement should be reached on this matter also.

The contract terms which have been agreed will dictate the basic documentary requirements and the demands of the credit should reflect this. For instance, an FOB contract will normally produce bills of lading which are marked "freight payable at destination" and no insurance document, insurance being the responsibility of the applicants. The importing country's regulations will dictate others, perhaps certificates of origin, customs invoices and so on. The type of goods and their proposed method of conveyance will impose yet more constraints. Where dangerous or bulky goods are concerned, it may be necessary for the credit to allow for stowage on deck. Where they are of a nature which is liable to produce clauses on the bill of lading which are acceptable to the applicants, the credit should state the clauses which are acceptable. If the journey is to be by more than one form of transport, or if the services of forwarding agents are to be employed, the credit should state that an "on board" bill of lading is not essential, or that house bills of lading are acceptable, as the case may be. Prior consultation between sellers and buyers will provide answers to all these questions and make completion of the application form a far simpler process.

The exact requirements of the sellers regarding the letter of credit should be noted. It is assumed that any credit requested by sellers will in normal circumstances be irrevocable, but if they wish it to be confirmed in their own country this fact must be advised to the issuing bank; it should be remembered that this will entail additional charges. If they wish it confirmed by, or advised through a specific bank, charges may be increased even more, since the issuing bank may have no correspondent relationship with that bank and therefore yet another bank will be brought into the transaction.

If a transferable credit is called for, it is almost certain that the sellers are not the actual producers of the goods. Many buyers are prepared to accept this, relying on the sellers' expertise to locate a suitable supplier and save them the expense of maintaining their own buyers or agents in overseas locations. Otherwise it is almost certain that the goods could be obtained more cheaply by buying direct from the manufacturers. Also, it should be borne in mind that unless transfer of the credit is suitably restricted, there is no control over the origin of the goods and a strong possibility that documents will be stale by the time that they are received.

If the sellers request a red clause credit, the applicants will find themselves liable to reimburse the bank for pre-shipment advances made to the beneficiaries. It is unlikely that such a request would be made in the absence of prior agreement but it is well to be aware of the meaning of the term just in case. Similar considerations apply to a revolving credit, in which the amount available for utilisation will be reinstated at preordained times or on payment by the applicants of previous drawings.

The application form

Most banks' credit application forms are preprinted, giving a range of options from which the applicants must choose and calling for specific pieces of information which the bank requires in order to complete the credit. Applicants should remember that the appearance of a printed

Documentary Credit Application

Documentary Credit Application / Demande d'émission de crédit documentaire

Applicant / Donneur d'ordre	Issuing Bank / Banque émettrice
	Date and place of expiry of the credit / Date et lieu d'expiration du crédit
Date of this application / Date de cette demande	Beneficiary / Bénéficiaire

☐ Issue by (air) mail / Emettre par courrier avion   ☐ With brief advice by teletransmission / Avec bref avis par télétransmission

☐ Issue by teletransmission (which shall be the operative credit instrument) / Emettre par télétransmission (qui sera l'instrument permettant l'utilisation du crédit)

☐ Transferable credit / Crédit transférable

Confirmation of credit to the beneficiary / Confirmation du crédit au bénéficiaire
☐ not requested / non requise   ☐ requested / requise

Partial shipments / Expéditions partielles
☐ allowed / autorisées   ☐ not allowed / non autorisées

Transhipment / Transbordement
☐ allowed / autorisé   ☐ not allowed / non autorisé

☐ Insurance will be covered by us / L'assurance sera prise en charge par nous

Loading on board/dispatch/taking in charge at/from / Mise à bord/expédition/prise en charge à/de

not later than / au plus tard le _____ for transportation to / à destination de _____

Amount / Montant

Credit available with / Crédit réalisable auprès de
☐ by sight payment / par paiement à vue   ☐ by acceptance / par acceptation   ☐ by negotiation / par négociation
☐ deferred payment at / par paiement différé à

against the documents detailed herein : / contre les documents précisés ci-après

☐ and beneficiary's draft at / et la traite du bénéficiaire à

on / sur

Goods (brief description without excessive detail) / Marchandise (brève description sans détail excessif)

☐ FOB   ☐ C&F   ☐ CIF CAF

Other terms / Autres termes

Documents to be presented within [____] days after the date of issuance of the transport document(s) but within the validity of the credit / Documents à présenter dans les [____] jours après la date d'émission du/des document(s) de transport mais dans la période de validité du crédit

Additional instructions / Instructions supplémentaires

We request you to issue your irrevocable documentary credit for our account in accordance with the above instructions (marked with an x where appropriate). The credit will be subject to the Uniform Customs and Practice for Documentary Credits (1983 Revision. Publication No. 400 of the International Chamber of Commerce, Paris, France) insofar as these are applicable.
We authorize you to debit our account

Nous vous demandons d'émettre pour notre compte un crédit documentaire irrevocable conformément aux instructions ci-dessus (cochées d'une croix dans les cases choisies). Le crédit sera soumis aux Régles et Usances Uniformes relatives aux Crédits Documentaires (révision 1983. Publication n° 400 de la Chambre de Commerce Internationale. Paris France) dans la mesure ou celles-ci sont applicables.
Nous vous autorisons à débiter notre compte

Name stamp and authorized signature(s) of the applicant / Cachet et signature(s) autorisée(s) du donneur d'ordre

Left margin: Consult the Issuing Bank for guidance if the completion of this form should raise questions. / Demandez conseil à la banque émettrice si vous vous posez des questions en remplissant la formule

Right margin: © Copyright 1985, International Chamber of Commerce / Chambre de Commerce Internationale option or document on the application form does not mean that they are obliged to exercise that option or call for that document, although some are of course essential.

The ICC has designed a standard application form for optional adoption by banks, which is designed so that the information given thereon by the applicants appears as nearly as possible in the same position as it eventually will upon the credit when issued, thus greatly facilitating the transportation and checking of that data. It removes any possibility of confusion or doubt by specifically referring to the issue of an irrevocable credit, and does not give the applicants the opportunity of nominating a bank through which the credit is to be advised. Both of these factors are considerable improvements on many older, non-standard, forms, which, in addition to giving the option of application for a revocable credit, invited nomination of the advising bank. This latter is undesirable since only in exceptional circumstances, such as at the specific request of the sellers, is it an advantage for the credit to be advised through a particular bank, which may in any case not be in correspondent relationships with the issuing bank.

Date and place of expiry

Near to the top right-hand side of the form the applicants are required to state the expiry date of the credit and its place of expiry. Some applicants base their calculation of the expiry date upon the sellers' stated ExWorks delivery date, adding suitable periods to allow for the arrangements for shipment and the obtaining and presentation of documents to the negotiating bank. However, to avoid the possible need for amendment of the credit at a later date it is probably preferable to base it on the applicants' own needs. The normal time taken in transit by goods between the two countries by the agreed means of transport can be ascertained and thus a latest date for shipment can be established. Similarly the average time for processing of documents by the banks and postal transit periods can be calculated and deducted from the goods transit period to give the maximum period which can be allowed for negotiation. Adding this period to the latest shipment date automatically produces the expiry date of the credit. The place of expiry should always be in the beneficiaries' country if the full advantages of the credit system are to be enjoyed. However, applicants should bear in mind that this may involve them in reimbursing the issuing bank in respect of interest on the amount of the drawing between the time when the beneficiaries are paid and the time the applicants' own account is debited.

Method of transmission

The applicants are next asked to indicate by what means the credit is to be transmitted to the advising bank, the alternatives being teletransmission or airmail, the latter with or without prior teletransmitted advice of brief details. Which alternative is chosen will depend upon circumstances in individual cases, but it should be remembered that there is little point in the expenditure of what may amount to a considerable sum on teletransmission when the time scale involved allows the possibility of a timely arrival if airmail is used. Conversely, such a saving is a false economy if the arrival of the credit leaves the beneficiaries with too little time to arrange dispatch of the goods, thereby giving rise to delay and to additional charges in extending the credit.

E-mail? Assuming the corresponding banks accept it and both parties agree then e-mail is acceptable.

Beneficiary

The beneficiaries' name and address should be shown completely and accurately — completely to enable the advising bank to carry out its prime function of advising the credit; accurately because any discrepancy may cause problems with payment at a later stage.

Transferable credit — confirmation of credit

To be completed as appropriate.

Amount

The amount of the credit, in words and in figures, follows; obviously, these should agree. If the quotation has been an approximate one, either because of uncertainty as to the exact quantities which will be shipped or as to the freight which will be payable, then the stated amount should provide for this, either by use of the word "about" or "approximately" in which case the bank will allow a ten percent either way variation in the amount drawn, or by expressing the amount as a maximum by the use of the words "up to" or similar.

Partial shipment/transhipment

Shipping details appear next on the application, with options for partial shipments and transhipments to be allowed or prohibited. Unless there are compelling reasons for the contrary, partial shipments should always be allowed to provide the utmost flexibility. Transhipment is a variable regarding which a decision can only be based upon the facts of each case. Such decision will take into account the frequency of direct sailings or flights between the two countries, the nature of the goods and the method of transportation which is to be used. Whether or not transhipment is to be allowed should emphatically be based upon a decision rather than the mental toss of a coin, as is so often the case. Often the provisions of UCP will have a direct influence on whether or not transhipment can be forbidden, and reference should be made to the particular article which deals with the type of transport document called for in order to ascertain the extent of such influence.

Insurance

The statement that insurance will be attended to by the applicants would normally only be appropriate where the terms of the contract are such as make those arrangements the buyers' responsibility, eg FOB.

Journey

The voyage details stated should take into account the known plans for carriage of the goods, and specific ports of loading and discharge should only be inserted if they are truly relevant. Where goods are to be taken in charge and delivered at inland container bases there is seldom any point in hampering the carriers with unnecessary stipulations about the routing of the cargo.

Drafts

Next on the application comes the way in which the beneficiaries will be paid. UCP requires each credit to nominate a bank with whom it is to be available for settlement, either by payment, acceptance, deferred payment undertaking, or negotiation. In the last named case availability may be with any bank. Where payment is authorised, the paying bank will expect to be reimbursed with interest for the period between the date of its payment and the date it obtains reimbursement from the issuing bank or its agent, and this interest will be passed to the applicants along with the claim for the principal amount. Where negotiation is authorised, this interest element becomes the liability of the beneficiaries.

The question of drafts needs to be considered carefully. In the vast majority of cases, a sight draft under a credit, whomsoever it is drawn on, is a totally functionless piece of paper and can quite easily be dispensed with. Where the terms of payment are at usance, the draft becomes rather more significant, but only if it is to be used for financing purposes. Where one of the countries involved applies heavy stamp duties on bills of exchange they are quite regularly abandoned in favour of deferred payment credits. If a usance draft is to be used, the credit should be made available for acceptance in the country of the beneficiaries, since this will provide them with a first class acceptance which they can have discounted in their local market if required. The question of interest need not arise with a usance credit, since the maturity date of the bill will be known in advance and the bank can be paid by the applicants on the same date as their account overseas is debited.

Goods

Next, the description of the goods is invited. As has already been said, both in the text and in UCP, this should be in just sufficient detail to ensure that the right goods have been shipped. The sellers should be required to certify that the goods supplied are in accordance with the specification given in the appropriate order or proforma invoice, which should be identified with a reference number. If unit prices are given, they should agree arithmetically with the credit amount, and if they or the quantity of goods are approximate it should be ensured that the credit amount is also stated as being approximate. The stated contract terms should correspond with the documents which are called for, or if they do not, the reason for such divergence should be made apparent.

Documents

Next, the documentary requirements must be considered. Again, many banks have preprinted lists of the documents which they consider will be necessary. As in other parts of the form, the inclusion by the bank of a particular document does not mean that it must be called for. A good example of a document which is frequently demanded without any justification is the packing list and applicants should ask themselves whether it is really necessary before placing an "X" in the box on the application. For instance, where a single unit, or a consignment of goods all of the same description and specification, is the subject of the credit, a packing list is likely to add nothing to the value of the documents and should not be called for. Another example, which has been mentioned more than once already in this book, is the frequent requirement for "complete set of not less than three original clean on board ocean bills of lading". As we have seen, modern methods of goods handling often makes this a handicap rather than an asset and it should only be called for if it is absolutely necessary. Even if it is necessary, only one original is required to be given in exchange for the goods, any other purposes served by the bill being just as easily covered by photocopies. It should be remembered that the insurance terms "all risks", "with average" and "free of particular average" have now gone out of use, yet many banks still incorporate printed references to them in their application forms. The applicable clauses are respectively A, B, and C, and these should be substituted.

Where any documents are required other than transport and insurance documents, the application should state by whom they are to be issued and what information they should convey, whether they should be legalised and so on; otherwise the banks will accept them as tendered. Applicants should take care not to call for any documents which will either be completely unobtainable by the beneficiaries or unobtainable within the time constraints imposed by the credit. Also, they should take care that the documentary requirements are not inconsistent with the contract terms as stated following the credit amount or, if they are, that a clear explanation of the apparent discrepancy is given.

Presentation

By restricting the number of days after dispatch of the goods which are available to the beneficiaries for presentation of documents, applicants are able to influence the likely time of arrival of the documents in their hands. This can be useful where documents of title are required in order to obtain release of goods, though usually only where the voyage is of a significant length. Where the time of arrival of documents is not significant in this way there is usually little point in placing any restriction on presentation — UCP will in any case regard 21 days as the maximum period allowable. Where the period allowed for presentation is restricted by the applicants, they should take care to see that it does not contradict what the credit says about the expiry date of the credit. For example, if the period allowed for presentation is 15 days and the latest shipment date is on the last day of the month, then the expiry date should be on the 15th of the succeeding month. Finally, the period allowed for presentation should be realistic, allowing the beneficiaries adequate time to obtain, prepare and present their documents, otherwise the credit may prove to be unworkable.

Forward cover

If the credit is in a foreign currency, either that of the sellers' country or of a third country, a liability will arise in the future to reimburse the issuing bank for drawings made in that currency. Since in free currency markets there is no way in which the applicants' liability in their own currency can be forecast, unless they have accounts denominated in the required currency, they should carefully consider the desirability of buying the currency in the forward exchange market, thus fixing the amount in local currency which they will be required to pay for the goods. Since the exact date on which payment will be demanded will be uncertain, such cover will necessarily be of the option variety, allowing the deal to be struck at the agreed rate at any time within stated limits.

Summary

Applicants should be aware that the success or failure of the credit will depend largely upon the expertise and consideration which they give to the completion of the application, and that failing the co-operation of the beneficiaries they will have to live with any incorrect or incomplete documentation which may result from errors in its completion.

Having gone to so much trouble to ensure the smooth operation of the credit, it may seem rather harsh that from the time of its issue the applicants take a largely passive role in future as regards the credit. As was stressed at the beginning of the section of this book dealing with credits, the instrument is an undertaking given by the bank to the beneficiaries and this undertaking forms the core of the transaction. When documents are received, the bank will, or should, make its own decision as to whether they are acceptable in terms of its undertaking and, if they are, the applicants' account will be debited without further reference. This does not, of course, mean that if real discrepancies exist in those documents which the issuing bank has failed to notice the applicants will have no remedy against the bank, but the latter is likely to give scant consideration to objections based on what it considers to be trivia. The spirit of the documentary credit is a benign yet demanding one — the instrument exists to oil the wheels of commerce, not to lock them solid.

Discrepant documents

Undoubtedly, despite all precautions, documents will sometimes be presented which are not in accordance with the credit terms. If discrepancies have been noticed by the negotiating bank they will often telex for authority to pay despite those problems. The applicants should consider their position carefully when asked by the issuing bank for such authority. The rules relating to credits being what they are, often the discrepancies will be trivial and may be dismissed out of hand but if they cast any doubt upon the condition of the goods or their ease of clearance through import formalities when they arrive, it is probably preferable to ask that the documents be sent forward on a collection basis, perhaps with authority to inspect the goods before a decision is reached on their acceptability. Careful consideration should be given before agreeing to pay under the protection of a bank indemnity. The validity of such indemnities is often strictly limited, the problem being that they tend to relate specifically to the discrepancy mentioned therein, without regard to its wider implications. For instance, an indemnity may promise that the amount of the drawing will be refunded should any loss be incurred by reason of late presentation of documents, but the intention behind the issue of the indemnity may be merely to cover demurrage charges incurred by the goods: payment may be disputed if the cause of loss is forfeit of an onward sales contract by reason of the absence of documents of title to the goods. When giving notice of acceptance of discrepancies to the issuing bank, applicants should make it clear to that bank that they are doing so in reliance upon the indemnity held by the bank, if such is the case.

Wherever possible, however, every effort should be made to assist the beneficiaries in obtaining payment for the goods which they have supplied, even if this means reaching a separate agreement outside the letter of credit to compensate for any loss incurred by the buyers. "Do as you would be done by" is a good maxim for anyone involved in international trade, despite what may be said to the contrary in certain circles. A co-operative attitude now regarding someone else's difficulties will probably pay dividends in the future. Whatever happens, the credit must never, ever, be used as a flimsy excuse for the buyers' avoidance of their responsibilities under the contract in the absence of genuine reasons for refusal of payment.

Sadly, once in a while and despite all precautions, the applicants will discover that they have been dealing with dishonest sellers. In such circumstances it will be very difficult to attach any responsibility to the banks involved for any loss incurred as a result, those banks being well protected by UCP against such charges. Where documents are obvious forgeries but are nonetheless accepted by banks, a case may exist. However, by far the commonest cause of loss is where genuine documents are presented which cover goods which, when received, turn out to be either substandard or simply "case fillers", such as the substitution of common salt for pharmaceutical chemicals or drugs, or of bricks for machinery spares. Against such frauds there is no protection other than the exhortation, oft repeated in this book, to "know your trading partner".

CHAPTER 15

The avoidance of loss: the issuing bank

The issuing bank is one of the two principal parties to the documentary letter of credit and its role is commensurately important in ensuring that, not only the individual credit, but also the whole credits system continues to serve the trading community in the way in which it was designed to do. That system has been subject in recent times to a variety of abuses, most of which stem from attempts by issuing banks to limit their liability under their letters of credit without reducing their income from that source. While this attitude may be supportable from the accounting aspect, it is certainly indefensible from a banking viewpoint and in many cases a choice must be made as to whether an organisation exists in order to operate as a bank or as a mere vehicle for the generation of short-term profits. These may seem harsh words but the choice is a simple one.

However, this chapter is intended to examine the documentary credit from the point of view of the issuing bank and to recommend courses of action to ensure that it protects its interest as far as possible when dealing in documentary credits. At the point of issue of the credit, the chief concern of the issuing bank is that its credit should present an image of competency and professionalism to all who subsequently read it. This involves many considerations; not least among these is the basic design of the letter of credit itself. The International Chamber of Commerce has designed a standard letter of credit form which, for simplicity, coherency and practicality, would be difficult to surpass; any banks which have not yet adopted it should do so without delay. Such adoption on a universal scale would greatly simplify the checking of documents against credits and any chauvinistic bias in favour of individual bank forms would quickly evaporate following even a superficial consideration of the advantages to be gained from adoption of a standard format.

Given that the letter of credit itself is presented in an easy-to-read format, the next important consideration is its content. This will depend upon a critical evaluation of the application form received. The overriding concern of the issuing bank should be to ensure that, when the credit in its final form is sent to the advising bank, it will not be a source of irritation or, worse, amusement, to either that bank or the beneficiaries. It should reflect the expertise of the bank which has issued it in a way which will engender respect for the name of the bank.

Applications for the opening of letters of credit would normally be received only from customers who have prearranged facilities with the bank for the issue of such instruments. Other applications of an *ad hoc* nature will occasionally be received, perhaps with full cash cover tendered as security for the credit. Experience shows that generally speaking the more reliance a bank has to place on such security the more chance there is of something going seriously wrong with the transaction and issuing banks are strongly recommended to have nothing to do with it.

Given that the application is from an acceptable source, that it is correctly signed in accordance with the mandate held and that the proposed credit can be accommodated within the customers' agreed facilities, the bank should then carefully check the customers' requirements, in the light of the aim stated above of producing a credit which is concise, straightforward and technically excellent. The application will normally be for an irrevocable credit and any departure from this is worth querying with the customers in case a mistake has been made, unless of course they are in the habit of initiating revocable credits. Past experience of the customers' normal requirements helps considerably in the checking of the form and if any specialised form of credit is requested, such as red clause, revolving, or transferable, it may be advisable to check that they are fully aware of the implications of what they are asking for. This applies particularly to transferable credits: the customers should be aware that they are not dealing with the manufacturers of the goods and that in consequence they may find that they could obtain those goods more cheaply elsewhere. They should also be aware that unless safeguards are built into the credit the goods could emanate from any country in the world, subject to the voyage details included in the credit, and that documents could well be stale when received, without any remedy against the sellers being available.

The beneficiaries' name and address should appear in full, since this will be needed by the advising bank in order to advise the credit. If the applicants have nominated an advising bank, such nomination must be complied with, although if the nominated bank is not a correspondent of the issuing bank the credit will have to be forwarded to them through a bank which is. Because such involvement of an extra bank in the process is inefficient both in terms of time and cost, applicants should not be encouraged to make such nominations and it is questionable whether the opportunity to do so should be incorporated in the application form.

Amount

The amount in words should agree with the amount in figures, if both are given, and the currency in which the amount is expressed should be clearly identifiable. The contract terms should be appended to the amount to make it quite clear exactly what that amount represents.

Expiry, latest shipment and presentation

The dates should be examined for their correlation with each other and for whether they appear realistic in view of the arrangements which the beneficiaries may have to make for shipment and documentation. In particular, the difference between the latest date for shipment and the expiry date should exactly equal any period after shipment which is stipulated in the credit for negotiation of documents. If the expiry date is not far distant, it is probably advisable that full details of the credit are sent by teletransmission, and if the applicants have not asked for this to be done their authority should be sought, since they are the ones who will have to pay for it.

Shipment

The shipment details should make sense in the light of the information available elsewhere in the credit. If places of dispatch and delivery are airports, a call for presentation of a bill of lading in the documentary requirements is obviously nonsense. If they are inland cities then probably a combined transport document will be presented and the documentary requirements should allow for presentation of this, or of a forwarding agent's house bill of lading. The journey which the goods are to undertake should also be considered from the point of view of whether it is feasible without transhipment, if this is prohibited. If the quantity of goods is a large one similar questions should be asked about partial shipments.

Payment

The manner of payment requested by the applicants should be considered and if they wish the credit to be available to the beneficiaries in their own country by means of either payment or acceptance, then drafts should be on a bank in that country. In the case of the former the applicants should clearly understand that they will be liable for payment of interest for the time which elapses between payment of the beneficiaries and reimbursement of the issuing bank by themselves. Where drafts are to be drawn on the issuing bank, the credit can only be available to the beneficiaries by negotiation. In the author's view credits should not be issued which state that they are available only at the issuing bank's own counters, since such instruments are scarcely worthy of being called credits, damage the issuing bank's reputation and bring the whole documentary credits system into disrepute.

Documents

The documentary requirements should be examined carefully for consistency with the contract terms (ie FOB, CIF, etc) and for compliance with current import regulations relating to the type of goods or to the exporting country. Applicants should be discouraged from asking for an excessive number of copies of documents such as invoices, packing lists and so on, since they are seldom really required and, even if they are, photocopies are perfectly acceptable for many purposes. Some documents may be unnecessary altogether, such as packing lists where only one specification of goods is ordered or where the goods form a single unit.

If documents other than those normally supplied by the sellers, and transport and insurance documents, are called for, the credit should make it clear who is to issue them and what they should contain. The issuing bank should also be alert for requirements for documents which will be impossible for the beneficiaries to supply — the so-called "built-in discrepancy". The credit should not prohibit short-form bills of lading, unless these are proscribed by regulations in the importing country, nor should it refer to such terms as "all risks", "with average" or "free of particular average" with reference to the insurance requirements; these expressions have long been superseded by the Institute of London Underwriters' A, B and C clauses respectively.

Goods

The description of the goods should be sufficient to enable identification but should not contain excessive detail. Instead, the applicants should be encouraged to call for the beneficiaries' certificate that all conditions of the contract (identified by its reference number) have been complied with. Under no circumstances should attachments such as proforma invoices, detailed specifications, etc be accepted for attachment to, or to form part of, the credit. Multi-paged credits are costly to process, greatly increase the chances of mistakes being made, do nothing to enhance the issuing bank's reputation and, above all, are almost always unnecessary.

A credit should not include vague terms in descriptions of issuers of documents such as "qualified", "first class", etc but should name a previously-identified party in the beneficiaries' country who has consented to issue them. It should also not contain unsubstantiable requirements such as "shipment by conference line vessel", but instead should call for a certificate to this effect to be presented with the other documents. Certificates issued by carriers or uncustomary declarations on transport documents should be called for sparingly, if at all. Carriers understandably do not like issuing them and will refuse if at all possible; in fact such certificates are seldom truly necessary. An example of such a document is the so-called blacklist certificate which, contrary to popular belief, is an official requirement only in very few countries.

If any unit prices are stated in the credit, multiplication by the quantity of goods, if known, should give the credit amount, or there should be a good explanation for any discrepancy. The application should state for whose account are bank charges, and any request for negotiable documents to be sent direct to any party other than the issuing bank should be considered very carefully, since this will mean that the bank has lost the security provided by its lien over the goods. Where goods are to be sent by post or air, the bank may wish to preserve its security by having the goods consigned to it, but such a course usually involves the bank in much unnecessary work on arrival of the goods, and is also undesirable because the bank becomes involved with those goods, thus negating one of the underlying principles of documentary credits.

Amendments

Any subsequent amendments should receive the same careful consideration, bearing in mind their effect upon the already-existing terms of the credit. It should not be assumed that, because the issuing bank's file copy of the credit has been amended, that the amendment is in force and operative. If the credit is irrevocable, the beneficiaries are under no obligation to accept amendments, although UCP obliges them to give notice of rejection.

Procedure after issue

When the issuing bank has satisfied itself on the above points, and on any others that may concern it (the list is by no means exhaustive), the credit should be prepared, checked, signed and forwarded to the selected advising bank. It should contain a clear indication to the beneficiaries regarding where, when and from whom they will receive payment, and a clear indication to the negotiating bank as to how it is to obtain reimbursement. If the advising bank is required to add its confirmation to the credit, this instruction should be given, along with any other requirements such as telegraphic advice of drawings.

Where the credit is transmitted, that must contain all the information normally appearing on a credit, including the undertakings regarding payment and the statement that the credit is subject to UCP (not necessary if the message is transmitted through the SWIFT system), which normally appear in the small print. Great care should be taken if less than full details are transmitted to state clearly that full details are to follow. Otherwise the transmission as sent will stand as the operative instrument and cannot be added to or altered without the consent of the beneficiaries. Where the credit is transmitted by airmail, it should be clearly typed in an easy-to-read format. In this connection, where a bank habitually uses preprinted credit forms it is a good idea to keep a small stock of forms which are blank, at least as regards the documentary requirements. Nothing is more confusing than a credit which consists mainly of deletions of preprinted requirements, with the actual terms inserted wherever there happens to be a little space on the form and interlinked by various reference marks such as asterisks. A standby credit is a good example of a credit which usually is better typed on a blank form.

It is not unknown for credits to be issued as "confirmed, irrevocable letters of credit". When this happens, it is a clear indication that the issuing bank has no understanding of the principles of confirmation and the probability is that this level of expertise has been applied to other aspects of the credit as well. The basis of confirmation is the addition by another bank of a promise which ranks alongside that of the issuing bank. Clearly, the addition of a second promise by the issuing bank conveys no further protection to the beneficiaries than they already had.

The credit having been sent, a copy should be sent to the applicants and another placed in the issuing bank's own files; its value should be recorded against the applicants' facility. Drawings received and settled by the applicants should be recredited to that facility, as should credits which have expired unutilised, but only when a suitable period has elapsed after expiry to allow for processing and transit of drawings negotiated up to its expiry date.

Discrepant drawings

On receipt of drawings, it is the issuing bank's duty, within a reasonable time but not more than seven banking days, to check the documents against the credit and to decide on the basis of those documents whether or not they comply with the terms of the credit. If it considers that they do not it must immediately advise the negotiating bank by teletransmission of its refusal, with reasons, and state that it is either returning the documents (seldom a viable option) or holding them at the negotiating bank's disposal. It is perhaps at this stage that the reputation of the issuing bank is most at stake, since it has made a solemn promise to pay the beneficiaries provided that they comply with all the conditions of the credit. If it now seeks to avoid the honouring of that promise on the pretext of trivial "discrepancies", it will quickly find that its credits are despised and rejected in the commercial world.

Frequently, the course of action taken is to refer the discrepancies to the applicants for authority to pay, but this does not absolve the issuing bank of its duty to inform the negotiating bank. Care should be taken not to give the applicants the opportunity of evading their contractual responsibilities by taking advantage of trivial discrepancies noticed by the issuing bank. In some cases it is probably better to ignore such discrepancies. This, however, presupposes that the issuing bank is using staff with sufficient experience and expertise to make decisions upon what constitutes a "real" discrepancy and what may safely be ignored. Unfortunately, this is not always the case. Where applicants do try to avoid payment without just cause, it should be remembered that it will not be their reputation which will suffer most, but the issuing bank's. Fortunately, an explanation of the bank's position will usually suffice to persuade most applicants to take up the documents: where it fails, a simple threat of withdrawal of facilities will often succeed.

Sometimes a negotiating bank's covering letter will state that it has negotiated under reserve or under the beneficiaries' or their bankers' indemnity for discrepancies which it has noted. This does not affect the position of the issuing bank in any way and it must still carry out the procedures outlined above. If the negotiating bank has in turn offered its own indemnity to the issuing bank, this fact may be advised to the applicants and may affect their decision as to whether or not to take up the documents. However, great care should be exercised in ascertaining that the wording of the indemnity is acceptable, that it is valid for a suitable period and that payment of claims under the indemnity are not likely to be prejudiced by, for example, adverse exchange control regulations.

On some occasions, goods will arrive before the relative documents. This may mean that the documents were presented late, which will enable refusal under the credit, but this cannot be relied upon as the delay may have occurred after negotiation, either in the negotiating bank or in transit. In these circumstances, the applicants, if they are aware of the goods' arrival, may ask the issuing bank to issue an indemnity to the carriers to enable them to take delivery of the goods without production of the relative bill of lading. Again, goods which are consigned to the bank may arrive before the relative drawing and, rather than take them into store in its own name, the bank may elect to issue a delivery order in favour of the applicants. In either of these circumstances it should be made absolutely clear to the applicants that, having taken delivery of the goods, they will be obliged to pay for the documents when they eventually arrive, regardless of any defect in those documents or in the goods. Such matters must be taken up direct with the beneficiaries under the sales contract.

Drawings which the issuing bank decides are in accordance with the credit terms may be paid or reimbursed immediately and the applicants' account debited without further reference other than forwarding the documents to them without delay. Suitable arrangements must be made to match up any duplicate documents with the originals when received and where documents which have been refused are held at the disposal of the negotiating bank every effort must be made to obtain their instructions.

Acceptances under usance credits must be entered into a diary for payment at maturity, and kept in a safe place until that time, when proceeds must be disposed of in accordance with the instructions held. Very occasionally it happens that an issuing bank is restrained by an order of the courts from paying such an acceptance, often because the applicants have found the goods to be defective. Whilst this affects the issuing bank's power to debit the applicants' account, it in no way releases it from its obligations under the credit and it must pay in the normal way from its own resources. This inequitable situation should be pointed out to the court if possible and the bank should always be represented at any such court hearing of which it is aware. It should protest most strongly if the court takes a decision affecting it when it has not been notified of the hearing.

Such, then, are the responsibilities of the issuing bank. They are without doubt the heaviest of any involved in the credit process:

(a) heavier than those of the advising bank, which has merely to verify the apparent authenticity of the credit

(b) heavier than those of the confirming bank, because that bank does not have to draw up the credit

(c) heavier than those of the negotiating bank, because that bank has freedom of choice as to whether it negotiates or not

(d) heavier than those of the applicants, because its promise is not conditional upon their agreement, or even their survival, in order for it to crystallise, and

(e) heavier than the sum of all these because it is upon the willingness of the issuing bank to make the unequivocable promise so essential to the documentary credit process, and its willingness to stand by it, that the whole future of that process depends.

CHAPTER 16

Loss avoidance: advising/ confirming/negotiating banks

It is convenient to deal with the responsibilities of these three banks in one chapter since they are often the same bank and the actions which they take at one stage may have a profound effect upon those necessary at a later time.

The advising bank

The advising bank is perhaps the party with the least responsibilities under a letter of credit. Only where it is asked to confirm the credit does its responsibility increase dramatically, both in its commitment to others and in its duty to itself to avoid loss, either of money or reputation.

The sole requirement of UCP which is specifically aimed at the advising bank, is to check upon the apparent genuineness of the credit which the bank advises. It follows that under no circumstances should a bank advise a credit which it has received from another bank with which it does not have a correspondent relationship. In such circumstances it should return the credit, or identify the issuing bank's correspondents in that country and pass it to them without responsibility, advising the issuing bank of its action.

Checking is normally taken to mean verification of signatures and in many cases this is sufficient. Signatures imply transmission of the credit by airmail and such credits are usually fairly modest in value, the tendency being for the higher value credits to be transmitted by teletransmission. Where this happens, the banks concerned will have testing arrangements between them and so can be reasonably secure in assuming that a message has emanated from the source from which it purports to have done. With airmailed credits, however, the only immediate check is upon the signatures. As is well-known, there are many who possess the talent of the accurate and virtually undetectable forging of signatures and there is no shortage of ways of obtaining specimens of the authorised signatures within banks. Suspicion should therefore be aroused when a credit for a substantial amount is received by airmail, particularly where that credit is in favour of beneficiaries who are unknown to the bank and about whom no information can be obtained. When this happens, it is advisable to contact the issuing bank, asking it to affirm, by tested teletransmission message, that the credit is a genuine one.

Although in no way the advising bank's duty, it is a good idea, on receipt of a credit, to give its contents a quick glance to ensure that nothing is obviously wrong with it. This is suggested for two reasons. First, the bank may not wish to advise the credit in the form in which it has been received, either because it is technically incorrect or because it is likely to cause problems at a later date when documents are presented for negotiation, perhaps because it contains excessive detail. Second, because, like all the banks involved, the advising bank is the agent of the applicants and this is the last stage at which the credit will be alterable without the consent of the beneficiaries. The advising bank is perfectly entitled to refuse to advise until it is satisfied with the terms of the credit and in many ways it is desirable that it should do so, since such action frequently ensures that the issuing bank alters its procedures to avoid a repetition of the cause for rejection in the future. The same considerations apply to amendments.

Teletransmitted credits

A credit which is received by teletransmission may be assumed to be the operative credit instrument unless it specifically states that it is subject to a mail confirmation to follow. The question sometimes arises as to what action should be taken when a teletransmission does not so state but a mail confirmation is nonetheless later received. This matter is covered by Article 11(a)(i) of UCP which makes it clear that the mail confirmation can be disregarded, and of course this must be so or the irrevocability of teletransmitted credits would be impossible to maintain. Possibly the most practical approach is to check the confirmation against the original teletransmission and if any discrepancies exist to teletransmit immediately the issuing bank advising them of the position, whilst contacting the beneficiaries to ascertain whether they are prepared to accept an amendment to the credit. This, of course, they are not obliged to do; if they refuse there is no more action which the advising bank can effectively take.

The confirming bank

The position is rather different where the advising bank is asked to add its confirmation to a credit. It is now required to take on a responsibility similar in extent to that of the issuing bank, in that, if it consents to confirm, it makes a promise to the beneficiaries that they will receive payment provided that they comply with all the terms of the credit. This promise is just that; a prime liability and not a guarantee that the confirming bank will pay if the issuing bank does not, as is often thought. It is tantamount, therefore, to the issue of the confirming bank's own credit, with the same implications for its reputation, but since the credit was drawn up by another bank it is in the confirming bank's interest to check the terms of the credit very carefully, applying the same criteria as were recommended for the issuing bank in Chapter 15. In particular, the method of obtaining reimbursement should be absolutely clear, since the confirming bank will be the bank which is called upon to pay.

Confirmation may be requested by the issuing bank or by the beneficiaries. If it emanates from the latter and no authority is held from the issuing bank, that bank's authority should be sought before complying with the request. So-called "silent confirmation" is to be discouraged, since the issuing bank is unaware that the advising bank has accepted any additional responsibility and will therefore not feel obliged to take any action to protect its interest. Even more dangerous is the practice adopted by some banks of giving silent confirmation at the request of the beneficiaries to credits which have not even been advised by them. Such a bank has given a commitment to the beneficiaries under which, whilst it will be obliged to pay the beneficiaries against conforming documents, in cases of dispute it will have no enforceable claim against the issuing bank. The beneficiaries may even have accepted amendments to the credit of which the confirming bank is unaware and then failed to take those amendments into consideration in the documents which they have presented.

Confirmation having been added, the obligations of the bank which has done so are just as severe as are those of the issuing bank and confirmation should by no means be undertaken lightly or viewed as an easy source of revenue. Indeed, the reputation of the confirming bank is more at risk than that of the issuing bank, since that risk occurs in its home market and repercussions will be more immediately and keenly felt. The confirming bank does, however, acquire additional rights under the credit, and it can decline to extend its confirmation to any subsequent amendments. This may be particularly useful where the credit is to be increased or extended beyond the desired limits of the bank's exposure to either the issuing bank or the importing country.

The negotiating bank

The term "negotiating bank" is used here in its wider sense of any bank in the beneficiaries' country which makes payment to, or accepts or negotiates drafts drawn by the beneficiaries under a credit. The stricter meaning of the word "negotiating" was discussed in Chapter 11.

Unless it has confirmed the credit, no bank is under any obligation to negotiate documents, although in practice banks seldom refuse where documents are in order, since to do so could cast doubt upon their competence. The position of the negotiating bank is, however, a difficult one. On the one hand it has a mandate to pay provided that certain well-defined conditions are met; if this is not so that mandate ceases to exist. It must therefore be certain that the issuing bank will have no cause to refuse the documents because of alleged discrepancies, a factor which militates in favour of extreme caution. On the other hand, the credit is intended to facilitate and not to hinder international trade; rejection of otherwise complying documents for trivial matters will damage the bank's reputation in its home environment by gaining it a reputation for pettiness and obstruction. If neither of these is attractive to it, the negotiating bank is forced to tread a dangerous path between the twin precipices and, to continue the mountaineering analogy, unless its staff are adequately trained, experienced, and confident in their proficiency, it is moreover treading that path in thick mist.

"What constitutes a discrepancy?" This question has been asked on countless occasions but has never been satisfactorily answered. One bank's view will differ radically from that of the bank next door, ranging from the organisation which will negotiate anything with barely a glance at the documents, to the one which will reject a drawing because the word "Limited" has been abbreviated to "Ltd". A list of the more commonly encountered discrepancies is given shortly, but this should be regarded as a sample only and not taken as a definite checklist.

Frequently encountered discrepancies in documents

Letter of credit:

expired
exceeded
short drawn
late presentation
partial shipment

Invoice:

amount differs from drawing
contract terms not as stated in credit
description of goods differs
does not certify...
insufficient copies
shipping marks differ from bill of lading
unit prices not as stated in credit
additional charges claimed

Bill of lading:

late shipment
not issued by carrier specified
not signed by or on behalf of carrier
claused...
not marked "freight paid"
unauthenticated alteration
evidences transhipment
not endorsed
subject to charter party
insufficient originals/non-negotiable copies
goods not consigned as specified

evidences shipment on deck
does not show goods shipped from…
does not show goods shipped to…
not marked "shipped"

Insurance certificate/policy:

open cover expired (certificates only)
shipment not covered (certificates only)
hull limit exceeded (certificates only)
location limit exceeded (certificates only)
not countersigned by assured (certificates only)
goods underinsured
…risks not covered
not endorsed
shipping marks differ from bill of lading
not in currency of credit
dated later than bill of lading (policy only)

Draft:

words and figures differ
not endorsed
tenor not as per credit
not signed

It is a common misconception that documents are checked against the credit and negotiated if they are in order. In fact they are checked in at least three other respects, although an experienced checker may well perform some or even all of these operations simultaneously.

Besides complying with the credit terms, documents must comply with the requirements of UCP and, as has been seen, many of these requirements will have no mention in the credit itself. An example of this would be where a set of documents, perfectly correct in terms of the credit, cover the second instalmental shipment under a credit, where the first shipment was made late and the credit therefore became invalid in terms of Article 41. A thorough knowledge of, and the ability to apply, the UCP is therefore essential in any document checker.

The documents must agree with each other, an aspect covered in UCP but nonetheless worthy of a separate mention here. As an example of this, where the shipping marks on an insurance document failed to correspond with those on the bill of lading, the document would be rejected.

252

Finally, they must stand alone as documents capable of fulfilling the purpose for which they were designed. Many documents carry their own requirements which must be adhered to before they may be considered as valid, such as the necessity for the countersignature of the insured party to appear on an insurance certificate.

The negotiating bank has a reasonable time in which to decide whether to take up or reject the documents. What constitutes a reasonable time will vary considerably between different countries and between different banks in the same country, but in any case must not exceed seven banking days from presentation.

Fraud and forgery

Although disclaimant clauses are incorporated into UCP to protect all banks against liability for the consequences of fraud and forgery of documents presented, this protection is by no means absolute. Where circumstances exist which should have served to put a bank on its guard it may be held to have been negligent in its duties as agent of the applicants, if it nonetheless pays fraudulent beneficiaries; negotiating banks should be ever alert for signs of possible fraud. In a work of this size it is impossible to enumerate all the possibilities which are open to fraudsters in their never-ending quest to obtain money to which they are not entitled and since they are always at least one step ahead of the banks, merely by virtue of the fact that they know that they are dishonest whereas the bank does not, it would probably be counterproductive to attempt to do so. There are, however, a number of factors which, although not in the least suspicious in themselves, gain significance where they exist in combination with each other.

The foremost of these is the amount of the drawing. When fraudsters go to considerable trouble and risk to obtain money by false pretences, they tend to look for substantial returns from their wrong-doing. What constitutes a large amount is for individual banks to decide and any attempt to define it here would merely serve to indicate to the criminal element what might be a "safe" amount to aim for. As was stressed at the beginning of this section, the size of the drawing is not important in itself but only assumes such importance when it coincides with one or more of the other factors to be mentioned below.

Almost as important as the amount of the drawing is the status of the beneficiaries. Where this party is unknown in the commercial world but is nonetheless apparently dealing in high value contracts, the question arises why they are not better known. Often the answer is that they are a company which has been formed with the specific object of procuring a large supply contract from an unsuspecting overseas buyer and then using the basic principle of the documentary credit, that banks deal in documents and not in goods, either by shipping worthless goods and presenting the resulting genuine documents, or by presenting documents which are wholly or partially forged.

Another factor which is often seen in cases of fraud is the involvement of numerous countries in the transaction. There may be good reasons for a credit issued in Bangladesh to be advised through London to beneficiaries in Greece covering goods being shipped from the USA, but another possibility is that fraudsters are trying to put as many national boundaries as possible between themselves and any pursuing police investigators.

Mention of Bangladesh leads to another, particularly deplorable, facet of international trade fraud, in that very often it is the poorer nations of the world who are the target of such deception, in reliance on their lack of resources to enable effective action to be taken to recover their loss. This lack of resources also makes such countries vulnerable to offers of cheaply priced goods, since criminals are easily able to undercut the quotation of genuine suppliers, as they have no intention of supplying the goods anyway.

Other signs of possible danger, if they co-exist with the above, are:

(a) the use by the beneficiaries of one of the recognised tax havens, which may be from financial motives but may also be from a desire to confuse the pursuit following a fraud

(b) use of a chartered vessel, since at the lower end of the market it is frequently possible to find owners or masters willing to collaborate in the production of fraudulent documentation

(c) the beneficiaries being traders rather than producers of goods, which, although an honourable and essential profession, can attract the less-than-honest by virtue of the ease with which a business may be set up without significant outlay of capital.

Where the suspicions of a negotiating bank have been aroused in circumstances such as those outlined above, or for any other reason, provided that it has not confirmed the credit it may exercise its option to refuse negotiation and it is not obliged to give any reason for such refusal. Where it has confirmed, its position is a little more difficult since it is legally liable under the credit, but if it has certain knowledge that a fraud is being attempted it would be in little danger from a similar refusal. Usually, of course, there is not absolute conviction but a nagging suspicion and the only course open to the bank is to make further enquiries. No-one is completely immune to fraud and, provided that a negotiating bank can show that it has done all in its power to verify the transaction, it should be well protected by UCP.

Fortunately, perfect forgeries of documents are exceedingly rare and the eye of an experienced checker will quickly identify anomalies in the document and departures from the usual format. In most cases the issuers of the documents can be contacted for verification of their authenticity, but some, particularly bills of lading, may prove more difficult. In such cases, publications such as *Lloyd's Shipping Index* can prove invaluable in checking on the existence, capacity and whereabouts of the vessel named in the bill, and may also provide information regarding the ship's owners or agents who can be contacted for further information. Failing this, resort may be made to the International Maritime Bureau, based in Barking, Essex, England, which is the arm of the International Chamber of Commerce specialising in the combating of marine fraud. The IMB may well be able to verify the existence of the cargo described in the bill of lading, and its loading on board the stated vessel.

Payment and reimbursement

Negotiation having taken place, the negotiating bank must then follow carefully the instructions contained in the credit in order to obtain reimbursement of the amount paid by it. If it is a paying bank it will have paid without recourse to the beneficiaries and will either debit the account of the issuing bank in its own books, thus securing immediate reimbursement or, if the credit is not expressed in its home currency, will claim such reimbursement, plus interest, from the issuing bank or from a third bank nominated in the credit. Such a reimbursement claim should not require to be accompanied by a certificate of compliance and should be honoured without delay. If it is not, the issuing bank is responsible for interest payable as a result of the failure of its paying agent to reimburse in good time.

Acceptance

If the bank has accepted the beneficiaries' draft under a usance credit, the accepted draft will, according to the instructions received, either be returned to the beneficiaries or held in a safe place until it becomes due for payment, either on a safe custody basis on behalf of the beneficiaries or on its own behalf if it has discounted the acceptance. In any case, acceptance and maturity must be advised to the issuing bank.

Disposal of documents

As regards the documents, unless the credit states otherwise, these will be sent to the issuing bank, which has a reasonable time (not exceeding seven banking days from receipt) in which to examine them and to decide whether or not it considers that they are in accordance with the credit terms. This, of course, is the crucial factor which determines whether or not the negotiating bank has been successful in keeping to the narrow path mentioned at the beginning of this section. It is not obliged to acquaint the issuing bank with any discrepancies which it has found in the documents, but in practice if it had considered them important enough it would have rejected the drawing.

Rejection by issuing bank

If the issuing bank refuses the drawing for reasons which the negotiating bank considers spurious and these objections are maintained after reference to the applicants without adequate justification being proffered for such rejection, then it is evident that the issuing bank is seeking to avoid its obligations under the credit in order to please its customers, the applicants. This may be because they have lost interest in the goods or because they are in dispute with the beneficiaries regarding this or another consignment of goods. Whatever the reason, this situation is one of the most deplorable which can occur in connection with a credit and resolute action is called for from the negotiating bank. Often communication at high level threatening to refuse in future to handle the issuing bank's paper and to make clear to presenters the reason for such refusal, will bring about an astonishing reversal of policy on the part of the offenders.

Where, however, the rejection is justified, the position of the negotiating bank will depend on its true status in terms of the credit. If it has paid the beneficiaries there is little that can be done other than to attempt to dispose of the goods which it has, by default, become the owner of, at the best possible price and to revise its procedures to preclude future repetition of the mistake which cause the loss. If it has negotiated in the true sense of the word, it may seek to exercise its right of recourse against the beneficiaries, but the attendant admission of incompetence and the resulting bad publicity may well lead it to dismiss this remedy.

Discrepant drawings

It remains to consider the position where documents are presented which do not conform with the terms of the credit and the percentage of all presentations which fall into this category is amazingly high (and one of the more important reasons for the writing of this book). Technically, the mandate implied in the credit is to honour the beneficiaries' drawings provided that all conditions of the credit are complied with: if they are not, then the mandate falls away and there is no obligation upon the bank to take any further action. In practice, however, there are a number of options which are open to the negotiating bank between the extremes of outright rejection of the documents and total disregard of the discrepancies.

The first of these, and the most satisfactory to all concerned, is to have the documents corrected. Whether this can be done will depend upon the nature of the discrepancy (nothing can be done to correct late shipment, for instance) and the time which remains available before expiry either of the credit itself or of the period allowed after the date of the transport document for presentation of complying documents. In most cases, correction will involve the beneficiaries taking the documents away again, although the bank may be prepared to co-operate in allowing properly authorised and identified persons to make and authenticate alterations to certain documents on its own premises. On most documents, authentication of alterations is essential, though minor alterations to such things as typing errors on purely commercial documents such as invoices and packing lists, may be made without such authentication and may even be made by the bank itself with the agreement of the beneficiaries. Obviously, great discretion should be exercised when such an action is considered, the criterion being whether the alteration is of a nature which could mislead subsequent holders of the document and whether it is relevant to the interests of such parties.

The next most practical action is to teletransmit the issuing bank detailing the drawing, the underlying shipment and the discrepancies found, and ask for its authority to pay notwithstanding those discrepancies. It is important that, when such a teletransmission is sent, it gives the issuing bank all information which will be relevant to its decision. For example, there is little point in telling the issuing bank that late presentation has been made without including details of the carrying vessel in order that the applicants may calculate whether or not the documents will be stale by the time they are received.

An alternative course which is often followed as a "soft option" is to pay under the protection of an indemnity, either from the beneficiaries or from their bankers, in which the givers of the indemnity undertake to refund the amount paid if the documents are rejected by the applicants on the grounds of the named discrepancies. This course of action has a number of drawbacks. Although it facilitates the processing of the drawing it is of no help to the issuing bank unless the negotiating bank in turn extends its own indemnity. This involvement in multiple indemnities creates much extra work at a later date in the monitoring of continued validity and release of the indemnities, and from the beneficiaries' point of view involves them in additional expense if the indemnity is required to be issued by their bankers. More importantly, it leaves the amount of the indemnity outstanding in the beneficiaries' books as a contingent liability. More than one company has had its annual accounts qualified by its auditors by reference to numerous such indemnities, casually given and unrecorded in its books. Similar considerations apply where the bank pays or negotiates "under reserve" in respect of the discrepancies found.

Finally, the option exists for the credit to be disregarded altogether and for the documents to be sent to the issuing bank on a collection basis. Where this occurs, usual practice is for reference to be made to the credit in the covering schedule and for the discrepancies which have been found to be listed. This is not really necessary, however, since a collection is a collection and should be treated as such. In this, full instructions should be given to the collecting bank (the erstwhile issuing bank) and the provisions of the Uniform Rules for Collections should be regarded as applying to the item. For full information on the treatment of collections, see Chapter 8.

CHAPTER 17

The avoidance of loss: the beneficiaries

It has been stated before in this book that the beneficiaries have less responsibility under a letter of credit than any other party and this is true insofar as it concerns their duties to others. If they so choose, they are perfectly at liberty to ignore the credit completely and this in fact happens on a surprising number of occasions. Their obligations under the commercial contract are, of course, an entirely separate matter. On the assumption, however, that they wish to carry the sale through to a successful conclusion, their prime duty is to themselves in making absolutely sure that they will be paid by the buyers.

We have already spoken many times of the paramount need in an international trade transaction for sellers and buyers to be in possession of the fullest possible financial information on their opposite numbers and for that information to be constantly updated. Sellers should not be under the impression that because the buyers have agreed to provide a letter of credit to cover payment for the goods that they have nothing further to worry about. Even with all the safeguards provided by Uniform Customs and Practice and by the banking system itself, abuses do occur whereby buyers find an excuse not to pay for the goods. The usual result of this is that the goods are eventually sold to the highest bidder, invariably at a substantial loss and frequently to the original buyers. The issue of impossibly complex credits, inclusion of "built-in discrepancies", equivocation over trivial discrepancies, all these are ruses which can be, and are, used by unscrupulous applicants to deny sellers the payment to which they are entitled and should have been certain of by virtue of the letter of credit.

We have seen that the chief advantages to sellers to be expected from the use of a letter of credit as the means of settlement are certainty and immediacy of payment, yet as much as 60% of all drawings under documentary credits are rejected by banks on first presentation and the time of payment is frequently postponed even from complying documents, by credits being made payable at the counters of the issuing bank and similar ploys. The purpose of this chapter is to put sellers in the position of being aware of these dangers and able to identify them in time to avoid loss.

Forged credits

Although there is nothing to prevent a credit being sent by the issuing bank direct to the beneficiaries it is highly unusual; the issuing bank normally employs the services of its agent in the sellers' country to "advise" the credit. This provides a great safeguard for the beneficiaries since it is the duty of the advising bank to check the apparent authenticity of the credit and if it transpires that it is a forgery that bank is liable for any loss which occurs if it has been negligent in such checking. Where a credit does appear to have been received direct, therefore, it should be viewed with suspicion, since such credits frequently turn out to be forged. The credit should immediately be taken to the beneficiaries' own bankers who should be asked to take steps to have it authenticated. Other tell-tale signs of a forged credit are repeated communications from the "applicants" stressing the urgency of the order and requesting immediate dispatch of goods, requirements in the credit that goods be sent by air and consigned direct to the applicants, requirements that any acknowledgement or request for amendment be addressed to the applicants rather than to the issuing bank, and the use of false or incorrect addresses or post box numbers (although this would not be apparent to the beneficiaries). The first two of these are, of course, not suspicious in themselves, but become so where the credit is received direct.

Checking the credit upon receipt from the advising bank

Though it might seem obvious, the single most important piece of advice which can be given to beneficiaries, and the most frequently ignored, is that immediately upon receipt of a credit they should read it. It is easy to breathe a sigh of relief at having received a "guarantee" of payment and to file it away until it is needed at the time when documents are ready to be presented to the bank. By this time, of course, it is far too late to do anything to remedy any deficiencies and the expected payment is postponed, perhaps indefinitely. A checklist, similar to the example shown here, is a good way to discipline the receipt of credits and verify the details.

Contract terms

Ideally, none of the requirements of a credit should come as a surprise to the beneficiaries, since the type of credit, payment terms, goods specification, contract terms, delivery dates, documentary requirements, responsibility for payment of bank charges, should have been agreed at the contract stage and the applicants should not have incorporated any additional requirements without first obtaining the beneficiaries' agreement. Provided that this has been done, it becomes a simple matter of checking the terms of the credit against the contract and requesting an amendment to the credit in case of any discrepancy. Such a request should be direct to the buyers, since the banks will in any case have to refer to them; a request routed through the banks will only be unnecessarily delayed. If a request for an amendment required to bring a credit into line with previously agreed contract terms is refused the buyers are already in breach of contract and the sellers would be well advised to take heed of this warning and refuse to ship the goods.

Type of credit

The first point of which to take note when checking a credit is the type of instrument which has been issued. A revocable credit can be amended or cancelled at the behest of either the applicants or the issuing bank without the agreement, or even the prior knowledge, of the beneficiaries. It is therefore of little use as a guarantee of payment and is normally used only where the buyers and sellers have a long-standing relationship or perhaps belong to the same group of companies and are obliged to use a credit as the means of settlement by regulations in one or other of their countries. Most sellers, in specifying a credit, will be expecting an irrevocable instrument, which cannot be amended or cancelled without their consent. The type of credit will be shown clearly at the top, usually preceding the credit number. If it says "confirmed irrevocable letter of credit", this is an indication that the issuing bank does not understand credits and great caution should be exercised with

Letter of Credit Checklist

LETTER OF CREDIT CHECKLIST	LETTER OF CREDIT NO.	
UNCONFIRMED/ CONFIRMED/ NEGOTIABLE	IRREVOCABLE ?	AMENDED?

Applicant:	Beneficiary:
Address:	Address:

Transport Document must be addressed to:	UK Bank Ref:
	UK Bank
	Telephone No.
	Issuing Bank:
Named Carrier/Forwarder?	Date of Issue:

Date & Place of Expiry	Last Shipment Date:		Presentation Days: 21/ 14/ other
Shipment From:	To:	By: AIR/ SEA/ ROAD	PREPAID/ FORWARD

DESCRIPTION OF GOODS:

VALUE:	Partial shipment allowed: YES/ NO	Transhipment allowed: YES/ NO

DOCUMENTS NEEDED:

No.	Original	Copy	Document Title	Special Clauses/ Instructions
1			DRAFTS YES/ NO	SIGHT YES/ NO
				DRAWEE:
2			INVOICE	
			COMMERCIAL/SIGNED ?	
3			TRANSPORT DOCUMENT	See above for delivery address.

ALL DOCUMENTS MUST SHOW: LETTER OF CREDIT NUMBER

SHIPMENT DETAILS MUST BE SENT TO BUYER/ INSURANCE COMPANY/ BANK?
COPY DOCUMENTS MUST BE SENT TO BUYER/ INSURANCE COMPANY/ BANK?   WHEN?
COVERED BY UCP 500 ?   YES/ NO if no, it must be rejected or amended
What costs are to our account?

the rest of the credit's terms. Other adjectives which may be used here include "revolving", "transferable", "red clause", and "standby", each of which was defined in detail in Chapter 10.

Time and place of payment

Probably the next most important matter to be checked is the terms of payment; these must be read carefully and understood and where any uncertainty exists the advising bank should be asked for clarification. If usance drafts are called for, their tenor should obviously be the period of credit agreed in the contract, but most problems in this area arise from the actual place of payment rather than the time. The majority of sellers expect to be paid under a credit by the bank in their own country to which they present conforming documents, but where the issuing bank has used words such as "available at our counters", or "payable on receipt by us of conforming documents", what should be a right is being denied to the beneficiaries. Unless such an arrangement has been previously consented to they should treat the credit with suspicion. In fact, such an instrument is flattered by being called a letter of credit at all; it is really a conditional guarantee of payment of a collection.

Amount

The credit amount is the next thing which should be checked. Not only should it be sufficient to cover the agreed price of the goods, including any variation in quantity which may have been allowed for, but it should also represent the full value of the goods under the contract terms which have been agreed. For a CIF contract, therefore, the amount must cover the full CIF value of the shipment, including freight and insurance premiums. If the quantity of the goods is specified as being approximate, then a variation of 10% either way will be allowed, but where the quantity is exceeded this will be of no use to the beneficiaries unless the amount is also expressed as approximate.

Dates and time constraints

Next, the dates stipulated in the credit should be examined and considered in the light of whether they can practicably be adhered to. The time required to procure or manufacture the goods and the frequency of sailings or flights to the specified destination will be the chief factors affecting whether or not the latest date for shipment can be met. If any doubt exists, it is preferable to obtain an extension now rather than to take a chance and risk delay in payment later. The other important time constraint is that which restricts the number of days after the date of the transport document which are allowed for presentation of documents. This should also be carefully considered in the light of the usual delay in obtaining the transport document and the formalities, such as insurance or legalisation, which will have to be attended to between that time and the stipulated date. If the credit does not stipulate this period of time, UCP automatically apply 21 days as the period allowed. The difference between the latest date for shipment and that for presentation of documents should automatically determine the expiry date of the credit if it has been properly drawn up, but beneficiaries should beware of credits to which such professionalism has not been applied. Many drawings have been rejected because the beneficiaries looked only at the expiry date of the credit without realising that the time allowed for presentation effectively nullified the credit several days prior to its stated expiry. Finally, while on the subject of time constraints, beneficiaries should be especially cautious where the credit provides for shipment in instalments at specified intervals. If one such instalment is shipped late, the credit becomes null and void for future drawings even though they represent goods shipped on time, unless it is specifically reinstated by the issuing bank at the request of the applicants. This can be a serious problem where shipping opportunities to a particular destination are few or where cargo space in the available vessels is heavily booked.

Goods and shipment

The description of the goods as given in the credit should now be considered and its exact conformity with the contract verified. Applicants are discouraged by banks from including excessive detail in the credit description, but instead should require just sufficient detail to identify the goods as those ordered and call for the beneficiaries' certificate that the goods supplied conform with the specification in the order. The brief description, however, should not indicate any deviation from the type or specification of goods which were actually contracted for. If, by their hazardous or bulky nature, it is likely that the goods will be carried on deck, the credit should specifically allow for bills of lading to indicate that this has occurred or the documents will be rejected. Similarly, if it is likely that the bill of lading will be claused by the carriers regarding defects in either the goods or the packing, the credit should specifically allow for this, provided, of course, that the applicants are prepared to accept such clauses.

The stipulated voyage should be considered, including whether it is in fact possible without transhipment, if the credit prohibits this. However, in many circumstances, such as where the goods are to be sent in a container or trailer and to remain in those conveyances throughout the journey, or where the goods are to be sent by air, provided that the journey specified in the credit is covered by a single transport document a prohibition of transhipment by the credit can be disregarded. The relationship of the stipulated voyage with the stated transport document should also be checked and if, for example, the voyage is between two points, one or both of which are inland, yet the credit calls for a marine bill of lading, this should be amended to a combined transport document.

Documentary requirements

The transport document is an important point to consider from other aspects. If the intention is to entrust the shipment of the goods to forwarding agents, they should be consulted in advance to ascertain whether they will provide the carriers' bill of lading or their own house bill. If the latter, the document must be signed by the forwarders either as carriers or as agents for named carriers, and such wording must appear on the bill of lading. If the credit requires any particular clauses or information to appear on the transport document which would not normally be present, the carriers should be contacted to ascertain whether they are prepared to comply. Generally speaking, carriers are unhappy about including information on bills of lading which they have no means of verifying. They quite properly consider that such information, if really necessary, should be provided elsewhere. They are also understandably reluctant to provide the many certificates demanded by paranoid buyers, or their governments, regarding the condition, age, flag and route of their vessels, and periodically rebel and simply refuse to issue them.

Regarding the other documentary requirements, it should be checked that they are in accordance with the contract terms, eg that an insurance document is not called for where the shipment is CFR, and that they will all be obtainable, since if one is missing or incomplete, payment will not be made. If any are to be issued by third parties, other than transport or insurance documents or regularly-seen papers such as certificates of origin issued by chambers of commerce, then the prospective issuers should be contacted at an early stage in order to confirm that the documents will be obtainable at the time they are required. Beneficiaries should beware of any credit which makes it a condition of payment that a document be presented which has been issued or countersigned by the applicants or their agents, since in such circumstances mere inaction on their part is all that is required to frustrate payment.

The credit should be examined generally to ensure that it contains no contradictory or nonsensical requirements. The beneficiaries' own name must be spelt correctly or this may cast doubt upon whether the right organisation is claiming payment. Any requirements for action such as dispatch of documents or telexing of shipment details "immediately after shipment" or similar should be reworded unless the beneficiaries are absolutely certain that they will be able to comply, since shipment details are rarely available in time for such compliance and interpretations of the word "immediate" vary. The advising bank's covering letter should also be read. This will often be the vehicle used for the addition by the advising bank of its confirmation of the credit and may also state for whose account bank charges are to be presumed.

Amendments

Provided that beneficiaries carry out all these checks, they should have little to worry about as the time approaches for negotiation other than gathering together all the required documents and remaining within the time constraints imposed by the credit. During this intervening period, or indeed at any time during the lifetime of a credit, they are under no obligation to accept any amendments which may be received, but should give formal notification to the advising bank of acceptance or rejection. Failure to notify acceptance does not actually nullify the amendment, and subsequent presentation of documents in conformity with the credit as amended acts as such notification of acceptance. However, it is advisable to give notification since that act will impart the quality of irrevocability to the amendment. The beneficiaries cannot, however, accept part of a multiple amendment contained on the same advice whilst rejecting the rest.

Presentation of documents

On the assumption that all the documents required by the credit have been obtained, if the procedures outlined so far in this chapter have been followed there should be a very strong chance of their being accepted by the bank and of negotiation being effected in consequence. It is not recommended, however, that the documents are simply lodged with the bank and the detailed checking left to them. Banks vary widely in the time they take to process documents under credits, some providing a same-day service whilst others take up to a week or even more, although the limit is seven banking days from the date of presentation. This means that if any discrepancies are found which can be put right, the time available for this to be done may be short or even expired; therefore it is very much in the beneficiaries' interest to check the documents themselves before they are presented.

Even though every care may have been taken to produce precisely the documents called for in the credit, it does no harm to check them once more when they are gathered together in the form in which they will be presented to the bank. Also at this stage it will be possible to check the documents against each other, for if they are inconsistent they will be rejected. This is particularly important in the case of the shipping marks, which in all other documents must correspond with those shown on the bill of lading. Any alterations which have been made to documents should be properly authenticated by the issuers and the documents themselves properly signed where necessary. The bill of lading, the insurance document and the bill of exchange, if any, will probably need the beneficiaries' endorsement, and if an insurance certificate is used it may need to be countersigned by the insured party on its face. It is as well to check that the cover is adequate, not only in terms of the credit requirements but also in the light of any restrictions on cover which it may itself detail in its preamble. These usually affect the type of goods, the value limitation on goods shipped together in any one vessel and the places of departure and destination. At the same time the expiry date of the open cover should be checked — these arrangements are normally valid over a number of years and the inadvertent continued use of out-of-date certificates is not unknown.

Any certifications which are required to appear on the invoice should be checked for their presence and correctness. Unless the credit says otherwise and the invoice is signed as a document it is not necessary to separately sign such certifications. The invoice description of the goods should coincide exactly with that in the credit, even to the extent of reproducing any spelling errors which appear in the credit version. Additional descriptive text may appear but care should be taken that no part of this seems to contradict anything in the credit description.

A credit should not make stipulations which cannot easily be verified, such as "shipment by conference line vessel". If it does, banks are instructed in UCP to disregard them. However, to be absolutely certain that no awkward arguments will ensue, it does no harm for the beneficiaries to provide their own certificate that such conditions have been complied with — assuming, of course, that the statement is true.

It is not a good idea to present any documents to the bank other than those called for in the credit. Any other documents should be sent to the buyers direct. This is because, although UCP provides to the contrary, some banks may nonetheless examine them in terms of the credit and, if they appear to cast any doubt upon the information contained in the credit document, will reject the drawing. The fact that they have no right to do so, and that this position would without doubt be upheld in a court of law, would be small consolation to unpaid beneficiaries in view of the expense and hassle involved in proving their case.

Discrepant documents

If, despite all these precautions, the bank discovers discrepancies which cannot be rectified, it may be prepared to take any one of a number of courses of action. Its mandate to pay has, of course, ceased to exist, because it depended totally upon the lodging of correct documents. However, most banks are prepared to assist the beneficiaries as far as they are able, bearing in mind that, even though they may be the beneficiaries' own bankers, they are in this instance acting as the agent of the applicants and their priority must be to protect the interests of their principals.

Unfortunately, all the options available where discrepant drawings are concerned are likely to cost the beneficiaries money. The quickest, and usually the most satisfactory, solution is to ask the bank to send a teletransmission message to the issuing bank asking for authority to pay notwithstanding the discrepancies. This will involve payment of the telex costs, possibly of both banks, but will usually provide a relatively speedy decision and thus reduce losses through interest charges. Much slower is the option of asking the bank to send the drawing to the issuing bank on a collection basis, which is in effect setting aside the letter of credit altogether. This option is not really to be recommended because it may involve a lengthy wait for remittance of proceeds and collection charges will be payable by the sellers whatever the credit has to say on the subject. It is sometimes unavoidable, however, as when in response to a request for authority to pay the applicants state that they wish to inspect the documents before reaching their decision.

The bank may offer to pay the drawing under the protection of the beneficiaries' indemnity, or one issued or countersigned by their bankers, in which an undertaking is given to refund the amount paid if the applicants refuse the documents by reason of the discrepancies listed. A similar alternative is for the bank to pay under reserve, which means that it reserves the right to reclaim the amount paid if the documents are rejected. Neither of these is very satisfactory, however, for although costs are limited to the commission which may be charged for a bankers' indemnity, plus a small interest loss whilst it is being prepared, it should appear in the beneficiaries' books as a contingent liability and the transaction cannot be regarded as finalised until the indemnity is released by the buyers taking up the documents.

If what takes place is a negotiation, ie the bank is paying the beneficiaries against a credit which is payable elsewhere, such as where drafts are on the issuing bank, the bank may deduct from the amount paid a sum representing interest for the period for which it will be out of funds. This also applies where a reimbursing bank is named in the credit if the credit states that reimbursing bank charges are for the beneficiaries' account (otherwise they are the responsibility of the issuing bank). In such cases, the bank has recourse to the beneficiaries if the draft is not paid. Where payment takes place, as where drafts are drawn on a paying bank nominated in the credit, or where the negotiating bank has also confirmed the credit, no such right of recourse exists and the transaction is completed when payment is made.

CHAPTER 18

Bank finance under bills and credits

In this final chapter we shall examine the various ways in which banks provide working capital to exporters and importers where such arrangements are directly related to either collections or to documentary letters of credit. Sellers of goods, particularly where a bill for collection is the agreed method of settlement, frequently require assistance during the period while the collection relating to those goods is outstanding, while buyers may wish to defer payment for the goods until they have concluded an onward sale.

Negotiation of collections

When a bank negotiates a bill or documents it in effect makes a loan to the drawers against the proceeds which they may expect to receive in the future. As with any other lending proposition, the bank will require negotiations to be part of a prearranged facility and, before granting it, will require its customers to provide it with full financial information in order that it may assess the extent of the risk which it is incurring by doing so. It will normally call for lists of drawees to be submitted in advance and will seek financial reports on them which it will continuously update, since they will be the prime source of repayment of the loan. It will exercise limits for each drawee, beyond which it will not be prepared to be exposed, and those limits may well encompass the collections of more than one drawer. It will often also be a condition of the facility that the customers' exports are covered by an appropriate export credit insurance policy.

Export credit insurance

It is perhaps appropriate at this point to include a few words of explanation of export credit insurance. While ordinary marine insurance can provide protection to exporters against maritime risks such as damage by fire or sinking, loss by breakage or pilferage and against the risks of war, perhaps the greatest risk of loss to exporters lies in the failure of the buyers, either through their own insolvency or intransigence, or through government intervention, to pay for the goods. Such risks can form a strong disincentive to companies to enter export markets, with a resulting adverse effect on a country's balance of trade and therefore on its balance of payments and its foreign currency reserves. Many countries, therefore, have established government-backed agencies which exist for the purpose of providing insurance cover to exporters against these credit risks which they are unable to cover under their ordinary insurance.

In the UK the government agency involved is the Export Credits Guarantee Department (ECGD), although following the sale to the private sector of its retail business this organisation's activities are confined to the underwriting of large-scale capital projects under lines of credit which might be established from time to time by the Treasury in favour of specific countries or groups of countries. Cover for retail operations of UK exporters is now provided by a number of companies, and for smaller exporters also by some banks. Many other countries have organisations providing similar services to their own exporters: COFACE in France, the Hermes organisation in Germany and so on. Although their prime consideration is facilitation of their own country's export trade, the commercial possibilities of the cover provided have been recognised and some of these organisations, such as that of Singapore, have begun to compete for export credit insurance business on a worldwide scale; commercial insurance companies also now offer competing cover in this field. Since the mid-1990s credit insurance companies do offer cover to exporters as a commercial package (companies such as: NCM, Tradewise, etc).

Negotiation or advance?

Many banks differentiate between collections against which they negotiate the full value and those for which they advance up to an agreed percentage of the collection amount. Technically, in the former case the bank may become a holder in due course of the bill whilst where less than the face amount has been given the bank merely has a lien over the bill to the extent of its advance and can only be a holder for value. In practice, there is really very little difference, since the bank will have taken a general right of recourse in its agreement with the customers and so does not have to rely on its recourse under the bill. The general right of recourse is necessary because this type of finance can be applied to collections where no bill of exchange is used, as is often the case where either the exporting or the importing country levies heavy stamp duty on bills.

Interest will be charged on the amount of the advance and may be debited to the drawers' account when proceeds are received, estimated and deducted from the amount paid at the time of negotiation, or deducted from the balance of proceeds if less than the full amount has been advanced.

Unless the drawers are absolutely undoubted and the bank is consequently content to rely solely upon its right of recourse if the collection is unpaid, it will consider the individual aspects of each collection against which it is requested to advance, taking into account the limits it has set for both drawers and drawees, but also looking carefully both at the documents and at the goods themselves. This is because it may have to rely upon its title to the goods to recover the amount of its loan if the bill is unpaid and the drawers are unable to repay when the bank seeks to exercise its recourse. To this end, the customer will normally be required to sign a general letter of hypothecation and pledge of goods, which gives the bank a right to sell its customers' goods if necessary in order to secure repayment of the loan.

Documents

The documents will be examined for the completeness in the light of the bank's knowledge of import regulations in the country to which they are consigned, for the security of title which they convey to the bank and of their adequacy for the purpose for which they are intended. In particular, the bill of lading will be examined to ensure that it is made out to order and is endorsed in blank, is not stale, does not bear any detrimental clauses relating to the goods or the packing and generally does not give any indication which might have an effect on the marketability of the goods. The insurance cover, if any, will be evaluated for its adequacy and the policy or certificate checked for any errors which might affect that cover.

Goods

The goods themselves are important and banks prefer to lend against collections covering shipment of merchandise which would be readily saleable in a stable and constant market. Goods which are subject to the whims of fashion, which enjoy only a seasonal demand, which are perishable, or which are of a highly specialised nature, are unpopular because of the possible difficulties in realising anything like their invoice value in a forced sale situation. For different reasons, banks are sometimes reluctant to be involved in the financing of transactions relating to commodities such as armaments, drugs and the like, particularly where those goods are bound for sensitive areas.

Discounting of bills

When a bank discounts a bill of exchange, it in effect buys that bill from the holder at a discount on its face value; the amount of the discount represents the interest from the date of discount until the maturity date of the bill. Unlike a negotiation, discounting is not possible when no bill of exchange accompanies a collection. Furthermore, it can only apply to usance bills and they must have been accepted. As was seen in Chapter 8, a bill drawn payable at a stated number of days after sight does not qualify as a bill of exchange within the meaning of the Act until it has been accepted and its maturity date can therefore be determined. Since with discount the source of the right of recourse lies in bill legislation, it is essential that the discounting bank acquires the rights of a holder in due course.

Because acceptance obviously takes place in the buyers' country, discounting of accepted bills under collections is usually carried out by the collecting bank acting upon instructions received from the remitting bank, which may also have negotiated the item. In most cases, the bill would be expressed in the buyers' home currency to enable the bill to be rediscounted in the local bill market, if one exists. If it does not, in very rare cases, and in total reliance on the standing of the drawers rather than that of the drawees, banks may agree that the collecting bank be instructed to return the accepted draft for discount by the remitting bank. Such a discounted bill would, of course, have no value for the purposes of rediscounting in the bill market, because the name of the acceptor would be unknown in the exporting country.

Exchange as per endorsement

A specialised form of discounting, this type of finance was developed to enable sellers to obtain finance for credit periods granted to their buyers whilst taking advantage of low interest rates applying in the buyers' country and putting the buyers in the advantageous position of having their liability denominated in their home currency. At the time of presentation to the remitting bank the amount of the bill, plus collection charges and interest, is converted into the currency of the importing country and the resulting figure endorsed on the face of the bill, which then becomes payable for this amount. The item is then sent for collection in the normal way, perhaps being negotiated by the remitting bank, and presented for acceptance. When this is achieved the collecting bank is asked to discount the acceptance and the proceeds are remitted back, either to be paid to the drawers or used to repay the loan, as the case may be. EAPE finance was once common in trade between the UK and Australia and South Africa, but tended to fall away as the interest rate differential was eroded. There is, however, no reason why it should not be used again where similar circumstances exist.

Á forfait finance (forfaiting)

As the name suggests, where *à forfait* finance is provided, something is forfeited, and that something is the right of recourse to the drawers which would normally be enjoyed by the discounting bank. This type of finance is generally reserved for larger contracts where buyers are obliged to request extended credit terms. It was nurtured in trade between the West and eastern Europe where the chronic shortage of hard currency with which to pay for imports was discouraging trade because of the huge contingent liabilities which would have arisen in sellers' books even were they able to finance the transactions. The geographical scope of forfaiting business has broadened considerably but the tendency remains for the buying country to be one with foreign currency reserve problems.

On receipt of an enquiry, the sellers approach a bank specialising in forfaiting business and request a quotation for a financing package, advising them of the full details of the proposed contract and of the credit terms requested. The forfaiters' quotation will be based on the sellers' basic price for the goods but will be increased to allow for the interest payable for the credit period requested and will be further loaded to cover various factors including exchange risks, credit risks, interest rate risks and political risks. The total price will be that quoted to the buyers for supply of the goods on the requested terms, with a stipulation that bills of exchange accepted, or promissory notes signed, in respect of payment for the goods will carry the aval of an acceptable bank in the buyers' county. The subject of avalisation was touched upon in Chapter 7, but what it amounts to is a guarantee by a party, otherwise unconnected with the bill, that it will be paid. Since in forfaiting the guarantee is frequently given by the central bank of the importing country the degree of security thus afforded the forfaiter is high and dishonour of forfaited paper is extremely rare.

Once the contract is signed, shipment of the goods and presentation of the required documents proceeds in the normal way. This may be by means of a collection but is more likely to be under a usance letter of credit. The resulting acceptances or promissory notes are presented to the avalising bank which adds its endorsement "por aval", whereupon the instruments are returned to the forfaiter, who then discounts them at the previously agreed rate which has been calculated to achieve payment of the sellers' basic price in full. As has been stated, the forfaiters surrender their right of recourse to the drawers, and thus the latter have no contingent liability and as far as they are concerned the transaction is at an end. From that point on the forfaiters carry all the risk, presenting the bills or notes as each falls due and taking the difference between the bill's face value and its discounted value as their gross profit before interest charges.

To summarise, the advantages to the sellers of using *à forfait* finance are that they are able to grant extended credit terms to their buyers whilst obtaining payment without recourse on, or soon after, shipment of the goods, without bearing the portion of risk which would remain uncovered if the deal were financed with backing from an export credit agency. The buyers have the advantage of being able to obtain the capital goods which they require on the credit terms which best suit their requirements.

Acceptance credits

An acceptance credit is an extremely simple arrangement whereby buyers or sellers of goods have the right to draw usance bills of exchange on the issuing bank in respect of payment for goods which is either awaited by sellers or due to be made by the buyers. The bank accepts the bills and then discounts them, the proceeds of the discount being paid to the drawers. The tenor of the bills will have been calculated to cover the required financing period but there is often a subsidiary agreement providing for maturing bills in respect of which covering funds have not yet been received to be provided for by a temporary loan. This type of credit is unique in that applicant and beneficiary are one and the same.

Back-to-back credits

Although a back-to-back credit is not necessarily a financing arrangement, this is in fact most frequently the case. It arises where merchants are buying goods from their suppliers and have contracted to sell those goods to the ultimate buyers. The merchants will usually have no physical contact with the goods, their function being to act as intermediaries between manufacturers and end buyers. Where the merchants are the beneficiaries of a letter of credit from the ultimate buyers and are asked by the manufacturers to provide them in turn with a letter of credit, the problem arises that because documents will have to comply with the terms of the first credit (the "master" credit) the back-to-back credit must be issued in such a way that it will produce such complying documents.

Where the merchants have a previously agreed facility with the bank for the issue of letters of credit, the issue of a back-to-back credit may be made under that facility and no financing is required. The technical problems remain, however, since it needs but one mistake to be made, or for documents to be delayed in transit, for the back-to-back issuing bank to be faced with an unavoidable duty to pay on the one hand and a non-complying set of documents on the other. Where the purpose of the transaction is not finance, however, this risk should be offset by the customers' creditworthiness, which it is to be hoped was taken into consideration when the facility was granted.

Most frequently a request for the issue of a back-to-back credit takes place in circumstances similar to those giving rise to many transferable credits, where the merchants in the middle of the transaction are not of sufficient standing to warrant the granting of letter of credit facilities and cannot cajole the manufacturers into parting company with the goods unless they can provide them with a credit as an assurance that they will be paid. Some countries' regulations do not permit the issue of transferable credits, or in some cases the merchants would prefer that the ultimate buyers remain unaware that they are not dealing with the manufacturers of the goods, lest in future transactions their own services are dispensed with.

They therefore approach a bank, usually either their own bankers or the advising bank of the master credit, and ask that they issue a credit in favour of the manufacturers, not under a facility but against the security of the money which will become due when they present complying documents under the master credit. If the bank agrees (banks' attitudes to back-to-back credits vary widely) a credit will be issued showing the merchants as applicants and requiring dispatch of the goods to the end buyers and presentation of the documents called for in the master credit. Unlike a transferable credit, it is essential that the dates for shipment, expiry and presentation of documents are earlier than those in the master credit, which must on no account expire before documents reach the issuing bank of the back-to-back credit.

Although each individual credit is subject to UCP, the back-to-back aspect of their relationship is not, and therefore banks indulging in their issue can look for no protection from the articles. Because of this they are not subject to the restrictions which UCP place upon transferable credits regarding requirements which may be altered. This gives rise to numerous requests for variations in the terms, all designed to prevent the ultimate buyers and sellers from being put in touch with each other. These only serve to increase the danger that a discrepancy will arise between the documents presented under the back-to-back credit and those required in order to obtain payment under the master credit.

For the merchants, the attractions of back-to-back finance are that it serves better than a transferable credit in enabling them to maintain their pivotal position in the transaction because it is potentially more flexible and it is far cheaper than the alternative, even were such a course open to them, of borrowing the money with which to obtain delivery of the goods.

For the banks, it is difficult to see what advantages could possibly accrue from this type of business. If a bank which issues a back-to-back credit has advised the master credit it is withholding information from its principals which may be of vital concern to them and therefore may be considered to be in breach of its duties as an agent. If it has not advised the master credit, the beneficiaries may accept amendments to that credit without its knowledge. It is frequently dealing with an organisation on whose behalf it would not under normal circumstances even consider the issue of letters of credit, yet it is implying to the suppliers of the goods that a very different relationship exists. Its "security" is subject to the possibility already referred to of being nullified by postal delays or human error. Its return is small, usually pathetically so by comparison with the profits which the merchants are making from the deal. The wonder is therefore that banks are prepared in any circumstances to entertain such business, but in many countries of the world back-to-back credits are quite commonplace; whether this stems from ignorance or optimism on the part of the issuing banks is impossible to tell.

Where a bank does agree to issue a back-to-back credit and reimbursement for drawings thereunder is obtainable from no other source than the proceeds of a drawing under the master credit, its first action should be to ensure that it remains in possession of the original of the master credit in order to make certain that negotiation of documents cannot take place through any other bank. Alternatively, the original should be marked indelibly, on its face, to the effect that it is the subject of a back-to-back agreement. The bank should then insist upon the first beneficiaries supplying, in advance of the issue of the back-to-back credit, their commercial invoices and drafts in accordance with the requirements of the master credit, fully completed as far as possible and signed. Careful consideration should then be given to the dates for shipment and expiry and the time allowed for presentation of documents under the back-to-back credit, to make it as certain as possible that the similar dates in the master credit will be complied with. It should always be borne in mind that any variation in the terms of the master credit may well put the bank in a position of total reliance on the ability of the first beneficiaries to rectify the differences before presentation under the master credit, and that if such differences relate to the bill of lading the bank may have no option but to release the bill (and with it, of course, *prima facie* ownership of the goods) to the first beneficiaries in order that alteration(s) may be made and authenticated by the carriers. Sometimes, requirements of the master credit, such as the sending of documents by the first beneficiaries direct to the applicants within a specified period from shipment, may make the issue of the back-to-back credit totally unviable, and the bank must weight up each of the master credit's requirements with this in mind.

Back-to-Back Credits

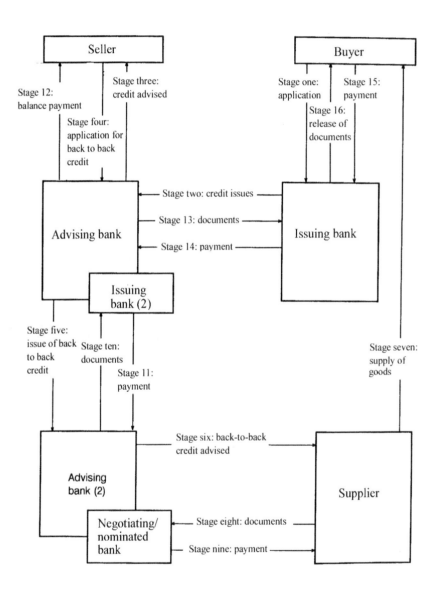

Usance letters of credit

Normally a usance credit is an indication that the buyers are being granted extended credit terms by the sellers, but they can be used for the provision of import finance to the buyers by the issuing bank. This is achieved by requiring the beneficiaries to draw usance bills under the credit but including a provision for those bills, when accepted, to be immediately discounted at the expense of the applicants. The sellers, therefore, are effectively paid at sight while the buyers benefit from the usance period in order to process and/or on-sell the goods. From the sellers' point of view there remains the question of recourse, but as the bills are usually drawn on a bank the likelihood of this right being exercised is minimal.

Buyer credit guaranteed by exporting country

In furtherance of their basic aim of encouraging their own country's exports, the export credit insurance organisations of many countries (including ECGD) are prepared to issue guarantees to overseas banks in support of loans made to buyers for the purchase of goods from the guarantor country. This means that the sellers receive immediate payment for their goods and do not need to concern themselves with such matters as the granting of credit terms and the contingent liabilities attaching to negotiated or discounted bills of exchange or promissory notes. Such arrangements may be either for specific projects involving one contract or may be under a line of credit involving multiple suppliers and buyers concerned in a particular trade, usually in goods of a capital nature.

Produce loans

A traditional form of finance provided by banks to importers is where the bank advances the money to the buyers which is required to pay an inward collection or a drawing under a letter of credit and as security for the loan retains control over the goods until repayment occurs. This means that the documents must include either a negotiable bill of lading made out to order and endorsed in such a way, either specifically in the bank's favour or in blank, as to allow the bank to take delivery of the goods on arrival, or a transport document showing the bank as the named consignee.

On arrival of the carrying vessel, the bank will arrange with its agents for the goods to be cleared, warehoused and insured in its own name. In effect, the bank is *de facto* the owner of the goods until they are paid for. When this happens, a delivery order will be issued to the warehouse keepers instructing them to release the goods to the buyers or their nominees.

Trust receipt facilities

Under a trust receipt facility the bank pays an inward collection or a drawing under a letter of credit in the same way as for a produce loan, but instead of warehousing the goods on its own account releases the documents to the buyers in exchange for their signature to a trust receipt. In this document the buyers acknowledge receipt of the goods, which are identified by shipping details and by a bill of lading number, and undertake to hold them in trust on behalf of the bank, whilst admitting the bank's continued ownership of the goods pending repayment of the loan, and to sell the goods and to account to the bank for the proceeds, in the meantime insuring the goods for the benefit of the bank.

This arrangement has the advantage from the bank's point of view of making it unnecessary for it to become directly involved with the goods. The disadvantages are that the buyers have physical possession of those goods and may abuse the bank's trust by selling them without its knowledge and without using the proceeds of sale to repay the advance. Alternatively, they may use the documents of title as security for further advances from other lenders. It is well established in law that in the latter circumstances the second lender's interest takes precedence over the first. The operative word in a trust receipt facility is therefore the first, the transaction being wholly based upon the degree of trust which the bank feels it can place on the buyers.

INDEX

295